MY F.

THE LOST LEGEND OF PEAR TREE

PART ONE

'A hugely important story, told with profound, sometimes painful honesty regarding a subject we all too readily shy away from. Kalwinder Singh Dhindsa captures the vibrancy, the reality, the complexity of every Punjabi family. And he shares the tragedy of his own. A brave and captivating read'

Hardeep Singh Kohli

'Anyone who has been stalked by the Black Dog, anyone who has had the shadows and tragedies of life growl at them, will recognize the brave brutal truth of this work. Kalwinder Singh Dhindsa moves with unexpected grace from the darkest places to cathartic moments of joy and insight. More sorrow, drama and redemption per page than I have read for a long time.

This is a voyage connecting Derby, India and the worlds of Doctor Who through all the stations of the human heart'

David Southwell

Part One
THE TROUGH
Kalwinder Singh Dhindsa

FOR

My PEopLe

To Liz

Best wishes

Cover design by Tamás Miklós Fülep

@TomFulep
www.fulep.com

Edited by Fine Point Editing

@FP_Editing
www.finepointediting

First Printing, 2016

ISBN-10: 1530819563 (PRINT)
ISBN-13: 978-1530819560 (PRINT)

@KhalSir

@PearTreeDerby

www.khalsir.wordpress.com

Year 1

John Port School

Chapter 1: D Day

It was Wednesday, March 1st 2006 and life was great. I had been married to Rav for almost seven months and not long after our marriage I began my first main teaching position as an NQT Science Teacher at John Port School in Etwall, Derbyshire.

This particular day of the week was always a good one for me because on Wednesdays I could feel the weekend drawing in that much faster. In general, school life as an NQT initially began quite positively and I was really enjoying the whole experience. Until, that is, a few weeks into the job, when I began experiencing more and more problems with some very difficult teaching groups that I had been allocated, which had particularly misbehaving students within them.

During these early weeks of my teaching career I would feel a lot of anxiety in the mornings because of the problems I was experiencing and the thought of the long day ahead of me. The anxieties would leave me with a serious case of butterflies in my stomach. Fortunately, the joy of finishing for the day would fill me with complete euphoria during the drive home. This would fade when the butterflies returned later in the evening when I would have to settle down to plan and prepare for the following day and all its potential tribulations.

It was a great shame that I should feel this way because when I was a student myself I never ever dreaded attending school. Unfortunately, this all changed when I began training as a teacher. As a student I used to actually dislike Fridays, but when I became a teacher I began to absolutely love them and the wonderful weekend they would inevitably bring.

On the whole, I was content with my life and things seemed to be ticking along reasonably well. Most things that is, except some serious concerns that were progressively beginning to rear their heads in my private life. Concerns that were really putting an added dampener on my health and well-being as the days and months went on.

On the morning of Wednesday, March 1st 2006, I woke up briskly and then hurriedly readied myself to make sure I was on time to drop Rav off at the train station. Having come down the stairs, I walked through the kitchen, past my mother at the sink and then through into the living room to retrieve my car keys. As I opened the door, to my surprise I saw my father sitting on a stool in the corner of the room looking straight back at me. We then both greeted each other with a nod as he momentarily stopped crunching on his cornflakes. I then began to think to myself, 'Why was he not at work?' As I picked up my car keys I noticed how smartly dressed he was. His hair was neatly combed back and he was also wearing a new pullover. Still a little puzzled as to why he was at home at this time in the morning, it then dawned on me that he must have taken a day off work from the Chaucer Bakery. It was the first time in a long time that I had not seen him in his normal work clothes and on this particular morning he looked in good spirits which was nice to see. Rav then came into the living room and told me that she was ready to leave for work. We then both left the house together.

Dropping off and then picking up Rav was a daily occurrence for me on weekdays. Having returned home from the morning journey I would settle down for a few minutes in front of the TV to catch up with the latest regional and international news whilst drinking my solitary cup of tea for the whole day before I would make the twenty-minute journey to work, in Etwall.

At school I never allowed myself any time whatsoever to eat. Sometimes I would take sandwiches in with me and then bring them back home to devour later in the afternoon. This routine would result in me becoming absolutely starved by the end of the school day. Although, the euphoria of finishing would temporarily supress the hunger on the drive home. However, once alone and at home, I would then feel more comfortable about wanting to eat and put an end to my self-inflicted starvation. Eating had always been quite simple with me, I never ate when I felt hungry; I only ate when I was starving. This particular issue I had with eating was down to a couple of things, but the main reason I wouldn't eat during school time was because I would always be using my break periods to either prepare myself thoroughly for forthcoming lessons or sitting-in on detentions I had dispensed. My fellow teachers in the very small and claustrophobic science staffroom at John Port School were always bemused at my inability to ever eat anything during the day. On some occasions they would be quite taken aback when they would see me take a bite from a sandwich and then swallow it. However, even then, I would only ever just take the one bite and then place the sandwich back in my school bag to be finished off later at home.

Another reason for my possible eating disorder could also be down to the fact that I've never liked eating in front of people. In my younger days, and still to this day, my mother would make a great fuss of my eating habits and how I should eat. On many occasions in the past, she had commented loudly on my eating habits in the company of family and friends, stating what I could eat and how much I should eat because I had a tendency to waste food I didn't like. Obviously, once everyone's attention had been drawn to me I would then be totally put off eating anything, in fear of being watched and ridiculed by those around me. For that reason, I preferred to eat in isolation, but in school there was no way of doing that as I was always in somebody's company.

My biggest single issue with food however has always been my inability to be able to eat anything in the mornings due to a lack of appetite. This added to my feelings of anxiety due to teaching and did me no favours at all for the rest of the day. This therefore explains the solitary cup of tea, which is the only thing that I can stomach during the early mornings; a routine that goes back to my own school days as a student. For many years this single cup of tea and a couple of teaspoons of sugar was the only thing that sustained me in the form of any nutrition throughout the morning to lunch. This continued to be the case when I began my new career in teaching.

Unfortunately for me, not eating in the mornings when I began teaching meant that the hunger pains would very quickly catch up with me later in the day; my stomach would begin to rumble ferociously. Throughout the day I would desperately hope that nobody but myself would hear the noises that erupted from the pit of my stomach. However, sometimes during quiet periods it could get quite embarrassing and I would try to dampen the noise by drinking from my water bottle.

Whilst taking morning exams at the Village Community School during my student days, I would sit uncomfortably through them for hours in the hope that my growling stomach would not embarrass me. Sometimes I would show up wearing a thick coat or pullover and force myself to sit in a position where my left thumb and knuckles would be firmly jammed into my stomach as I bent over in my chair so that I could muffle any noise that could be emitted. On one occasion I even asked a teacher if I could be excused so that I could go to the toilet even though I didn't need to relieve myself. It was a relief to give my left hand a rest from pressing against my stomach for so long.

The most embarrassing recollection regarding my growling stomach occurred during my PGCE course at the University of Leicester. On one particular day it struck with a vengeance and of all the places it could occur, it had to strike in the most awkward public building of all, a library. As a large group of us were about to enter through the front doors of the Studies Building for a tour, my stomach roared like Vesuvius. 'Guess I better get myself something to eat,' I said. Every person in front of me now stood staring straight back at me. As I sheepishly smiled back at them I couldn't help but chuckle at the thought that they probably thought I soiled myself, having heard my thunder. I made an awkward about-turn and then walked away. I joined up with them all a few minutes later after I had filled my empty stomach with the emergency sandwich I was saving for later in the day.

Fortunately during my teaching days, nearly all the rumbles from my stomach would be drowned out by the sound coming from my own mouth or the volume of noise from background chatter that the students engaged in during lessons.

On returning home from the train station I went straight back into the living room where I once again found my father sitting in the corner of the room next to the heater. He was now watching the news having finished his bowl of cornflakes. During the time I was away my mother had also left for work too, which was a short walk to B&B Fashions at the Cotton Brook Industrial Estate.

As I have said, I would have normally sat down and drank my cup of tea whilst watching the news. However, today I was in a rush to get out and away from the house as quickly as possible. So I picked up my school bag off the floor where I had left it the night before and swung it over my shoulder. I then picked up a box of exercise books that I had been marking the night before and took them into the kitchen. After placing the box of books on the kitchen worktop I proceeded to pour myself my solitary cup of tea.

The books in the box were an absolute pain to mark. Most of them were in a pretty awful state and it really annoyed and frustrated me that I had to stay up late the previous night to try and mark what was handed back to me. This particular Year 8 group was a real handful on most occasions, and the state of some of their books showed how very little some of them cared about their education or school at the time. At one point during the night whilst I was marking these books, my father came down the stairs, opened the living room door, looked straight at me, shut the door and then went back upstairs. He didn't utter a single word. He was probably just checking to see if I had forgotten to turn the heater off again, not realising I was still downstairs. One more thing for him to moan about in the morning, I thought to myself as I reached for another book.

As I began to pour my tea I noticed that my father was now standing beside. Again I felt that there was something about his appearance today that I just could not quite put my finger on. He just seemed to be different, as if he was about to go on some kind of trip that he was looking forward to. I had not seen my father like this for a while. Could it have been that he was finally beginning to show some signs of positivity? It was good to see this change from his usual behaviour; for the first time in a long time he was radiating positive vibes towards me and he looked very relaxed within himself. 'I wish I had a free day,' I thought to myself.

Having poured out the tea that my father had made for me a few minutes earlier, I took a little sip from my cup and realized that it was still too hot to drink. As I was in a rush to get away I needed to cool it down quickly. My father took out an almost empty four-pint bottle of milk from the fridge and offered to pour some milk into my tea. I took the bottle from him and began to pour some milk into my cup, whilst trying to avoid any overspill. I gave it back to him with the smallest amount of milk still left inside. It was just about enough to fill the stomach of a little dormouse. 'Pour it all in, there's only a tiny bit left' he said to me in Punjabi. 'No, that was enough' I replied, stubbornly. He placed the milk back in the fridge and I quickly drank my cup of tea in front of him then placed the empty cup on the worktop. I repositioned my school bag on my right shoulder and picked up the box of books. My father opened the back door for me and I stepped out of the house to make my way towards the car.

I must have looked like the ultimate science teacher with my brown blazer, full beard, brown sweater and dark brown trousers. I actually liked to dress this way for work. It was almost like a costume and I was happy to dress up and play the part of the stereotypical physics professor: it was my uniform. On occasions I even wore my geeky Clark Kent glasses. However, this was a little dangerous because the rims on them were a bit too thick and this would sometimes

affect my field of vision whilst I was driving so I stopped
wearing them. I loved playing up to the stereotype, but it was
more than a uniform to me. I was, in effect, putting on a
disguise by trying to act the role of a teacher as well as
trying to be one; then again, maybe I had seen so many
episodes of Doctor Who that the Doctor's exuberant dress
sense had also rubbed off on me too.

My father spoke to me one final time that day. 'Shall I hold them?' he asked me in Punjabi, referring to the box of books I was carrying. 'No, it's Ok. Bye!' I said, as I made my way to the car, leaving him behind at home with my grandmother and brother who were still asleep in their beds.

I was becoming progressively more and more snappy on
weekday mornings, as I knew another long school day was
ahead of me. It was not only my father who would feel my
temper, but Rav and others members of my family at home.
Fortunately for me, my temper at school was the complete
opposite as my fuse was very much longer and better
controlled. My short temper at home was mainly down to two
things that were seriously bothering me and both were very
much linked to my father and my ongoing quest to lift his
spirits as well as to ultimately please him.

One of these things was due to the fact that a couple of months previously I had been told by my NQT coordinator at John Port School that if I carried on the way I was going I could find myself in a position where I may not pass my NQT year. This assessment of my progress seemed to be based on the observation feedbacks he was getting from his colleagues and also the feedback he was receiving from me. Not passing the NQT basically meant that if I failed, I would not be able to become a fully qualified teacher and there would also be no second chances to try and do it again. This really unsettled me and I remember thinking quite frequently, 'What else would I do if I didn't pass?' I remember thinking at the time that it would be a great failure in my life if I didn't succeed in becoming a teacher. Not only would I have let my wife down but also my father and my family. Rav and I had only been married for just over half a year and we were banking on a lot of things with my new teaching career. For this reason, I did become a little alarmed and distressed by it all. 'What else could I do if I did not pass?' I kept thinking to myself. 'Was I really failing? Or was it the NQT Coordinator's way of alerting me to what could happen if I didn't pass? Was it a ploy to show the pitfalls of not succeeding? What a cruel thing to do.' I later found out that I was not the only NQT who was told about the dangers of failing. The damage had been done though, and once the fear of failure had been put into my mind there was no other option than to pass my NQT year. My life depended on it and the last thing I wanted to do at the end of the academic year was fail to succeed.

The second thing that bothered me more than my job itself was my father's apparent lack of happiness in the preceding weeks. My annoyance and frustration at home was mainly down to the fact that I couldn't do anything to lift his spirits during the previous few days in which his unhappiness had dipped drastically. During these days, every time he was down in the pits, I tried my best to cheer him up. I would try random wisecracks and engage in silly behaviour just to make him smile. On one occasion I actually managed to raise a smile, however it was a very quick one that disappeared as soon as it had flashed across his face. It was a small victory for me though and I felt a bit happier as I saw him smile like in the days of old.

As the initial days of the 2006 New Year ticked along, my father's predicament began to make me feel more and more miserable. This resulted in a knock-on effect on my school-

life too. As time went on, it seemed that I just could not do anything for my father, to lift his spirits. Sometimes, at school, during quieter periods, I would try to think of ways to make him snap out of the darkness that had engulfed him. I was constantly thinking about my father. He was always on my mind but I just couldn't get through to him.

In the week before Wednesday, March 1st, I had been on a half-term break and it would have been the ideal opportunity for me to have spent some time with my father. We could have gone for a walk, or a drive to talk, to do something, but I was unable to as it was prearranged that Rav and I would go up north to see her parents. I remember both my mother and father came out of the house to see Rav and I off on the day we departed. As I sat in the car, I noticed my father was very withdrawn, almost standing in my mother's shadow. He asked a few questions about the state of the car, petrol and washer fluid before they both bid us goodbye. On the day we arrived back into Derby I was very happy: I was back home again for the weekend before I was to return to school on Monday. I had planned to use these two days to again make efforts to try and cheer him up and spend more time in his company. My joy however, was short lived as he quickly snapped at me for no apparent reason when I entered the house on our return. I became increasingly annoyed and frustrated with his behaviour but I decided to bottle it up over the weekend. 'I would be back at school again on Monday and I would be away from all his negativity again. The students would do a fine job of distracting me from my unhappiness at home,' I thought to myself.

The final days that led up to Wednesday, March 1st were very strange days for me. I had only been back at school for two days having had a week-long break, yet I returned home on each of these days very tired and absolutely worn out. Monday and Tuesday followed the exact same pattern. On returning home, I would first make myself something to eat alongside the sandwich I inevitably brought back and then I would slouch on the sofa watching children's TV for about an hour. At about ten minutes past five I would get back in my car to pick Rav up from the train station.

In the previous weeks, I would normally have picked Rav up, returned home and then driven out again just after six o'clock to collect my father, when he would finish work at the Chaucer Bakery at about six thirty. On this Monday and Tuesday however I didn't pick my father up from work because I was too tired to drag myself off the sofa again. So, he would make his own way back to Pear Tree, either walking or getting a lift back with a colleague. I was just too tired to do anything and would fall asleep very quickly on the sofa as soon as I got back from picking Rav up. A few months previously, my father wouldn't have relied on me picking him up, as he would have used his own car for work.

When I began teaching at John Port School my father had given me his blue Ford Mondeo and he ended up buying a green Daewoo for himself that he would use for work and give lifts to his work colleagues. However, around the turn of the 2006 New Year he decided to sell his Daewoo and from then on he would either walk to and from work on Bracken's Lane, near the Spider Bridge, or get lifts from the people he worked with. I still managed to pick him up on some occasions though, unless he told me otherwise. Sometimes I think he would tell me not to pick him up because he knew how tired I used to get, having come back from a long day at school and also because he felt bad as it was his decision to sell the Daewoo.

I remember the day before Wednesday, March 1st when I temporarily woke up from my slumber on the sofa, to see my father at the living room door looking at me. Having seen I was there, he shut the door behind him and I nodded off again. He would always check up on me to make sure that I didn't have my boots on whilst slouching on the sofa even though no part of my boots ever touched the fabric of the sofas because I would hang my legs over the armrests. On this day like the one before it, I didn't have the opportunity to engage in any talk with my father and I went back to sleep and awoke later on in the evening to begin marking the box of Year 8 books that I had brought home from school earlier in the day.

In these last two days prior to Wednesday, March 1st, all my father would do when he got back from work was eat very quickly, alone, in the front room and then go straight up to bed for a very early night.

On the morning of March 1st 2006, I was still annoyed with the previous weekend's bad feelings between my father and myself. I had tried my best for weeks to make him smile and lift his spirits, but I had failed miserably.

This was my account of the final days of February 2006 and the first day of March 2006. Little did I know that those words said by my father to me regarding the box of books on that morning of Wednesday, March 1st 2006 would be the last spoken words the pair of us ever exchanged. In his last efforts to help me before we were both to be parted forever, he had offered to pour milk into my hot cup of tea and then carry my box of books to the car.

Although I refused them both, it was his final act of love and fatherly kindness that will remain with me till the day I die.

Chapter 2: High Rising Spirits

Only four months previously, my father had been in high rising spirits, Charhdi Kala as us Sikhs would say. Rav and I had been happily married since August and everything was going well. To this day I still don't remember much about our wedding day but I'm certain of one thing. My father had the time of his life. It was obvious to all who saw him on the day how much of a good time he was having. I'm sure the wedding film will provide all the evidence required to confirm this but to this day I've still not watched it. Maybe that's also why my memories of the day have faded as time has passed.

I've never liked watching myself on video and the same applied after I got married. The fear of ridicule if I happened to be caught doing something others perceived as a little embarrassing was always something I liked to avoid.

Sunday, August 7th 2005 was the day Rav and I got married and it was a wonderful day in my mother and father's lives. It was obviously a great day in my life too but to be honest I've never liked these sorts of big occasions. The gathering of hundreds of people and the painfully loud noise and alcohol-fuelled excess that would inevitably come with it, was just not my solitary cup of tea.

Something I do vividly remember about my wedding day though, was trying to keep track of the drama that was unfolding at Edgbaston on the final day of the 2nd Ashes Test between England and Australia. Amazingly, as the day went on Australia rallied defiantly with their last-wicket pairing, to get into touching distance of an unbelievable victory. However, euphorically, the match ended when Michael Vaughan's England team managed to snatch victory from the jaws of defeat. England had managed to miraculously record a two-run victory, which became the narrowest result in Ashes history.

As a family, we had never seen my father glow with so much pride. He also had another reason to be extra happy that day too. His older brother Mohan Singh Dhindsa had managed to make his way up north with his family, to celebrate my wedding in Thornaby, Stockton-On-Tees. The reason why this was such a big deal for my father was because Mohan had, until then, spent the last few months of his life in a very depressed state which had resulted in him detaching himself from anything and everything he had ever once cared for.

In late November 2005, only a few months after my wedding my father decided that it would be the perfect time for him and my grandmother to go on a little break back to his homeland in the Punjab region of North West India. Once everything had been booked and arranged, his excitement and anticipation at the thought of the journey ahead couldn't be contained. My father and his mother would be returning home to their small village of Ram Rai Pur, in Nawanshahr.

Having seen Rav and I get married in the company of the English side of his family, my father thought it would now be a good idea to spend some time in the company of the Indian side of his family. He loved the fact that he was going back home. He had always been very proud of his roots and the place where he was born. He never allowed anybody to speak disparagingly about it, nor did he ever hide the pride he felt for his little village of Ram Rai Pur. In the weeks before his departure, he would make sure to mention his trip to every person he would meet. On some occasions he would get very animated about his imminent trip and his excitement would overflow, especially when he had been drinking.

Two days before he was to depart, my father decided to pay one final visit to the younger of his two surviving brothers.

My father, Mohinder Singh Dhindsa, was the youngest of four brothers. The eldest, Sohan Singh Dhindsa, had passed away in August 2002 having succumbed to heart disease and angina. This then left three remaining brothers, my father, Mohan Singh Dhindsa and the second eldest, Major Singh Dhinsa.

Since the wedding, Mohan had fallen further and deeper into the clutches of depression. My father had been trying for months to make him snap out of this dark spell, but nothing would lift his brother's spirits.

My mother and grandmother joined my father during this final visit. It was their hope that they would see Mohan one last time before my father and grandmother departed so that he could pass on any news or good wishes. Also, more importantly, they all wanted to finally get to the bottom of what exactly was making Mohan feel so unhappy. The question, which was on all our minds. 'Why had Mohan's spirits sunk so low? What had got in to him for him to suddenly want to give up on life?'

During that visit, my father spoke to Mohan about his forthcoming trip and asked him if he wanted to pass anything on to their three sisters back in Punjab. Mohan didn't respond to these offers from my father and just kept repeatedly stating, 'I'm not well.' 'Tell us what's wrong then?' my mother asked, but Mohan had by now withdrawn so far into himself that it was impossible for anybody to get any answers out of him. My father began to persist with the same question, but again the only answer Mohan kept replying back with was, 'I'm not well.' This resulted in my father becoming more and more frustrated with himself and his inability to help his brother. My mother then suggested to Mohan that it might be a good idea if he joined his brother and mother on the journey as the little break might allow him to take his mind off the things that were so obviously bothering him here in England. My mother also suggested that he could go back to Ram Rai Pur and do something about his share of land that had been passed down to him by his own father.

In previous years, Mohan had always been very keen on establishing how much of the family land he was allotted alongside his three other brothers.

Mohan wasn't interested in the slightest and again refused the invitation. When my mother and father finally realized that they were not going to get any further information out of him they decided to leave and bid him and his family goodbye.

Things didn't go to plan for my father that day. By all accounts he tried his best to lift his brother's spirits. But my father had left his brother that day feeling unhappy and frustrated. He had failed miserably. That was the last time my father saw his brother alive and unwell. It would be the last spoken words the pair of them ever exchanged.

On Friday, November 18th 2005, my father and grandmother were ready to depart for India. My mother had already packed all the luggage that they required for the trip the night before. The next day my brother had organized a van that a friend of his used, to drop them off at Birmingham International Airport.

Ram Rai Pur Calling

My father and grandmother arrived in Amritsar, Punjab on Saturday November 19th. Their first port of call once they had made their way towards Nawanshahr was to stay at my father's eldest sister's, Simo's, village of Rakhar. They stayed there for the next two days and during this time my father also managed to meet his middle sister, Rivalo, who came to visit them. On the second day the pair of them visited their home village of Ram Rai Pur in Nawanshahr. Once there, he first checked in on his old family home, which now stood vacant. He then went to visit his surviving uncles, my grandfather's brothers, and a few of the village locals.

Ram Rai Pur is only one square mile in area so it did not take my father long to meet all the people he wanted and needed to see. My father and grandmother then went to visit my mother's village of Sahabpur, which is only about a three-minute drive from Ram Rai Pur. In Sahabpur they then met my mother's side of the family and my mother's elderly father, Munsha Singh Thiara who lived with his eldest son, Joginder Singh Thiara and his family.

My father had only been in India for two days when on Monday, November 21st he received a phone call from England that would change all our lives forever.

During this call he was informed that his brother, Mohan, had been involved in a serious accident and that it would be a good idea for him to return home to Derby. After further questioning from my father, it was later revealed in the conversation that his brother had unfortunately died.

At around the same time that this call was being made to India, I was at work. Later on in the day, as I made my way back to Pear Tree, I sensed a cold chill in the air. As I finally arrived home I noticed that the darkness had consumed the remains of the afternoon light. Having parked my car in our driveway, I made my way through the back gate. I was so happy, I couldn't wait to get into the warmth of home and tuck into my sandwich. So with my school bag over my shoulder, I quickened my stride and skipped over the last little step that led to the back door with a huge grin on my face.

I would always skip that last step due to the excitement of finally finishing another long school day, and having returned home.

However, this time I nearly slipped as my foot touched down on the ice that had formed beneath me. Fortunately, I quickly adjusted my balance as I lunged towards the back door. As I looked up, I immediately noticed my sister, Daljinder, at the door to greet me. 'I nearly broke my neck there!' I said to her. 'I wouldn't be saying that' she snapped back. 'Mohna's killed himself!' It wasn't a greeting it was a death knell.

Once I had got inside, I quickly learned from my sister that Mohan had hanged himself. My father's brother had killed himself. Suicide! Suicide? He had quite literally broken his neck. I just had one thought in my mind on hearing this news, 'my poor father'. As the news of his death began to settle into the corners of my mind I could not help but be preoccupied by the thought, 'What a completely selfish person he had been all his life.'

I found out more information from my mother that cast further light on to Mohan's suicide. It turned out that during the previous night, Mohan had wanted to go out for a late evening walk with his wife, Reshmo. However, his youngest son picked up on this strange behaviour and refused to allow his mother to follow his father out of the house. Having not been able to take his wife with him, Mohan then began to walk and walk as far as he could, away from his home on Cromwell Road, Derby. As he did so, in the dark and cold of the night, he managed to cover nearly nine miles until he reached his final destination of Weston Underwood in

Ashbourne, Derbyshire. Mohan had returned to the site of what was once his place of work, Richard Lees Ltd. It was there, the following morning, that his body was found hanging inside one of the buildings and later identified by a cousin of mine, Jujhar Singh Thiara, who just so happened to be working there as an employee of Tarmac Topfloor at the time.

Mohan had decided to end his life by hanging himself using the fabric of his own turban. Of all the places he chose to take his life, he decided to do it at the place where he and his brother spent over a decade working together, side-by-side.

It had only been three days since my father and grandmother had been dropped off at the airport. Knowing my father so well, I knew he would have only one thought in his mind as soon as he was told that his brother had an accident: home.

My father had barely had any time to spend with his family and the local villagers before the call came for him to return. He was also unable to meet his youngest sister, Sisaw. It was initially decided that Mohan's death would be kept from my grandmother, considering her already frail state. So on the day of return, it was decided that it was best to tell her that they were actually going to Jalandhar to get her eyes checked. Later on in the day my father eventually revealed to her that Mohan had a minor accident and that they were actually returning home to England. But I'm sure that even she would have realized that was not the real story and there was something seriously wrong for them to have to come home so suddenly.

After hastily making plans to come home, they made their journey back to Pear Tree on the 21st November.

As soon as my father got that very first call, I'm sure he would have immediately feared the worst. That phone call all but destroyed him there and then. After pressing for further information it would not have taken him long to work out that his brother had really died.

'What must have been going through his mind in those seconds and minutes after hearing the news?' I thought to myself. He must have been in absolute shock. Only he would ever know. It was something that I just could not have comprehended at the time.

Even worse than this must have been the utter desolation he would have felt on the plane journey back. 'What must he have been thinking?' I'm sure that two thoughts would have rested heavily upon his mind: the heartache of losing his brother and the guilt he would have felt that he was unable to do anything to save Mohan's life – the guilt being the most destructive thought of all. For the whole journey back to England, these thoughts must have been the only things passing through his mind. Yet he could not talk to a single soul; not even his own mother. He must have been absolutely eaten up inside.

His first chance to really talk to anybody once arriving in England would have been during the time spent travelling back to Derby in the car. This would have given him a couple more hours to assimilate the news having been told additional details of what had actually happened whilst trying to make sure that my grandmother did not overhear.

Pear Tree Calling

On Tuesday, November 22nd my father and grandmother returned home to England, just four days after departing for India.

I had been sitting in the living room with my mother, Rav and my sister, waiting, when we heard the doorbell ring. We knew immediately that it would be my father and grandmother at the front door. I decided to stay put and let my brother, who was in the front room, answer the door with my mother. After a minute or so my father apprehensively entered the living room with his head bowed. 'You all right Dad?' I asked, as I offered him my hand and then placed my other hand lightly on his back. He returned a gentle nod but not a single word was spoken. I shook my father by the hand; I released my grip and scanned his face for any signs of emotion. It was then that I noticed the sheer devastation in his face, which now looked much darker in appearance. The glow that had emanated from him only a few days earlier had been completely extinguished, forever. It was not the light of the Indian sun but the darkness that had consumed him. I did not say anything else to him after my initial greeting. I really did not know what to say. I could see that he was upset and I did not want to upset him any further. His brother dying was more than enough to occupy his mind. My grandmother then entered the living room. As soon as she saw me, she began to cry. 'Mohan is dead?' she said, half asking, half telling. I gave her a comforting hug as I had no other response.

Over the years, I had noticed that out of all my grandmother's four sons, she seemed to have been the closest to Mohan, even though she had never actually lived with him and his family in Derby. This may have been because of the amount of time she and Mohan had spent in each other's company. When she was alone at our house on Portland Street, Mohan would come around frequently to visit her during the mornings.

After greeting us all, my father left the living room and made his way upstairs. Within half an hour he had freshened up and then decided to make his way to his late brother's house.

My father's face that day was a tragic one. He had lost another brother. However, this time the brother had not gone naturally as Sohan had done so previously. Mohan had decided to take his own life with his own hands. My poor father did not deserve this. 'How could his own brother have put him through this?' This was a thought that refused to leave my mind for many weeks, months and years after Mohan's death.

The following couple of weeks were a very difficult period in my father's life. Every day, without fail, he would go to his brother's house during the grieving period prior to the funeral. Throughout this time, he had all but lost his appetite and was not eating well.

He was now considered to be the head of the family; the head of the Dhindsa family even though he still had one remaining older brother who was still alive at the time.

My father had been the youngest of four brothers. However, the eldest brother, Sohan, had all but passed the authority and responsibility onto my father after his passing. My father knew full well what was expected of him and what he had to do. Up until his death, Sohan was the head of the Dhindsa family, but after his passing my father effectively took over all duties. My father never liked the label, but he was always honoured to carry the responsibility and duty that came with it. Because he was the youngest he would still, on all possible occasions, try to put his two older, surviving brothers before him. Unfortunately, these two brothers were just not cut from the same cloth as my father and Sohan. Growing up I could see that both Major and Mohan were very different in the way they behaved and conducted themselves around other people.

There were many people who visited Mohan's house during the grieving period and a few of them of them indirectly put it across to my father that he was now effectively the head of his whole family. This intensified the burden on my father's shoulders, as well as the toll all of this was having on him. My father now had the extra pressure of not only looking after his own family but Sohan's, Mohan's as well as his final surviving brother, Major and his family. It was a lot to take in and a lot to take on.

Sohan Singh Dhindsa was an elder figure for the Dhindsa families in Derby. When he passed away on Friday, August 9th 2002 it left an enormous hole, not only in my father's life but in my own too. Sohan was my eldest thiah but he was also like a second father to me. He was a good man who also became my best friend. I was heartbroken when he passed away. I was not the only one.

When I was born in September 1979, Sohan and his family were living together with my mother and father at 160 Portland Street in Pear Tree, Derby. The occupants of the house at the time were Sohan, his wife my eldest thiee, Manjit their eldest daughter and Jasbinder their son: a few months after my birth their other daughter, Jastinder, arrived. My sister Daljinder and brother Manjinder would then arrive within three more years to add to the household. That would make ten of us in all, by 1983. So it was no wonder that Sohan and my thiee decided to give up their share of the home to my father and his new family and move out to Cameron Road.

Due to this closeness between both families I effectively had two sets of parents: a big dad, big mum, mum and my father, who I used to call chacha. This was because my cousins would call my father chacha (a father's younger brother): I began to follow suit. It was only when my thiah moved out that I finally began to stop calling my father, chacha. I can still recollect a strange feeling of embarrassment I had when I called my father 'Dad' for the first time.

Sohan was born in 1945 and my father was born in 1954, resulting in a nine-year age gap between them. When my father first arrived in Derby in 1967 he was only 12 years old. In Sohan's final hours of life, he revealed to my father that during their early days in England he had always treated my father as if he was his son.

During the period of mourning after Mohan's passing, I only ever made one visit to his house to pay my respects and offer my condolences to my thiee and his children. I was very reluctant to go. The long school days and the tiredness I felt on returning home initially kept me away. I was also not very keen on taking time out during the afternoon because I would normally use this period for a little rest or a nap. Only after this rest and after I had picked Rav up from the train station would I begin planning for the following day, in the late evening. The thought of taking time out to visit Mohan's house just made me feel even more anxious and uncomfortable.

To further add to my worries, not long after Mohan's death I was informed by the school management that the headmaster would observe one of my lessons. Clearly, recent events did not do anything to increase my confidence or decrease my nerves. The pressure on me began to intensify.

At the time I also honestly felt that visiting Mohan's house would do me no benefit whatsoever. The last thing I wanted to do was go there and sit, silently, for hours on end and listen to the same story being repeatedly told time and time again about how he had died. The inevitable question that would be asked when people would come in to pay their respects is, 'What happened?' I did not want to hear it. I wanted to remain positive. I had no other choice if I wanted to avoid failure at school. I could not afford to be dragged into the darkness of unhappiness.

Or maybe, I just had another pressing, niggling thought that refused to leave my mind. After Mohan's death I felt very angry towards him and because of the anguish he had put my father through. 'Nobody deserved that amount of pain and torment in their life,' I thought to myself. Having to listen to people talk about Mohan in a favourable light after his death did not appeal to me because all I kept thinking about at the time was what a selfish thing he had done and what a selfish person he had been all my life.

I eventually did visit Mohan's house a few days after his death but only because I persuaded myself to believe that the only reason I was attending was to make sure that I did not upset my father any further.

I felt that my father did the best he could do to help his brother, under the circumstances. However, I also recognized that he would forever regret the decision he made to leave his brother so that he could travel to India with their mother. There is no doubt that the following thoughts would have crossed his mind.

If he been in England, in Derby and by his brother's side he could have saved him. Did he give his all? To give your all you would have to give your absolute best. Mohan died: he could not have given his absolute best. He had let Mohan, Sohan, himself and all his family down; most of all, he had let his own father down.

Mohan died and my father had failed. It would have been as simple as that for my father to admit to himself.

From a very early age I began to gradually appreciate the kind of person Mohan was. From hearing stories about him to seeing with my own eyes how he conducted himself; I quickly formed my own impression of him. This was probably another reason why I didn't immediately hurry to his house to mourn his death. I was too aware of his past to want to start hearing stories about what a good man he was in death. But then again maybe there once had been another side to Mohan that I had never got to see. A side that was very different to what he later became and that I later saw. Maybe he had not always been the person he was, in my lifetime. Maybe he had another side to him before I was born. He may not have been the person I thought he was all his life. At the time I didn't care much for either side; all I could think about was my own father and the hurt that his brother's death had caused him. The fact that some people could have changed the way they once behaved in their life was just not on my radar.

Irrelevant of whatever anybody else thought of Mohan, deep down, nothing could change the fact that my father and Mohan were brothers and my father would have always tried his best to look after him. My father was always loyal. Family or friend, he was always there for you. If you shared his friendship, then he was by your side and on your side.

My eldest thiah, Sohan, didn't have the greatest relationship with Mohan. Just before Sohan passed away there had been some friction between Mohan and his brothers as to how my grandfather's plot of land in India should be divided between the four of them. During one particular period, Mohan started to frequently make a fuss about the whole issue, which then caused a build-up of tension amongst the brothers. Mohan always seemed to be a constant thorn in his brothers' side, especially Sohan – the eldest – and my father – the youngest. Mohan would always want to be involved in everything but he would be the last to show his cards, or in most cases, his money when it came to the crunch. It was obvious to us all that he liked to look after his money and material possessions as he would always try to keep a strong grip on his assets and make sure that they were looked after, first and foremost. I also remember the cars he used to buy over the years. He would like to buy the latest model but then always be careful to make sure that he did not clock up too many miles on it. To get around this problem he would have two cars; an expensive model as well as a battered banger, which he would use nearly all of the time. The good car would only ever be taken out on really special occasions. There was no hiding the fact that Mohan liked to cut corners. Unfortunately, on most occasions it was at the expense of his own immediate family.

It was common knowledge in my family that on a couple of occasions Sohan had to literally slap some sense into his younger brother when he tried to get above his station.

Apparently, these slaps were in the days before Mohan had made his conversion to become a baptized Sikh. But even when he did become a baptized Sikh I sometimes felt that his behaviour at times was not befitting of a Sikh. To some people it was an absolute shame what he was reduced to at the end of his life because from what I heard after his death, it seems he was not always the man I thought he was. Apparently, during his younger days before he got married he was quite a character. He used to like looking smart and impressing people with his Mr Cool persona. So maybe this person who I had thought was quite selfish all my life was not the selfish man I thought he was during all of his own life. Maybe it was only after he quit drinking that he transformed into the miser-like character that we all later got to know.

Towards the end of Mohan's life, all that he ever cared for just seemed to dissipate from his existence; even the material possessions had lost all their attraction and charm. He seemed to have given up on everything. He seemed to have given up on life.

During my younger days my father would take me on walks around Pear Tree. On some occasions we would pass the old

Co-Operative Peak bakery, where my father and Mohan used to work together only a few years previously. Sainsbury's and B&Q now occupy the site of the old bakery. I used to love passing by over the bridge and taking in the aroma of the comforting and homely freshly baked bread. As we would look into the distance over the brick wall, we would spot tiny little rabbits jumping in the long grass. He would then tell me stories about the time he used to work there. As well as the story about the trouble he once got himself into when his brother Mohan found himself in some hot water.

This particular incident occurred during one break period when they were both in the canteen of the bakery together. As my father was tucking into his sandwiches, an argument broke out between Mohan and another man. Before my father could do anything to diffuse the situation the other man had thrown a cup of hot tea into Mohan's face and then began to throttle him. My father, upon seeing what was happening to his older brother, grabbed the nearest thing to hand – a stool, which he then swung, striking the man over the head and knocking him out cold. In an attempt to loosen the man's grip around his brother's neck, my father spent a night in a cell at a Derby police station. Thankfully, he was quickly released as the victim, or should that be the attacker, decided not to press any charges. To this day I'm not quite sure what it was all about or who started it. Fortunately, nothing more became of it, although the bakery did reward my father and Mohan with the sack.

It is these acts of loyalty that my father displayed to his family and friends that I am most proud of. However, over the years I felt that sometimes his brother Mohan and other members of the family that he would often help out, would not always reciprocate these selfless acts. This is what annoyed me the most about my father when I was growing up; he would do anything for anyone without hesitation, yet when he needed help, some of these same people he helped were nowhere to be seen. 'Why would he keep going back for more?' I would think to myself. He used to give a lot of his time and kindness, but some people just took advantage of his goodwill. Maybe people just got used to his good nature? My father would never forget these metaphorical slaps in the face. He could never let these thoughts go. The niggling anger in his heart would build up over time and be released during periods of drinking. Yet he still continued to look after his own.

I used to have quite a blunt attitude to loyalty when I was growing up. You were either with me or you weren't. If not, then forget about it. 'I don't need you in my life.' Yet, I could never understand why he could not do the same. Maybe he owed it to his own father to respect the family name by doing all he could to be good no matter how others treated him.

The day before Mohan's funeral was a Monday, and in the last lesson of this particular school day I was going to be observed by the headmaster. For all NQTs, the school's policy was that the headmaster would make at least one lesson observation of all new starters. The Year 7 science lesson that was being observed went reasonably well, I thought, even though I did initially worry about how some of the students might behave during the observation. Fortunately, having the headmaster sitting in the corner, watching on resulted in everyone being on their very best behaviour. How different they would have been had he not been present. It was a good class overall but for a handful of students who would find it really difficult at times to remain focused. I managed to get through it, though, even with all the thoughts and images that were still overshadowing me in relation to all that had occurred in the previous week. It was a great relief to finish the day, especially now that the dreaded headmaster's observation was finally over and done with. Once again, the anxieties and build-up of stress throughout the course of the day were completely overtaken by the euphoric journey home. As I drove home that afternoon I sensed my world becoming a darker place.

Mohan's funeral took place on Tuesday, November 29th 2005. Having initially had serious reservations about showing up, I decided to go with my gut instinct. Although I was still irritated by what he had put my father through, I knew very well that I had to go to his funeral for my father's sake. Deep down, I also knew that if I had not gone I would have regretted it for the rest of my life.

Another reason for my reservation was because I really didn't want to see Mohan's face in his open coffin knowing how he had died. A few years earlier another relation, Kevin Singh Dhindsa had also taken his own life. At the age of 20, he decided to end it all by laying himself under a passing train at Pear Tree Train Station. Although I attended his funeral I decided not to pass his open coffin.

Having worked a half-day at school I decided to finish one lesson early so that I could make my way towards Markeaton

Crematorium just after midday. A lot of people attended Mohan's funeral, which was good to see. During the service I watched on, as my father remained by his brother's side throughout. From the crematorium all the mourners made their way to the Guru Arjan Dev Gurdwara, on Stanhope Street. Mohan had been sent off in honour. At the end of the day I was glad and relieved that I had attended the funeral service, not only for my father but for his beloved brother too.

Mohan's death did not seem to affect me that much at the time. Maybe I was too distracted with school life. Maybe I was too distracted by my father's own upset and pain. It could be said that I didn't show much emotion. However, the night before the funeral I did shed a tear or two. Maybe I had finally become overwhelmed by Mohan's passing. Although, I would have immediately convinced myself that the tears were actually for my poor father and not for his brother. At the time I had not given too much thought to what Mohan must have been going through when he decided to end his life. All I could think about was the consequences of his actions and what he had put my father through. I did have sympathy for his three sons and his wife. She had also been suffering illness for some time before his death. I did feel sadness towards Mohan but these feelings were clouded by more prevalent thoughts of what a truly selfish act he had committed. 'Selfish right till the end,' I initially thought at the time.

My resentment towards Mohan was not to subside either when a few days after his funeral his wife came to our house. My father, Mohan's wife and myself were the only three people in the living room when she turned to my father and said in Punjabi, 'You will also die too.' I remember looking at my father just after she had spoken. He didn't reply. We both knew she was not well. But still, what a thing to say. I did not forget the look on my father's face as he seemed to accept the inevitably of what he had just heard.

Mohan's wife had been suffering from a schizophrenia-like condition for a number of years. Maybe this was also another major reason why Mohan's overall health began to decline so alarmingly towards the end of his life, which then lead to his own eventual death.

My father had spent his whole life looking after his family. He tried his utmost to break the shackles of Mohan's depression, but it was to no avail. My father would have done anything for his brother, Mohan. But the most important thing he could have ever done for him was the one thing he could not: save his life.

Chapter 3: The Gathering Storm
The Black Dog Prowls

In the subsequent days and weeks after Mohan's funeral, my father's whole outlook on life changed dramatically. As the New Year of 2006 approached, he began to progressively become more downbeat as the impact of his brother's death led to a noticeable detriment in his well-being. Around the festive season of 2005 I was to witness just how quickly things had deteriorated for him. From almost glowing a couple of months previously to now being reduced to a dark shadow of his former self.

December 15th 2005 was my father's fifty-first birthday, so Rav and my sister tried to make an occasion of it. In an attempt to lighten his mood, they decided to place some magic relighting candles on his birthday cake. However, when he tried to blow them out without success, he became very frustrated. When the joke was revealed to him he was not at all amused. Watching on, I could almost sense his disappointment having once again failed to accomplish something that should have been fairly simple. On this day, like many before, he clearly gave us all the strong impression that he had effectively stopped caring for occasions like this.

In his mind he saw no purpose for celebrating anything in his life any longer. He was just not at all interested. He also began to complain about how the smoke from the candles was stinging his eyes. By now he had become so withdrawn that this new negative and distorted attitude towards his life led him to become more and more irritable as time went on.

I really could not stand this behaviour that he was displaying towards us all. At the time I was still having my own difficulties at school with the management and misbehaving students. For this reason, at home, when he behaved in such a manner I didn't like to be in his company. The last thing I wanted to do when I returned home having finished a long day at work was to be subjected to his irritability. I just wanted to relax and switch off when I got home, but it was impossible for me to do so.

This was all a far cry from the same day, one year previously, when he had celebrated his fiftieth birthday. On that day, my father had returned home from work at the Chaucer Bakery in a very excited state. He then began to tell us all how surprised and a little embarrassed he was to have seen his birthday notice pinned on the canteen notice board. My sister had booked the notice a few days earlier in the

Derby Evening Telegraph. His colleagues had then stumbled across his youthful picture and shared it for all to see. My mother, who was in the process of cooking, then reminded him that they were expecting visitors from Leicester, so she ordered him to freshen up before they arrived. When he finally came downstairs having taken a shower he entered the front room and to his surprise there we all were, waiting for him. The room was filled with his family, including my eldest phua and phuffhur from India and my eldest thiee Chindar, Sohan's wife. Also with us that day included my cousin, Jastinder, her brother, Jasbinder, and his wife, as well as Satnam and his wife, Natasha. Many photos were taken that day, including one of my father and myself.

A year later he would barely crack a smile.

I felt for my father but there just seemed to be nothing I could do for him. In the previous days and weeks, he had begun to complain about pains in his head. He would tell my mother that at times the pain was so intense that it was almost as if someone was striking him with a hammer from within his head. Whether this could have been a result of conflicting messages and emotions in his mind or his earlier brain injury in February 1993, we would never know. When we did ask him to elaborate on what he was feeling he would on most occasions quickly close up and not respond any further. Sometimes when he did try to explain he would find it very difficult to communicate and put his thoughts across. A problem my father had all his life. He was just unable to express himself clearly enough for us to understand what he was going through.

Time and time again he would grumble about the pains he was feeling, but as we could not see anything physically wrong with him there was nothing we could say or do for him to put his mind at ease. Due to this apparent lack of empathy we displayed, he might then have concluded that maybe it really was all just happening in his mind. Unfortunately, the mind was an area that we just could not access nor could he comprehend.

He began to make visits to his GP very soon after Mohan's death. A mental health therapist was then consulted who decided to put him on a course of medication when it became clear that he too was now suffering from depression. He was also told that due to the strong side effects the tablets could provoke in him he would have to stop drinking alcohol too.

A storm was gathering and he knew he would have to face it all, alone and single-handed if need be: just like he had always done. After losing his brother, Mohan, I feel the stress and pressure that he felt in trying to keep things together for his family began to gradually overwhelm him. The enormity of trying to live up to the expectation began to overshadow him. He missed his brothers terribly as well as his own father who had passed away in January 1997. His family was breaking apart right before his eyes and he knew full well that there was nothing he could physically do to prevent it from occurring.

My father always liked a good drink, whether it was a quiet casual one at home or a noisy few in a social setting. In the evenings he loved nothing more than to settle down in front of the fire with a garish bottle of alcopop. During these occasions he would become quite jovial whilst sipping away on the lurid contents of the bottles, which he used to have stocked in the pantry. On most occasions, during these periods of drinking his mood would mellow. 'Fair enough, he was a bit drunk but at least he was happy,' I used to think. However, this began to change when his brother passed away and sometimes his anger and frustrations would simmer to the surface instead. When he was finally told to give up drinking for good due to the medication he was taking, the alcohol that he had used for many years to let off some steam was no longer an outlet for his feelings to be released. Consequently, his mood became darker and his spirits shrank. As the 2006 New Year came and went my father quit drinking for good, or in his case, for bad.

I had given up on drinking a few years previously, around the end of January 1999 during the early months of my university life in Leicester. When my father quit, I was initially quite happy about it but as time went on his mood and self-esteem began to drop lower and lower. I subsequently then began to wish that he would resume drinking, if only to release the anguish that would build up within him. Without the drink he was unable to express and vent his anguish.

I guess it was also unfortunate that I had given up on the drink when I had too because in the years that passed I was unable to use the act of social drinking to develop a closer relationship with him. Before I had given up drinking, it was not possible to have shared a drink with him anyway. The reason for this was because I only really began drinking when I was seventeen, during my time at Mackworth College and I had all but given up by the time I was nineteen when I was at the University of Leicester. So, because of that short time period I had never really had the opportunity to drink socially with him. The only time we ever did spend any time in each other's company, when drink was involved, was when we went to the pub or a special occasion, such as a wedding. During these occasions I would always try and sit with him or my eldest thiah, Sohan. If I was not able to sit with my father, I would always have him in my peripheral vision in case anything ever happened to him when he had drunk too much. I wish I had spent more time in his company over the years, but drinking was not my scene any more. To get smashed out of my head for no apparent reason or benefit was just something I felt was totally counterproductive to the person I wanted to be. I just did not want to entertain that thought any more.

During my college years and then my very early university days there were only ever a handful of occasions when I really did get totally drunk and out of my mind. I quickly realized that it was almost impossible to put your point across when you'd had a drink. This was because when other people saw you were drunk they were then more likely to not take you seriously or listen to whatever you had to say and if you were in the company of other drunks you had no chance of being taken seriously at all as your views would have no doubt been dismissed entirely. The biggest problem I always had with drinking, though, was the Jekyll and Hyde nature of it, whereby perfectly good and decent people, when sober, would become quite unrecognizable in their character and manner when drunk. This was definitely not the kind of persona I wanted to show to others. I just wanted to be myself at all times. In my mind, I felt drink just led to another persona, a fake persona totally against my nature and the person I am.

I gave up drinking because it was my intention to be myself at all times: what you saw was what you got and expected. I do know that even during my most inebriated periods, I always had some awareness of what I was doing, even if my legs didn't. But the amount of times I've heard people saying that they have had no memory of what happened the night before just didn't sit right with me. All it suggested to me was that the drink was a great foil, to lie and to deceive, most of all to be dishonest. I felt that saying you had no memory of an incident after a bad experience was just an excuse to hide behind the alcohol. I just found it quite impossible to believe and if it was the case that you had no memory, then maybe it's not a good idea to be in that state of mind ever again. For this reason, I felt sometimes people would take advantage of the drink and do things that they knew they would never attempt or get away with when sober. I really did not like this aspect of drinking, and the trickery and deception that came with it. The dishonesty, hate and pain people inflicted on others is why I didn't want any part of it any longer.

On many occasions, I would see my father getting very frustrated with himself and others around him when he was under the influence of drink. As he would try to explain himself, I would notice how people around him would brush him off, assuming it was just the drink talking. However, had they actually listened to what he was saying they would have realized that on a majority of occasions he made absolutely perfect sense. In my father's case, on most occasions a drunk man's words were indeed a sober man's thoughts. Unfortunately for my father, even when he was sober he would sometimes still have the same problem in relation to expressing himself clearly without getting agitated in the process. 'Why would he drink if it caused him such difficulty like this? Maybe it was just his way of letting go and releasing some steam,' I would think to myself.

As a child I never liked my father drinking and I would become increasingly upset and concerned for him when he would drink too much. On these occasions the quantity of drink inside would result in him becoming quite incapable of looking after himself, never mind my mother, my siblings or myself.

It makes me think back to the early days when, as a family, we would have to go to weddings together. At these weddings he would get very drunk and I would then begin to worry about whether we would all be able to get home safely. Sometimes he would get so drunk that I would try to keep my eye on him so that he didn't fall or stumble into anything. Looking back, I feel that it was an unfortunate undertaking for someone as young as myself to play the role of a carer for a supposed grown-up, who also just so happened to be my father.

Some of the most worrying experiences as a child, in relation to my father's drinking habit, were when he would try to drive our family back home in the car whilst being totally drunk. Fortunately, he always managed to get us home in one piece, as well as miraculously avoid any police intervention in the process. The feeling of discomfort in the pit of my stomach on the long drive, all the way back, is something I've never forgotten. On some very rare occasions he would get so intoxicated that he would be unable to even lift his head, never mind drive. On these occasions my mother would then have to drive us all home in her bare feet because she couldn't drive in her heels. The added thought of my mother trying to drive us home was even more terrifying. Although my mother did have a driving license and could drive, she was never really too confident in her own abilities as a driver or her ability to work out which route was the best way home. During these times, when my mother would drive, my father would be slumped in the front passenger seat and every now and again he would lift his head to give my mother some directions whilst biting at his bottom lip. As he would do this, my mother would throw some insults his way as they argued amongst themselves as to how drunk my father really was and how displeased she was that she had to drive us all back home. This display of childishness would also keep my younger sister and brother quite amused in the back of the car. I was never amused. The long and painful journey home would also take forever because my father would constantly need to take toilet breaks at the service stations when he would shout, 'coffee'. I really didn't like seeing my father in this state. He wasn't an alcoholic, he just happened to get very drunk on occasions like this because he could never refuse someone's hospitality. To refuse would be like disrespecting the other person, or even worse that these other people would think badly of him and his family. That was just the way he thought and was brought up to behave.

Drinking and driving was obviously not a wise thing to do. I learnt this valuable lesson at a very young age. I'm not making excuses for my father and my people but that was Punjabi culture back then and unfortunately, on occasions, still is now. It was a very dangerous, silly and selfish thing to do and something that I feel is totally unacceptable. Any parent continuing to do so in this day and age is an absolute disgrace, in my opinion.

Many years later, after I passed my driving test my father once put me in the same uncomfortable situation as he did my mother all those years previously. I let it pass once but quickly put my foot down when I thought he might try it on again. I told him, quite clearly, that I would not be used as his personal chauffeur so that he could get drunk and then use me to drive us all back home. Especially if I was still not the most confident driver in the world. I wasn't trying to be selfish, you could say I just hated being taken for a ride and I finally knew exactly how my mother felt when she had been put in the same situation.

To this day I very rarely go to Punjabi weddings. I don't mind going to the actual wedding ceremony in the Gurdwara, but I try and avoid the party at all costs.

Maybe they remind me too much of my father and the memories of the past. Maybe it's because when I'm sitting alone and bored out of my mind, I sometimes feel the urge to raise my head and have a quick look around to catch his eye and see him smile again; to make sure that he is ok.

On the rare occasions I do go to a Punjabi wedding I actually enjoy sitting alone in silence at the Gurdwara. However, I become really uncomfortable when people around me chatter or try to talk to me. In my opinion, Gurdwara halls should not be places where you should engage in conversation. I find it extremely rude and disrespectful, especially when the Guru Granth Sahib is being recited. I have the opposite problem in the party venue. Due to the incessant loud noise pumped out at intolerable decibels, it is almost impossible to have a proper and meaningful conversation with anyone. It is completely unnecessary in my opinion. Why Indian weddings must include excessive quantities of drink and very loud music is beyond me. It is certainly not my idea of having fun. I preferred the old days and the bhangra tunes of yesteryear.

The University of Leicester

In late September 1998, my father and I set off for Leicester, where I would spend the next three years of my life studying for a BSc in Physics with Astrophysics at the University of Leicester. It was perfect for me in terms of its location as it wasn't too far from home and not too close either. I had just celebrated my nineteenth birthday and it would be the first time in my life that Pear Tree, Derby would not be my permanent home.

On entry into my new room at U1, Mary Gee Houses on Ratcliffe Road, my father and I began to quickly transfer all my belongings from his burgundy Ford Escort Eclipse. It was a surreal moment as for the second time in my life it felt like my father was dropping me off for my first day at school. Just like he had done at Pear Tree Infants about fifteen years previously.

On that day just like this, the butterflies in my stomach returned knowing that my father would be leaving me once again, but this time to fend for myself as an adult. My father and I were just about to explore the rest of my block, when there was a knock on my door. Three young men came into my little room to greet me. Neeraj was the first to introduce himself with a handshake. 'Hi I'm Nij,' he said. 'Hi, my name's Kal,' I replied. Ather then shook my hand, 'Short for Khalid?' he asked. 'No! Kalwinder Singh Dhindsa,' I replied. 'Nice to meet you Kal, my name is Ather Ul-Haq Sarwar, At for short.' Finally, Jaskirat introduced himself with a handshake, 'Call me Jas.' I then introduced them all to my father who stood beside me as further handshakes were exchanged. My new friends then left and said they would return in half an hour so that we could then further explore our surroundings together. Having spent a few more minutes with my father making sure that everything had been transferred from the car into my room he decided it was the right time for him to head back to Derby. As he was about to leave he pulled out his wallet and handed me some money. On saying goodbye to each other we shook hands. Strangely, up to that point it was the first time in my life that we had ever shaken hands. He then told me that he would return to collect me the following Friday so that I could spend the weekend in Pear Tree.

In terms of drinking, within the first few weeks of my time at the University of Leicester I had seen and done it all as well as lost the t-shirt. My whole initial experience just seemed to revolve around alcohol and getting drunk. As the New Year of 1999 approached, I began to drink less and less until eventually on January 27th 1999 I quit – full stop. I was nineteen years, four months and fourteen days old and I'd realized that drinking was just a massive waste of money and time.

When people now ask me why I gave up drinking, they assume that it must have been because I had ONE really bad experience. In fact, it was a collection of incidents that changed my ways; two in particular. During these early university days, I unfortunately, through no fault of my own, managed to get myself involved in a few unsavoury altercations. The first incident occurred in Leicester and the second, in Derby. On both occasions my friends at the time got themselves into a bit of trouble that I had no choice but to involve myself in too.

Leicester Royal Infirmary

In my first week at Mary Gee Houses I began making new friends. As the days went on, new circles of friends emerged which increased with further additions from other halls of residence. In late November it was decided that we would all get together and meet up at the Hangar nightclub on Yeoman Street in Leicester City Centre for a night out.

On that particular Wednesday evening I was already familiar with most of the people I was going out with. Once inside the nightclub, I gradually began to lose myself in all the alcohol I had drank earlier. This then resulted in me making an uncharacteristic move towards the dance floor. Something I would never have done whilst sober. Being very self-conscience, I had always hated dancing and throwing myself into the limelight. After an hour or so the group of people I had initially entered the nightclub with were finally joined by more people.

As I continued to try and make out that I knew what I was doing on the dance floor, my attention was drawn to a shaft of light that pierced through the darkness behind me. As I turned to get a better look, I noticed a group of young men that I didn't recognise, burst out of the toilets and then down the stairs. The door quickly closed behind them and the shaft of light quickly vanished into the darkness. However, as soon as it disappeared it reappeared just as quickly and my attention was once again drawn towards the door. However, this time I just about recognized the first person who had come out, followed quickly by another.

On my first visit to the University of Leicester campus during Freshers' Week I had made friends with a fellow student, Ranbir, who studied Computer Science. Earlier on, during the day of the Hangar's night out he had introduced me to his friend, Sukh.

Ranbir and Sukh both lived in the same accommodation block as neighbours at Digby Hall and they shared the same Bharat coach when they would return home towards London. Between us we decided that my group of friends would join with Ranbir's small group of friends at the Hangar nightclub later in the evening. On that night Ranbir and Sukh were accompanied to the nightclub by Pav and Aman.

I quickly recognized the first person as Sukh and the second person behind him as Pav. Rather unsettlingly, in that split second I also noticed that Sukh had quite obviously been glassed. Blood was now streaming from his face and dripping down onto his Argentina football jersey. As Sukh's large frame stumbled out of the men's toilets he then began to give chase to his attackers, quickly followed by Pav.

As this was all cracking off, Ranbir and Aman had been buying drinks at the bar in the back of the club. As soon as they saw Sukh they realized that something was seriously wrong so they quickly dropped their drinks and left in hot pursuit of Sukh and Pav. All four of them were now making their way down the stairs and out of the club.

All of this occurred very quickly as I looked on from my position on the dance floor, but in my drunken state it all seemed to be happening very slowly.

Just before the incident took place I had been with my own group of friends on the dance floor and was a little bit detached from Ranbir and his friends. However, as soon as I noticed what was happening I had a split second to make a decision and react to what I had just seen. I knew very well that if I left it any longer to make my decision, my drunken state of mind would no doubt have tried to convince me that I didn't really see what had occurred. But I knew exactly what had happened as I had seen it all with my own eyes. Drunk or not, I wasn't going to lie to myself just to keep out of any potential trouble that Ranbir's friends had now gotten themselves involved in. I liked Ranbir and I could see that he and his friends were now in some serious trouble. In that seemingly long and drawn out moment I knew I had to make my decision. 'Do I leave my group of friends and follow Ranbir's friends out or do I stay on the dance floor?' It was an easy decision to make. There was absolutely no way I was going to pretend to myself that I hadn't seen anything. Having seen Sukh's face in such an awful state, I knew that he would need to get immediate medical attention. I made my decision without any further hesitation. I stepped off the dance floor and followed them all out, down the stairs and out of the club.

My fellow U-block residents, Neeraj and Jaskirat had first introduced Ranbir to me. For some reason I have always believed that Ranbir was wearing a cream coloured turban on our first meeting. Something he has always vehemently denied. Maybe it was a cream shirt he was wearing or a cream bag that he was holding. I'm not sure, but the confusion still amuses us to this day. Ranbir was always a chameleon-like figure. Earlier on during the day of the Hangar's night out, Ather and I noticed two suspicious characters sharing a drink from a Bacardi bottle just outside U-block. It was only when the shorter of the two called out my name that I realized it was Ranbir. I hadn't recognized him because he'd decided not to wear his turban. Instead, he was wearing a blue and white patterned bandana with his hair dangling loose. He was quite obviously trying to emulate Jazzy B, the Punjabi bhangra singer (Not Jazzie B the founding member of Soul II Soul). He would have pulled it off had he not been squinting like a mole because his contact lenses were causing him such irritation. Ranbir then introduced Ather and myself to his taller friend, 'This is Sukh, he lives with me,' he said. Sukh put his hand out and said 'All right?' as Ather and I then took it in turns to shake his hand. He then took a long drag of his cigarette as he scanned us both up and down. He then looked away to blow his cigarette smoke out from the corner of his mouth. At this point I noticed Sukh's immaculate Argentina football jersey and his incredibly white Ellesse trainers that he was carefully trying not to drop any cigarette ash on.

On seeing the damage to Sukh's face, I just wanted to make sure that he was ok and that Ranbir and his friends would not get themselves into any further trouble. All five of us were now making our way down the stairs, through the front entrance doors and then out of the club.

As I made my way out of the front door, the cold chill of the outside air immediately hit my face. A fraction of a second later I was then hit again, but this time it was by the closed fist of one of Sukh's attackers. It was certainly not my intention to get involved in a fight when I left the club to follow my new friends out, but that is exactly the situation I now found myself in. I had no idea there would be a welcoming party for us all. As soon as I had stepped out onto the pavement two of these attackers had set upon me; I was not expecting it at all. The first punch came with a ring attached to a fist, which crunched straight into my right temple. I wobbled but did not fall; a split second later I was pushed to the ground by the other attacker. I quickly got up having avoided any further strikes as they tried to stick their boots into me. I hardly had any time to think, but I quickly recognized that I needed to regain my senses and get out of this situation otherwise I too would find myself in the same predicament as Sukh. Back on my feet now, having quickly sobered up, I looked around to see that Sukh, Pav and Ranbir were also involved in scuffles too. We had all been quickly set upon by about five or six young men who had originally left the club after attacking Sukh and then waited outside for us. A couple more people had also joined in the mêlée after they had seen what had originally cracked off inside. Sukh was now on the ground, getting a good kick-in. As the rest of us pushed our attackers away, we all turned our attention to Sukh and rushed towards him. As we charged, his attackers dispersed and gave Sukh some valuable seconds to get back on his feet and out of harm's way. At this point I noticed that Aman had now also joined us.

Once Sukh was on his feet we were all able to make our way further down the road. As I ran past the last of our attackers one final boot was swung in my direction, and it brushed against my hip. Having regrouped, we decided immediately that Sukh needed to get down to the hospital as soon as possible. He was still bleeding, but some of the blood was now drying on his face. It was obvious that he had been targeted because of his large frame and demeanour. As I carefully scanned him up and down, I first noticed how badly his face was cut up. I then noticed his bloodied Argentina football jersey and then finally as I looked down at his feet I was shocked to see the incredibly red Ellesse trainers he was now wearing. I too was bleeding after taking the initial punch to the side of my head. Although I felt a stinging pain I was still buzzing with the adrenaline rushing through my body and out of my mouth. Pav then suddenly realized that I too was in their company, because of all the noise I was making. At this point they all burst out laughing, with the exception of Sukh who was unable to do so. As they continued to laugh at me, none of them could understand how and why I had managed to get myself involved in their punch-up. Only then was it pointed out to me that I was bleeding as I touched the side of my head with my finger, and felt the trickle of warm blood slowly making its way down my face and neck. Once we had reached a safe distance from the nightclub we stopped walking and called for an ambulance. After a few minutes it arrived, and Sukh was taken to the hospital. Now that he was in safe hands the rest of us made plans to join him at the Leicester Royal Infirmary to make sure that he was ok.

Nobody else in my original group of friends had followed me out of the nightclub that night. Had Ather chosen to join us all that night, I have no doubt he would have followed me out too, but he was not well and decided to rest at home.

Although, he did make his own way down to the hospital in his red VW Polo, after I had called him to let him know about what had occurred.

After everything that had happened Pav, Ranbir and Aman had got away with zero to minor scratches. But for the first time in my life I required a few stitches for the cut to the side of my head. However, this was insignificant compared to the amount of stitches Sukh received.

I later learned that the reason I had not initially seen Aman when the fighting first kicked off outside was because he had briefly stopped at the cloakroom to collect Sukh's jacket. Sukh had asked Aman to collect it for him just before he stepped out of the nightclub to pursue his attackers. Pav, Ranbir and myself didn't need to stop at the cloakroom as we had all gone out that night without jackets. It was only after Aman had stepped outside that he too was set upon. In the exchange of kicks and punches he managed to lose his green pager, which fell out of his pocket. To further add to Sukh's misery, as well as Aman's immense irritation, Aman then also had Sukh's expensive jacket ripped from his grasp in the scuffles outside.

I doubt Ranbir or any of his friends ever expected me to follow them out that night. Why would they? They hardly knew me, but I made my decision and I stood by it. It was an honest and correct decision. Although I may not have fought off the attackers as well as I could have, I am sure of one thing; just being there as another body to be pummelled, saved my new friend, Sukh, from receiving any further strikes to his body and face. 'So be it. We were all safe. No one died,' I remember thinking to myself as I waited to be stitched up in the hospital.

The incident at the Hangar's nightclub was reported to the police during the early hours of Thursday morning. All five of us were then interviewed at our separate halls of residence, however Ranbir decided to do his interview with me at Mary Gee Houses. Quite wonderfully, a police officer was quickly dispatched to meet with Ranbir and myself about the attack on Sukh. 'What a fantastic response,' we both thought. What followed, though, shocked me to the core when I realized the real reason for the prompt police response. We both thought that the police were going to ask us about our incident. However, what they really wanted to investigate was another incident that occurred not long after ours, regarding another young man who was also in the club at the same time as us.

As our interview began, Ranbir and myself were immediately shown a photo of this young Asian man's face. We were then asked if we knew who he was. We studied the picture carefully. 'No, we did not,' we both replied. We were then told the name of the young man and that he had lost his life in the early hours of the morning after falling from a bridge in the city centre. At that point, neither of us could bear to look at the picture any more. But the image had been forever imprinted in our minds. He looked to be the same age as us, but unlike us, he was now dead. We told the police officer that we were very sorry to hear about his death but we knew nothing about this other incident and therefore were unable to help with their investigations. After hearing about how the poor young man had tragically died, only then did we both realize what a lucky escape we all had that day.

My greatest frustration after the Hangar's incident was that once again, and twice in the space of as many months, I had damaged my Ericsson GA628. The attacker, who had aimed that last boot at me as we were making our way down the road, had in the process snapped my mobile's aerial off.

A further annoyance the next morning was the stinging pain on the side of my head where my newly acquired stitches were now pulling at my skin. I later found out that I had a hairline fracture of the skull. All said and done, I definitely saw the stars come out during that Hangar's night out. Unfortunately, though, it was not through the Manor Road Observatory telescope that I normally observed them through.

On the Friday afternoon my father picked me up from Leicester, as he would always do every week, during my first year. By now I wasn't in any great deal of pain but the stitches did still sting a bit. Fortuitously, they were all located on a part of my head where they were not visible to the naked eye as my hair and baseball cap covered them up very well. I have no doubt that had my mother seen them on any other part of my face she would have slapped me first then asked questions later. Fortunately, nobody noticed them. I had got away with it and a few days later I had them removed; the stinging pain subsided.

To this day you can still see the scar when I cut my hair really short, it's situated on the right side of my head just near the temple, close to my ear. A hairline fracture indeed, a feature that will remain with me forever like the dimple on my right cheek when I smile and the little hole on the top of my right earlobe, which I was born with.

One final thing I needed to make sure I dealt with before it landed me in any more hot water was the need to get my bloodied, blue shirt washed as soon as possible. I offered this task to my cousin, Satnam. In the process, I also had to reveal to him what had happened for it to be in such a state. I presented him with a plastic ASDA carrier bag with my shirt within it and he told me he would have it washed for me within the week. Satnam was the only family member I told about the incident. Nobody else knew what had happened. I even kept it from my cousin, Kully and her husband, Harry, in Syston. I didn't want to worry them.

Kully was the middle daughter of my eldest English mamma. She married Harry in October 1989 and then moved from Derby to live in Syston, Leicestershire with Harry and his parents. She had lost her mother, my eldest English mammi, Harbans, in April 1995. By the time I began university, they were already parents to two young daughters. When I was younger, I always got the impression that Kully didn't like me much, because of the way she would look and shout at me for no apparent reason. However, when I began university in

1998, Kully and Harry always made me feel very welcome when I visited them at their home. They looked after me very well and invited me around regularly, to eat with them. On some occasions I even stayed overnight. It was through Kully and Harry that I was later introduced to my future wife, Rav.

About three weeks after the Hangar's incident, when I was back in Derby again, I asked Satnam if I could have my shirt back. As he sheepishly handed it back over to me, I noticed that it was still in the same plastic carrier bag I had originally put it in. On closer inspection, I realized that he had not even touched it, never mind washed it. So I snatched it back off him and decided to take a huge risk. I handed it over to my mother to wash instead. 'Whose blood is this on your shirt?!' she asked in Punjabi. I then began to tell her how I had lent it to Satnam. His mum then washed it and put it on his washing line. However, Nazim the builder then cut his hand in the garden. So he used my shirt to stop the bleeding. My mother accepted my explanation without any question.

I once trusted my washing to my good friend, Ather. On one particular occasion at university, he happily agreed to wash my clothing in with his bed sheets. However, about a week later he got up early one morning and found my underpants tucked inside his duvet cover which he had snuggled into the night before. In a fit of rage, he swiftly jumped out of his bed and burst into my room, next door, where I was still sleeping. Having been abruptly awoken, I was smacked in the face by my newly found underpants. As we both chuckled, I thanked him for their safe return. He knew they were mine straight away. My chaddis were unique.

Not long after the Hangar's incident, Sukh and Ranbir decided to move away from their original Digby halls and join Ather in H-Block at Mary Gee Houses. I doubt their decision had anything to do with the pair of them wanting to be any closer to Ather, Jaskirat and myself. I'm guessing it was more down to the fact that by now Sukh had found himself a new girlfriend who would look after him and who just so happened to live within walking distance.

Derbyshire Royal Infirmary

Another violent confrontation that took place not long after the Hangar's incident occurred whilst I was in Derby during my Christmas break.

It was a Friday night and a large group of us had decided to go out to celebrate a friend's birthday. I was quite familiar with most of them because a few months earlier I had spent a few occasions in their company during my time as a student at Mackworth College in Derby.

That night, I once again found myself in the wrong place at the wrong time. However, after the previous incident in Leicester I had become a little more aware of the dangers that lay ahead of me if I was not fully switched on.

On this evening I really did not feel comfortable with the company I was in as I could sense something sinister in the air. I was definitely not the kind of person who would deliberately go out to look for trouble, but once again I found myself deep in it. Having gone from place to place during the night in our large group we finally settled upon the Eclipse Club, on Babbington Lane. To be honest, by then I was quite bored with it all and I just wanted to go home. But I chose to stick around for the sake of a couple of close friends. As the hours ticked slowly by, nearly all the people in the group that I had gone in with began to get progressively more and more drunk. As I had decided to hold back on my drinking I was now effectively babysitting my closest friends. Fortunately, another close friend had already gone home earlier in a taxi, completely legless, as he had foolishly gulped down a whole can of super-strength Skol Super. This left me only having to look after two of them. One of them, was by now almost paralytic and the other was drunk too, but less so. This then led to the inevitable; the very drunk one then decided to get into an altercation with someone else inside the club.

Fortunately, this 'someone else' that my very drunk friend had managed to get himself into an altercation with was somebody I had known from my old school days at Village Community School. Unfortunately, he was also heavily under the influence of drink or maybe something even more potent. As the atmosphere between the two groups of friends began to get more and more heated, a few attempts were made to cool things down by mutual friends on both sides. I also tried to calm down my fellow Village alumnus but it immediately became evident to me that he didn't recognize me when he began to threaten me too. I didn't take too kindly to this as I shook my head in disappointment and then stepped backwards, away from him.

A few seconds later the two of them finally met head on, reminiscent of rutting stags clashing their antlers together. A couple of bouncers who had been watching on from a few feet away then rushed in to separate the pair. Having intervened, one of the bouncers began to usher my very drunk friend out through the side fire exit. I had wanted to leave the club for some time now so this was an absolute blessing in disguise for me as I happily watched him being escorted out. My other drunk friend and I then followed our very drunk friend out through the side exit to make sure he had some company on the other side. Once outside, I tried to calm the pair of them down in the hope that all three of us could now start making our way home. I was fighting a losing battle though. There was no way we were going home early as both of them wanted to go straight back into the club – we were celebrating a birthday, after all.

As it dawned on my very drunk friend that there was no way he would be allowed back in he began to get even more aggressive and angry at being thrown out and having his night ruined by my fellow alumnus. Both my friends now began to get really worked up in the realization that their night was over. The three of us were now alone outside in the cold whilst the large group we had initially entered the club with remained oblivious, inside.

Having learnt my lesson from a few weeks previously, I felt quite empowered that I had decided not to drink so heavily that night.

A year before, the three of us had visited the Showcase Cinema in Foresters Leisure Park to watch 'Tomorrow Never Dies'. In preparation for watching the latest James Bond offering, we made sure to buy our tickets a couple of hours in advance whilst still sober. As we were celebrating a birthday there was only one thought in our minds. Get smashed. With my ticket placed safely in my trouser pocket we began the evening with a few drinks in the Oast House. We then moved on to the stronger stuff, gulping down straight shots of Bacardi along the short walk down to the cinema. Once inside and seated, it was only a matter of minutes before the evening's excesses caught up with me. No longer able to focus on the screen and completely intoxicated with drink, my head flopped back and I was knocked-out drunk. To this day I still don't remember anything about the film. I do however vaguely remember spotting a Pavarotti-like figure onscreen, on seeing him I then began trying to sing Nessun Dorma. I also remember swearing at Pierce Brosnan and then getting into a disagreement with someone behind me who kept telling me to shut up because of the noise I was making. When the film finally ended my two friends escorted me home.

Fortunately, I only lived around the corner. Unfortunately, my legs had all but deserted me. As I stumbled my way down Portland Street I realized that I had lost my baseball cap and became extremely irritated. When I finally reached home and rang the doorbell, my mother was waiting for me with a slap. She was not impressed. Having sat down and put the TV on, my mother then began laying into me because of the state I was in. I was then suddenly overcome by sadness that was linked to the death of my eldest English mammi who had passed away a couple of years previously. When I woke up the next morning, I felt quite ashamed of myself; I didn't know whether I was genuinely upset about her death or whether it was the drink that was playing around with my emotions. I began questioning my honesty and integrity, as it seemed that these feelings had been flushed out with the drink. To add to this, I was further ashamed because of the abuse I had directed at Pierce Brosnan. To finally cap it all off, I eventually realized what I had done with my baseball cap. As a series of flashbacks from the previous night came trickling back, I recalled Pavarotti, Brosnan and then what I had done with my cap just before I passed out. Prior to the film beginning I had astutely taken it off and shoved it down my coat sleeve so that I wouldn't lose it later in the night.

All three of us had been outside the club for a good few minutes now. In my elevated sober state, I again suggested that now would be a good time to make our way home because there was no way we were going to be let back in.

Unbeknown to me and my other two friends, when the three of us left the club, the alumnus that my very drunk friend had had the altercation with inside, had also been ushered out via another door. He was now also just as disgruntled to have had his night ruined. All four of us were now outside together and it didn't take long until we all eventually caught his eye. I first spotted my fellow alumnus as he was rummaging for something in a large wheelie bin, in an alleyway. As he walked towards me I noticed the two-foot long piece of wooden carpet grip that he had now acquired, and was now obviously on his way to show us. Having met each other's gaze, once again both of the warring parties confronted each other. 'Here I go again,' I muttered.

Since I knew of my fellow alumnus from my school days I didn't expect him to want to make any trouble with me whatsoever. So I got in between the two of them to make sure nothing else happened outside. However, neither of them wanted me to intervene as they both took it in turns to keep pushing me away. As they continued to square up to each other, like they had done inside the club, I sensed immediately that it wouldn't be long before the first blows would be exchanged.

Once again I found myself in an undesirable position; do I turn my back on the situation and walk away or do I get involved? Once again I chose the latter.

My very drunk friend was already having trouble standing up straight when suddenly he was pushed and then struck down by the makeshift weapon. I watched on as he crumpled to the ground. The other drunk friend who was also in close proximity was then just as quickly struck and knocked to the ground. However, this drunk friend immediately got up and began to stagger his way up the road as the alumnus then turned his attention back to my very drunk friend who was still lying on the pavement. As he then tried to strike a few more blows with the carpet grip he inadvertently snapped it in half.

Fortunately for me, as I was very much sober this time around compared to the last time out in Leicester. I had planned ahead when I first saw my fellow alumnus rummaging through the bins.

Although I was wearing a kara during the last incident, on that occasion I was unable to make any use of it having been unable to react quickly enough to the trouble I found myself in. However, on this occasion knowing that something was going to kick off as soon as I saw him approaching with his weapon in hand, I decided to take some preparatory action to defend my friends and myself.

As I was I being pushed away by the pair of them during their initial confrontation, I had the foresight to slip off my kara from my right wrist and place it in my back pocket for easier access, should I be required to make use of it later on. I was fully aware that if I had kept it around my hand and then tried to throw some punches with it, I would have done more damage to my own wrist than the person I was aiming my punches at. Now that my half-inch thick steel kara was in my back pocket, I felt safer in the knowledge that should my friends be attacked I would be in a better position to defend them and myself should things turn nasty.

Unfortunately, this is exactly what happened, but this time I was lucky to have my senses about me. In the previous incident I was far too groggy to have even thought of anything like this as I made my way out of the nightclub. I quickly learned from my past mistake after that punch, with ring attached, crunched into my right temple in Leicester. A painful lesson had been absorbed. Fortunately, this time I was sober and fully aware of the trouble I could get myself in if I was not fully switched on. I immediately sensed that trouble was going to strike that night and I prepared for the foreseeable.

At the exact moment the carpet grip snapped in half I stepped forward towards the alumnus to confront him. He then momentarily stopped hitting my friend, turned his attention to me and began to move towards me. At this time, I had not taken my kara out of my back pocket to defend myself as I still hoped and held out onto the belief that he would not want to engage in a fight with me. How wrong I was.

Surprised by his sudden turn towards me, I quickly overcame my surprise as he charged at me. So I ran and as he tried to chase me down I led him up the road away from the town centre and also away from my very drunk friend. After a while it dawned on him that he could not catch me so he stopped chasing me and turned around to walk back down the road. I followed him back down the road, keeping a good few steps behind him as he continually kept turning his head to look back at me in the hope I would be foolish enough to get too close to him. As he slowly panted his way down the road I noticed that my very drunk friend was unfortunately still lying close to where he had fallen.

Having realized that my fellow alumnus would do me no favours, I decided to abandon my plan for peacekeeping. By now I had followed him all the way back and confronted him for the second time. Since he had dispensed with the piece of carpet grip earlier, he decided to place a couple more, well-directed boots into my very drunk friend. 'Leave him alone!' I shouted. Having got his attention, he turned around and glared at me. However, this time the look on his face was of someone who was unequivocally enraged. He'd had enough: enough of me. I could see it in his eyes. He was going to sort his problem out once and for all. He was going to sort me out once and for all. I knew exactly what was coming. But I would not run, not again.

Like an antagonized raging bull, he charged at me once again, absolutely livid. This time however, I was adamant that I was not going anywhere. I would fight my corner. I would stand firm and strike hard. Waiting for him to come even closer I firmly planted both my feet on the ground. As he continued to advance I remained rooted and just as he was within six feet of me, in the blink of an eye I pulled out my kara from my back pocket. I had given myself just enough distance and time to pull it out and wrap it around my right fist. Another three feet closer and both of my fists were raised towards him. As soon as he saw the thick flash of silver wrapped around my fist he immediately stopped, dead, in his tracks.

As I confronted my friend's attacker, who was now on the verge of becoming my own attacker, I realized that all my acts of diplomacy had failed. Diplomacy had well and truly gone out of the window even though I had tried my best to reason with him. I therefore felt I had no choice but to bare my kara and make use of it. It was definitely not my intention to attack him with my it. My only intention was to scare him off and in the process defend my very drunk friend. There was no choice about the matter; I had to look after him. As soon as the alumnus saw my kara he aborted his charge towards me. My plan had worked.

'Come on then!' I yelled out just as he was forced into an abrupt halt. I regretted it as soon as I said it, as it was absolutely not the wisest thing to say to an antagonized raging bull. As he checked his charge towards me on seeing my kara, he fortunately made a slight stumbling movement forward. Just as he did this he put himself in the perfect strike zone for my next impromptu surprise. As he inched in closer and closer I was able to line him up and then release a mighty right boot that smashed him straight in his pelvic region. Fortuitously, the follow-through meant that he collapsed to the floor like a sack of sodden potatoes. Now laid out on the floor in front of me I had not planned for my next step. There was no way I was going to beat him whilst he was on the floor like he had done to my friend. However, there was no doubt that had the roles been reversed he would have quite callously tried to flatten me into the ground I stood on. It was not in my nature to kick a man when he was down. So I just waited for him to get back up in the hope that I may have changed his mind about wanting to attack me whilst he was in the process of rearranging his privates. Unfortunately, he got back up quicker than I expected. I had by now well and truly destroyed his night by striking a blow to his manhood. There was no time to think. So I ran. Again.

I knew very well that had I used my kara I would have cut him up real bad. There was absolutely no way I was going to do that. He now also knew that there was no way I was going to use it and together we both now knew that once he got his hands on me he would have given me the greatest damn thrashing of my life. So when he then began to charge towards me again for the second time, I ran for my life. Having outrun him on previous occasions I set off very swiftly back up the same road that he had chased me on previously. It was all very bizarre and quite surreal being chased by him because as I was running away I reminisced about my old Village School days and how my fellow alumnus would always do very well in the short distance events at Moorway's Leisure Centre on the school sports day. He was obviously not the same athlete now. I guess that's what alcohol does to you in the long run. So much for those sports days, yet again he was unable to catch me. At first he chased me up the road then he stopped again, I then followed him back down to stall him further and annoy him even more. He then began to chase me down the road around the railings near the entrance of the nightclub where the door staff had been watching the whole saga for the last few minutes. At no point whatsoever throughout the whole duration of the event did they do a single thing to intervene or offer assistance. But then again they might have seen me with my kara wrapped around my fist and thought that I was the aggressor and the kara was my weapon of attack rather than it being something to defend myself with. After I had rushed past the door staff and around the railings one last time I then ran back up the road one final time with him still trying to catch me.

This had all been going on for a couple of minutes now. Being chased around like a headless chicken was a good thing though, as during that whole period of activity that the two of us shared, I had taken all his attention away from my very drunk friend who was still on the floor. I had made up some valuable time for my friend to get up and get out of danger.

Finally, my fellow alumnus just gave up and then started to slowly hobble and pant his way back down the road towards my friend to try and finish off what he'd been denied earlier. I could no longer get him to chase me around the cars and up and down the road any more. Thankfully though, by this point more and more people had begun to start leaving the club because it was now chucking-out time. Amongst these revellers were also what remained of the original group of people that we had initially gone into the club with that night. As they began to come out of the club one by one, even more worse for wear, they noticed their friend, who was still on the floor in an absolutely terrible state. As I made my way down towards them all, more and more people began to flood the previously deserted roads. My fellow alumnus had by now run off into the night.

At this point I placed my kara in my back pocket and then turned my attention to my very drunk friend who was still on the floor. As I ran towards him a crowd of people had gathered around trying to work out what had happened to him. Just as I was about to bend down to speak to him a very tall man within the gathering, upon seeing me rushing towards them all, unexpectedly elbowed me straight in the jaw. Obviously thinking that I was the attacker coming back to do some more damage? 'He's my friend,' I groaned, as I stooped down and reached for my stricken jaw. I didn't retaliate. I let it go, he was only protecting my friend. I had no ill feelings towards him, other than a sore jaw.

Fortunately, the only strike I took that whole night to my own body was an elbow to the face by a Good Samaritan. There was only one other upside to the whole night's farce. Amazingly my Ericsson GA628 had survived unscathed.

My very drunk friend who had spent the last few minutes flat out on the floor finally managed to get back on his feet, with a little assistance. Then surprisingly out of nowhere our other drunk friend then suddenly appeared back on the scene, quite bizarrely, with a bag of chips in one hand and a can of pop in the other. On seeing his friend in such a terrible state he dispensed with the can of pop by slamming it into the ground in a fit of rage.

My very drunk friend was in a really bad state. His face had now ballooned and his speech was even more slurred due to the bruising and cuts around his mouth. An ambulance arrived and quickly took him away to the Derbyshire Royal Infirmary, which was only around the corner. My other drunk friend and I then walked the short distance to the hospital leaving behind the group of friends we had initially gone out with that night. It did not take long to walk to the hospital. I used the time to reflect on another fine mess I had gotten myself into. Another fine mess that could have so easily once again turned so badly in my favour.

The medical staff began to promptly treat my friend as soon as he had arrived. Not long after, his mother and eldest brother quickly arrived to be by his side too, after they had been called to tell them what had happened. No doubt they too would have been very shocked on seeing the state of his face when they realized just how badly he had been attacked.

I later found out the actual reason why his face was so distressingly beat up. As his attacker was chasing me for the second time, my friend who was now concussed from the original blows tried to get back on his feet, however, as he tried to do so he faltered and fell, head first, into a roadside curb that resulted in him obtaining a hairline fracture of the jaw.

I decided not to call my own parents. I saw no point; other than my sore jaw I didn't have a scratch on me. I was completely fine, so there was no need to worry them. Another reason for not calling home was because earlier in the day my father had advised me not to venture into town because of all the trouble that frequently occurs. How right he was.

As I lingered around the accident and emergency waiting area in the early hours of that cold dark morning, something happened to me that changed me forever. Reflecting on everything that had happened to me within the last few weeks it suddenly dawned on me that, once again, my life had been spared. I had got away with it, again. 'But how many more chances would I be given? I could have been the person who got badly beaten today. I could have been the person who tragically died, just like that poor young man in Leicester.' I also thought about how fortunate I was that night to have been wearing my kara. It seems my faith had saved me.

The kara is a sacred article of faith in Sikhism. It is a constant reminder to all Sikh disciples to do God's work and to remind them of what their mission on earth is. To remind the wearer that he or she must carry out righteous and true deeds and actions that are in keeping with the advice given by the Guru.

It can come in many forms and sizes, but the one I was wearing during that period in my life was a very heavy thick steel bracelet with sharp edges.

The kara can trace its history back to the brutal and deadly Sikh martial art of shastar vidiya, which was used to settle disputes. This art of combat was known in the Punjab as iron fist fighting or loh mushti a form of boxing that, instead of using gloves, would use steel or iron bracelets worn on both hands. It was also historically used like a knuckle-duster for hand-to-hand combat but can also just as effectively be used in self-defence.

I used it entirely for self-defence purposes during my altercation in Derby and fortunately for me I didn't have to strike my fellow alumnus with it.

Suddenly in one vast collective moment of reflection it all just got too much for me. I became overpowered by all of the thoughts swirling through my mind from the previous night's events in particular. My whole life began to flash before my eyes. My father was right. Alone and still seated on my own I began to feel weaker and weaker. Finding it difficult to breathe, I lost the ability to even speak. My energy was draining away from me; my head flopped forward as my eyes caught sight of the solid, white floor beneath me.

Almost six years previously on Tuesday, February 9th 1993, my father had been in the same Derbyshire Royal Infirmary accident and emergency waiting area, sitting most probably in the exact same seat as myself as he waited to be seen by NHS medical staff.

Earlier that night he had visited his elder brother, Major, who lived on Willn Street, Derby. That night, as my father returned home to Pear Tree, he parked his car around the back of the house on Pear Tree Crescent then began to make his way towards the front of the house so that he could enter through the back door. As he was doing so he was involved in an altercation with a group of young men who were passing the front of our house. Having exchanged a few words with them, one of these young men pulled off a wooden panel from our side fence and struck my father with it, down the right side of his neck. The group of young men then ran off along Portland Street. Immediately after the incident my father rushed into the living room of our house, where we had all been sitting. In a very agitated state he stepped towards the living room mirror then began to pull at the neck of his shirt to look at the abrasions he now had on the side of his neck. He then decided to make his own way to the Derbyshire Royal Infirmary. On arrival he checked himself in, sat down and waited to be seen. However, as he waited, something happened to him that changed his life forever.

I can only speculate as to what occurred, but I'm quite sure that recent events in his life at the time would have weighed heavily on his mind. My father who had been sitting patiently, waiting to be seen, began to feel lightheaded and faint. As the night's events began to overpower him he gradually began to lose his balance and composure. Suddenly, his upper torso began to alarmingly lean forward; within a split second his head smashed into the waiting room's solid, white floor.

He would spend the next week of his life in a coma: I was thirteen years, four months and twenty-seven days old and I was about to lose my father.

As I was sitting down in the same accident and emergency waiting area I too suddenly began to feel lightheaded and faint. One-minute I was fine then the next the enormity of the whole situation and the memory of what had happened to my father in the exact same locality struck me like a thunderbolt.

Fortunately for me though someone was looking down on me. 'Are you ok?' he asked. I couldn't utter a single word, but fortunately I had enough strength to feebly shake my head dismissively. That was his cue to grab me by my jacket collars and pull me up towards him and then drag me out of the waiting area and out into the dark, where I was immediately slapped in the face by the beautiful chill of the cold night air.

Thankfully, I was helped out of the waiting area that night by the eldest brother of my hospitalized friend. On seeing me in such a state, he immediately realized that I was not well and instinctively took me out for some well-needed fresh air, then placed me on a bench and went back inside to get me some water. I was lucky that I had someone there for me that night, to help me. If only there could have someone there for my father almost six years previously. If only I could have been there. If only I could have been by my father's side.

As soon as that cold air hit my face, I immediately began to feel better. The dry mouth that I had only moments earlier suddenly began to slobber in the cold night. I then had a strong urge to remove the mouthful of spit, which was accumulating fast. I needed to get rid of it, so with all the strength I could muster, I began to roll my neck back and try to spit it out all in one go. And spit it out all in one go I did. Unfortunately, though not very far. It just so happened that it landed smack splat a few inches from my mouth, on my right thigh. I tried to wipe it off my jeans with the sleeve of my jacket but I just made it worse. My friend's eldest brother then returned with a bottle of water in hand and tried to make out he had not seen me smearing saliva all over my jeans. Although I still felt quite drained by what had just happened, I still managed to raise a little chuckle at my incompetency. Still dehydrated, I gulped down every drop of water as if I had been a stranger to it all my life. It was almost as if my body was trying to reject the last drop of alcohol within me with the ultimate expression of disgust whilst expelling it.

A few weeks later in Leicester I would see the same predicament fall at the feet of my friend, Sukh. A group of us had been waiting on the forecourt of a petrol station on Narborough Road for a couple of taxis to take us all back home to our halls of residence. As we all waited, Sukh and a few others were a little worse for wear, as well as very cold. So we all decided to step into the warmth of the petrol station. On entry, Sukh's eyes immediately fixed their attention onto a Cadbury's Creme Egg. He then asked Ranbir to buy him one, and then he gleefully stepped outside to devour it. Once outside, he realized that to fully appreciate the moment he would first need to vacate his mouth of all the slobber. The Creme Egg was then passed on to Ranbir to pick away at the foil wrapping. We all watched from inside as Sukh began to roll his neck back whilst straightening his large frame. We then heard a very loud and disgusting noise that emerged from the back of his throat. He threw his head forward and spat all of the contents of his mouth out. Unfortunately, it didn't go very far. It just so happened that it landed smack splat on his right foot. After a quick chuckle and a shrug of his shoulders he took the now unwrapped Cadbury's Creme Egg from Ranbir and thrust it, whole, into his mouth.

A few years later, I saw a piece on the news about my friend's elder brother. Alcohol had all but consumed him and he was now a shadow of his former self. It was a great shame as in his younger days he was a very good football player and coach and it was sad to see how his life ended. He was a good man.

In the days, weeks and months after the Derby incident, I began to detest drinking and certain types of drinkers that I was still associating myself with. It especially made my skin crawl, being in the company of drunk people who were behaving in, what I deemed to be, a silly or embarrassing manner that could no doubt lead to more unpleasant altercations.

In late January 1999, about a month after the Derby incident, I gave up drinking in excessive quantities just for the sake of getting smashed. I've not really touched it again in the same manner. Since then I have on a couple of rare cases celebrated very special occasions in my life but only when I have been in the company of people I trust absolutely.

I had only been at university for a couple of months or so now, but I had wasted so much money on drink. Most of it was my own money from my time working at Kwik Save in Littleover during my college days, however, some of it came from what my father would give me at the end of every weekend. It was not fair on my father that he should be providing me with this money, only for me to waste it on drink. I was not being fair on him or my family. They deserved better. After the day of the Derbyshire Royal Infirmary incident I made sure never to accept any money from my father ever again, if I knew it was likely to be wasted. From an early age he had instilled into me the importance of money and how if it was spent on important things, like food, then you could never truly waste it. My father supported our little family all his life, and he never ever asked for any repayment. Providing for his family was his life. That was his duty as a father – to act in the best interests of all his family.

As I sat on the bench that day, contemplating my near out of body experience, I couldn't stop thinking about my father and how relieved I was that he was still in my life.

Chapter 4: Catch-51
The Black Dog Barks

As the New Year of 2006 commenced my father's mood had become lower and darker than any other time before. From the beginning of January to the end of February, his whole outlook on life became apathetic. Life just didn't interest him any more. The little favours he would once happily do for family and friends were now all well beyond him.

At this point it should have become quite obvious to me that he was surely losing his passion for life. However, throughout this whole period, not once did I ever consider that my father would contemplate or carry out anything as desperate or destructive as his late brother, Mohan. When speaking about his brother's death he once told me that what Mohan had done was very wrong and that he should never have taken his life in the way that he had. This naturally led me to believe that my father could see and appreciate the selfishness of the act and the consequences it had for the bereaved loved ones who were left behind.

During these early months of 2006, my father would sometimes engage in little conversations with Rav as he would try to tell her that in times gone by he would have done anything to help anyone, but recently he just could not muster the energy to do so any more.

Before Mohan's passing it was my father who took responsibility for all the grocery shopping and other little jobs, which needed be done in and around our house. I was quite happy to take a step back as it was his domain. That was the niche he had created for himself. He was the man of the house who would take care of everything and everyone. All that had now completely changed for the worst. He was no longer able to function as the man of the house. Something had quite literally broken within him. However, before his depression hit rock bottom he was still able to carry out some minor tasks, such as, bringing home cheese-topped baps and buns from the Chaucer bakery and buying Yazoo milkshakes and snacks, just like he used to in the old days. I guess making even the smallest of contributions like this around the house was his way of fighting back. It could be said that maybe he was also regressing into earlier happier times in his life. It is quite true that in the end you start thinking about the beginning. He could obviously sense the darkness slowly encroaching and this was his way of defying it. His private battle against the darkness that was depression had begun.

During my younger years at Pear Tree Junior School and then later at Village Community School, every day without fail, my father would buy my brother, sister and myself three packets of crisps and leave them on the kitchen worktop for teatime. Sometimes he would even buy bottles of Yazoo strawberry milkshake for us all to drink too. On the rare occasion when he was not able to do so, he would leave some money near the cooker. I would then go to my mamma's shop on Balfour Road to buy some snacks with the money. I can't remember a single occasion when he let the three of us down by not providing for us. I also remember another occasion when I was very young when he had to leave me at my little masser, Darbara's house on Harrington Street. As he left me that day to play with my cousins, he made sure to provide us all with a large pack of pink wafers that we could all share at teatime.

Another incident of his kindness and love for his family occurred during a blizzard many years ago. On this occasion my eldest English mamma's daughter, Jazz, and her sister-in-law, Penny, went to Nottingham for a shopping trip.

However, as they tried to make their way back to Derby, Penny's car broke down. Penny called home to inform her husband, Jasbir, who immediately decided to call my father for help and the use of his burgundy Ford Escort. On arrival into Nottingham my father and Jasbir were able to get the broken-down car started again. Penny and Jasbir then made their own way home in their car and Jazz decided to keep my father company and return to Derby in his car. The now dark dangerous conditions and the whirling snowstorm didn't help their sense of navigation, though. Jazz later told me it wasn't the best decision she ever made because on the drive back home they got a little lost and instead of turning off the M1 they continued going straight on until they ended up in Sheffield. She laughed it all off though as they eventually reached the safety of Derby, more than grateful that my father had come to the rescue. It was a typical gesture of kindness from my father. On receiving the call for assistance he agreed without hesitation to come to their aid. It was from the goodness of his heart that he tried to help them, as always.

It was due to one incident towards the end of 2005 that I realized just how bad things had become for him. On this particular day he was preparing to go to work at the Chaucer bakery in his Daewoo car when something happened to him that left him pretty petrified and quite visibly shaken for days after.

During this period, we had two family cars, not including the one that my brother would have permanently parked in the back garden, unable to move it as he was either fixing it or looking after it. The blue Ford Mondeo belonged to myself and the green Daewoo belonged to my father.

On this icy-cold winter morning he had managed to get into his car, but when he turned the key in the ignition nothing happened. Having tried again a few more times to get the car to start he decided to give up and head back into the house. However, as he tried to get out he found that he was unable to do so as the door would not open. He tried the other door too, but again it didn't open. On realising he couldn't get out he became stricken with panic as he began thumping the car horn in the hope that somebody would notice him. Eventually my masser, Darbara, from across the road heard the noise and came to my father's assistance.

My little masser, Darbara, and his family had originally lived at 83 Harrington Street before they moved into 34 Pear

Tree Crescent, where both my mamma's had originally lived with their families before they moved to a shop in Addison Road, Derby.

On seeing my father stuck in his car, my masser was able to rescue him by helping him out through the back of the car via the boot. This incident really shook my father to the core because a couple of days later he sold the Daewoo. At the time, everyone in my house apart from my father, found it all quite funny.

Now, if the same thing had happened to me I would have assumed that either the doors had frozen shut or the electrics had failed. I would then have tried to find a way of escaping and no doubt in the process chuckle to myself at the ridiculous predicament that had befallen me. On recounting the incident, I would have self-mockingly turned the whole story into a yarn about my great escape. But not my father, he just seemed to think that the whole world had it in for him and that nothing was going his way.

The act of decision-making had just become too much of an encumbrance for him. Life and everyday living was a burden he could do without, as every little decision became a great exertion. What once came naturally, became so extremely difficult. Even the minimal demands of shopping became chronically overtaxing. Making decisions seemed to panic him, especially when he thought it was all getting too much. It was just easier for him to walk away.

My mother and sister also picked up on the strange behaviour he was now displaying when the three of them went grocery shopping in Sainsbury's. On this particular occasion as my mother and sister finished placing the items on the conveyor belt, my father had positioned himself far behind them and completely out of the cashier's sight. When the cashier informed them of the amount to be paid he just offered my mother his wallet and asked her to count the money out for herself. This was very out of character for him as previously he would have been the first in line to take charge of situations like this.

The glow that had emanated from my father only a few months previously was lost forever: absolutely extinguished. In my eyes, this sudden darkness that now took its place manifested itself as a constant form of moaning and whinging that progressed into severe withdrawal.

Throughout my whole life I have detested joy-sappers. The negativity and bad vibes they give off was something that I just couldn't bear to associate with. The mere sight or presence of these people in my company would make me feel quite deflated and demoralized. I hated negativity and this period in my life was the worst for it. For my father to then be constantly moaning and whinging in my presence at all times frustrated me beyond belief. Not only did I have it at home, but I also had to deal with it at school from students and on occasion from members of staff and management. I tried my utmost best to distance myself from all the negativity, but I was now getting it from all sides and from both barrels. It was all just becoming too much for me. I knew things were not going to get any better for me if they carried on as they were. Something had to give.

As my father's mood began to dip further he also began to suffer from uncomfortable dreams that no doubt stirred a lot of emotions when he would awake from them. My mother was the only person in the house who was aware of these dreams. Whether he told her first or she figured it out, I'm not sure, but he did disclose to her that he would keep having dreams about his past and his younger days. My mother also informed me that he would see his brother, Mohan, in these dreams too. 'Could constantly dreaming about his brother have led my father closer to him?' It was just a thought I had, but never for one moment did I take it seriously.

Dreams can be awful, especially when they involve loved ones that have passed away in the real world. It is almost as if you want to remain asleep to catch a glimpse of their face one last time. But the more you want to see them, the longer you have to sleep. Maybe this was also another reason my father spent so much of his time sleeping during the first couple of months of 2006, when he would come back from work and immediately go to bed. Another awful thing about dreams, especially good ones are that sooner or later you have to wake up. Those that know they are in a dream state know that there is nothing you can do to change anything in the real world. However, those that don't know they are in a dream-state get lost in the dream world, this then obviously results in a lot of confusion as to what is and what is not real when they wake up.

This first major episode of depression that my father experienced occurred about five years after the 1993 incident outside our Pear Tree home. After my father came out of his coma in mid-February 1993, he had to claim invalidity

*benefit for many years after. This period of redundancy
really knocked his confidence and self-worth over the next
five years that followed. During my time at the University of
Leicester, he finally began to get back into work and regain
his lost self-reliance thanks, in no small part, to his good
friend, Nazim. Prior to him beginning work again, I had
become quite troubled by his whole predicament as it began
to dawn on me just how much he was struggling to cope. I
found it quite unbearable to have to come back to Pear Tree
and see him in such a distressed state. His health had a
profound effect on me at the time and I feel my own studies
and general behaviour were also deeply affected by what he
was going through during these dark days. Fortunately,
throughout this whole period of depression my thiah, Sohan,
and my immediate family back home in Derby managed to
guide my father safely through and beyond this dark chapter
in his life. I was very grateful to them all for always being by
his side as he defiantly emerged from the darkness that had
engulfed him.*

My father once tried to disclose to me that there was
something on his mind that was seriously concerning him. I
immediately sat down next to him to hear what he was about
to tell me. However, as soon as he began to share his

thoughts with me it became quite obvious that the act of explanation was quite impossible for him to do. He just didn't have the words to express what he needed to say. Or maybe he felt that whatever was going on in his mind was something a father should never have to share with his child. Maybe he thought I wouldn't believe him. Or maybe he thought I too would dismiss him. The only thing I got out of him that day was that he was experiencing a throbbing pain in his head. He tried to describe this pain by jabbing at his right temple with his finger. As he did so he told me that the things he kept experiencing were also driving him crazy. Unfortunately, as I tried to ask him for further information in the hope of supporting him and seeking more answers, he closed up and revealed no more. At this point I also became extremely frustrated. I wanted to help him but there seemed to be nothing I could do for him. What else could I do if he refused to talk?

I was not the only one to become frustrated with him during this time. As the days went on, most of us in the house if not all, felt the same way. His whole outlook on life now just sounded like he was constantly moaning without any real reason for it. From this point on he just began to constantly complain about feeling unwell. The worst part of seeing all this was that physically, on the outside, he looked perfectly fine, but mentally, inside, he was not. He had always found it difficult to express himself, especially when frustrated. But it had now become even harder for him to tell us all what was going on inside his mind. He was quite obviously seeking attention, but we just could not provide him with the attention he required. This then resulted in a build-up of frustration on all sides. It eventually reached the point that most acts of engagement with him would result in some form of irritated reaction.

By now this perceived negative behaviour wasn't just confined to our own house; he would also display it to the outside world too. It wasn't that he was being nasty, it was just that whatever came out of his mouth would always come across as very pessimistic.

In vino veritas? In wine [there is the] truth?

'A drunk man's words are a sober man's thoughts', well at this point in my father's life he had given up drinking so whatever was coming out of his mouth had nothing to do with that. Could it therefore have been the medicine he was taking?

Whatever the cause of this depressed state, he now began to truly believe that he had been hard-done-by in life. Usually, in the past he would only ever talk about this during drunken periods at home. But now he was doing it everywhere, without the drink. He was not the man he used to be.

His childhood friend and relative, Major Singh Dhindsa, tried in vain to pull him out of his depression by taking my father on long walks so they could talk. Nazim, another of his long-standing good friends also tried to preoccupy his mind and keep him busy with work too, but nothing would change my father's state of mind. When friends and family once again tried to involve him in community matters, his stock answer would always be, 'Ask someone else, I'm not well.'

It was becoming evident to all who had seen Mohan struggling with depression that my father was now also beginning to show the same signs that Mohan had displayed before he took his own life. Had I visited Mohan prior to my father and grandmother departing for the Punjab, I too would have also picked up on this similar depressive behaviour. However, at the time, I chose not to go because I felt Mohan was just being his normal selfish self, as usual, and caring for no one but himself.

Towards the end of February, I also picked up on some very strange behaviour that my father was now beginning to project towards me. This behaviour was in relation to the questions he would annoyingly ask me. Questions, which I thought at the time, were quite random and irrelevant. 'Do you know what the alarm code is, if it goes off? Do you know where to pay the gas and electricity? Do you have the key to the upstairs bedroom window, the one facing the garage? Have you done this? Have you done that?' These questions would drive me crazy. 'Does it really matter?!' I would snap back in irritation.

As all this was happening he also began to stop assisting his tenant across the road. She was an elderly Scottish lady who lived opposite our own house on Portland Street. He'd reached the point where he just could not be bothered to deal with her any more. Over the years he had set her up very well. She didn't pay much rent, but my father didn't mind, as he knew the house was in relatively safe hands. However, as his depression got worse he used to become quite agitated with her constant requests and demands. He was just not concerned any more, even when she had tried to get him to replace a once perfectly functioning fireplace that had to be condemned because she painted over the brickwork.

'Maybe a life of giving too much and not getting enough back in return had finally sucked him dry? It just didn't matter any more. Life wasn't worth the struggle?' The enjoyment and satisfaction of helping others had been completely snuffed. He had reached the point where he was no longer able to accomplish even the most minimal tasks any more. This dragged him deeper into his depression and darkness. It is also quite possible that after the trauma of not being able to save his brother, his whole mantra in life no longer mattered.

Did he now think that he had failed his own father and his eldest brother?

After a lifetime's self-service to his family and his community, in his mind the one time he really needed to be there for a loved one, was the one time he couldn't. He wasn't able to save Mohan. If only he had shared my thoughts at the time. I felt stubbornness and a misplaced sense of pride took his brother and there was nothing anybody could do when he made his mind up to take his own life. But what did I know.

His whole mantra in life was to help other people, most of all, his family and close friends. Once this was effectively broken I feel his whole life just imploded. As his mantra could no longer sustain him, his spirit inevitably broke with it and in life there is nothing worse than an amputated spirit. Even Mohan's two youngest sons had picked up on my father's familiar behaviour and tried to talk to him. Both sons had seen their own father going through exactly the same as what my father was now going through.

The elder of the two sons even emailed me on the 21st February 2006.

'Hi Kaly [sic],

Please can you email us the details (i.e name/description) of all the medicine Chacha (your Dad) is taking related to his head/depression... I wrote something when I was in Derby.. can't find that paper .. I would like to enquire further re: these products.

Also please confirm if you got the email with the docs attached relating to depression..

have a good day...'

To be honest, at the time I really didn't know what medicine my father was on and when he should be taking it. He just didn't share that information with me. Maybe I didn't ask. Maybe I didn't want to know. Maybe I truly believed that he would never follow in Mohan's footsteps.

One particular question my father asked me towards the end of February really made me lose my temper. He had moaned at me because the toilet roll in the downstairs toilet had not been replaced. At the time, it was not the most important thing on my mind so I snapped back with a smile, 'Nobody's going to die!' He glared back at me with intense irritation and then muttered, 'You'll find out when I'm gone.'

During the last couple of weeks of February 2006 I honestly felt that he was deliberately trying to wind me up and get under my skin. It was as if he was genuinely trying to make me dislike him. But, I couldn't put my finger on why he was doing this. I have to admit, during that period there were many times I didn't like him because of what he would say or what he would do, but that never stopped me from loving him. He was my father and I loved him unconditionally. It was almost as if he was doing his utmost best to push me and other people away from him, to try and distance himself from us all.

One issue that drove a serious wedge between my father and myself at the time was in relation to the purchase of a new car. As he no longer had a car, I was hoping to give my Mondeo back to him and buy a new car for Rav and myself. My father loved his Fords throughout his life, but I had my eyes set on an Audi A2. However, he was quite against the idea of me buying the Audi. This resulted in him constantly bringing up the topic every time we were in each other's company when other people were around. His main reason for not liking the idea was that he felt Rav and I should buy a larger car in case we had any children later on. We were both as stubborn as each other but I wanted to get a smaller car because at that point in my life I had no need for a larger one. When bringing up the topic I felt he would deliberately try to belittle and undermine me in front of my own family and friends when he was trying to explain the errors of my ways. It began to really upset me a great deal. I didn't want to fight with my father and disrespect him in front of others so I would just get up and walk away from the conversation. Why was he doing this to me?

On February 9th 2006, about three weeks before March 1st 2006 and thirteen years to the day he was left in a coma, I came across an article in the Derby Evening Telegraph about a competition to design a monument that was to be built at the site of the former Baseball Ground in Pear Tree.

The Baseball Ground had once been the home of Derby County Football Club from 1895–1997. The club's reserve and youth sides continued to use it until 2003 when it was finally demolished. Originally called the Ley's Baseball Ground, it was used as a sports stadium for 113 years (108 of them as a football stadium and five of them as a baseball stadium when it first opened in 1890). In 1997 Derby County Football Club moved to the Pride Park Football Stadium, located on the Pride Park Business Park, on the outskirts of Derby.

Due to my obvious connection with Derby, and in particular the Pear Tree area in which the Baseball Ground was once located, I decided to have a go at submitting a plan for a monument. When I first stumbled across the article, I was really drawn into the idea of submitting a proposal. Something deep inside me wanted to create a piece of art that would be a lasting reminder of happy days. I also wanted to help create something that would make my father proud of me, to make him happy and to make him smile again. On the day I read the article my father was in the living room beside me. As I began drafting some thoughts and ideas together my father sat silently on a stool without taking the slightest bit of notice in what I was doing.

At the time I realized it was a good thing for me to get involved in because I felt it also allowed me to preoccupy my mind with good thoughts and not be distracted by all the negativity in my life that was gnawing at me. My plan was to create not just a monument, but a memorial to all those people connected to Derby and Derbyshire whose lives were made all the more joyful for supporting Derby County Football Club and all the success that the club brought to the area.

My original proposal:

'I believe that any memorial erected to commemorate the former home of DCFC would have to be something

associated with the club and also have some sort of connection to a significant and special part of Derbyshire and the city of Derby's history and heritage.

Therefore, I feel there would be no better commemoration than to erect a statue of the Rams insignia intertwined with a legendary Rolls-Royce Merlin engine as the internal body and soul of the Ram.

The Merlin engine, developed by Rolls Royce, played a fundamental role in the 'Battle of Britain' and helped secure our shores (Spitfire and P-51 Mustang).

If I was to be successful I would be quite happy to hand over the £1,000 prize and have it shared by John Port School, where I am currently a science teacher, and Pear Tree Junior School where I was once a pupil.

I lived in the shadow of the former Baseball Ground for much of my life and continue to do so even though it is no longer there. Therefore, I would love for there to be an everlasting reminder to my beloved home city and 'forever great' football club.

A couple of days later I showed my father my plans for my proposal on my little PDA, but when he turned his head away it was obvious that he was not at all interested in what I was up to. I felt disheartened by his reaction, so I tried to cheer him up by showing him a picture of the two of us I had stored on my PDA.

The photo was taken in the early 1980s at a Christmas party that we had both attended at his place of work at the Richard Lees Factory in Ashbourne, Derbyshire. In the photo I was wearing a paper hat from a Christmas cracker, which obscured my topknot. I would have only been about two years old at the time, as my father held me in his arms as we both smiled for the camera.

He glanced at the picture, but nothing. No reaction at all. I wanted to cry.

Unfortunately, I never got to submit my proposal before the deadline.

On the previous weekend before March 1st 2006, I sat down to watch the Six Nations Rugby in the living room. My father sat beside me, and Rav and my sister were also in the room whilst my mother was in the kitchen. It was Saturday 25th February and Scotland were playing England at Murrayfield. As an avid Rugby Union fan I watched on as Scotland outplayed and outfought England to beat them 18-12. I wasn't too disappointed with the result, as I've always liked a good underdog victory against the odds.

During the match a relative came to visit my father and see how he was doing. I was sitting on the sofa watching the game next to my father when the visitor stepped into the living room. As he came in I said hello and nodded my head in acknowledgement. I then moved my position on the sofa to sit closer to my father so the visitor could sit to my right. However, what happened next is something I didn't expect nor could ever have envisaged. As I moved to my left, my hand briefly brushed my father's thigh. Instantaneously, his body recoiled in repulsion as he pushed himself away from me. His convulsed reaction and resulting facial expression surprised me a great deal. Something was seriously wrong. Something was horribly wrong. 'How could he react in such a way? Why would he react like this? He was my father and I was his son!'

I remember happier times before his depression struck, when we would rest on the sofa together just like we used to when I was younger. I would use his legs as a headrest with a pillow placed on them so I could watch the TV in my elevated position. Sometimes he would nod off and go to sleep as I continued watching TV and listened to his loud snores.

On the last two days before March 1st 2006 I remember watching two films, which were on TV very late at night. At the time I was finding it difficult to sleep at night. Something was on my mind. It was almost as if I could feel something was keeping me awake, and I don't mean my father's snoring.

Or maybe my father's snoring was keeping me awake. Not the noise, but the person it was coming from.

One film I remember watching was called *Suicide Kings* starring Christopher Walken. The other film that was on the day before March 1st 2006, was called *Catch-22*, the 1970 satirical war film adapted from the book of the same name written by Joseph Heller. Now obviously *Suicide Kings* is a film that will stick in the mind, not for what it was about but for what it was called. Catch-22 however, stuck in my mind because of the term coined by Joseph Heller in his novel.

A Catch-22 is a paradoxical situation in which an individual cannot avoid a problem because of contradictory constraints or rules set upon them. Often these situations are such that solving one part of a problem only goes on to create another problem, which ultimately leads back to the original problem. Catch-22s often result from regulations, rules or procedures that an individual is subject to but has no absolute control over.

I feel my father was in the ultimate Catch-22 situation. His whole life mantra was to look after his people. After Mohan's death there was never any more desire for him to look out for others. Yet even when he defiantly tried to do so he would still be drawn back to the original problem that was tormenting him; his inability to save his brother's life.

I read Joseph Heller's Catch-22 novel whilst working at Toyota Manufacturing UK in Burnaston in late 2003 and early 2004. It was a great read but unfortunately I also found myself in a similar Catch-22 situation every day for a month, whilst working there. My Catch-22 involved my production line team constantly trying to beat the previous day's car production target. A target that was forever increasing shift by shift and dangled in front of us on the large computer screen above.

I began my time at Toyota in late 2003 with great expectations. I had originally got through the recruitment via the direct channels having passed all my tests and interviews and was then placed on a three-month probation period. It was always my intention not to stay for too long, but the money was a driving factor in wanting to stay for as long as I could. I also hoped to use the time to make my mind up as to whether I really wanted to become a teacher or not. However, on my second full working day there I was shifted to another team on the radiator assembly part of the production line whose team leader just didn't get on with me. From that day on it just became a long drawn out nightmare. A vicious circle of noise and mounting car numbers that never seemed to stop. As the long and draining days slowly crawled along just like the cars on the production line, I found myself becoming increasingly miserable in my predicament. I would come in day after day with my pencil and notebook. Within the notebook was a year planner. Every lunch break, I would find myself pulling the notebook out of my bag and then circling new end dates on the year planner to signify the day I would eventually leave. Every day, without fail, for almost a month, I struck off months, weeks and then eventually days to bring my end of employment date even closer. I finally decided that working in such an environment was just not for me and that what I really wanted to do was become a science teacher and carve out a career in education. I eventually circled a day that I knew would be my last to set myself free from this hellhole I had fallen into. Once I had circled that particular day into my notebook I began to bring university application forms in to fill out during my lunch breaks so that I could apply to PGCE Secondary Physics courses. However, there was only one place in my mind where I wanted to return; Leicester.

Even though I was on my probation period I realized that it would make no difference whatsoever if I left after one month or three months, because in either case I wouldn't have been there for very much longer anyway. Another thing that really annoyed me was that even though I was a full time employee, I had never been given my complete company uniform like others who had started at the same time as me. I really liked the company jacket that employees wore as I felt it looked very much like something Captain Jean-Luc Picard would have worn on the main bridge of the Starship Enterprise. I never received one though and had to make do with wearing *white t-shirts day after day. It was not all bad though, because I actually got on well with nearly all the people I worked with and it was great chatting to them during break periods. However, when returning back to the moving production line after the breaks, the conversations would terminate and the noise would take their place. The constant never-ending targets at Toyota and my new production line team leader became too much for me in the end so I knew I had to get out. It was unfortunate as had I stayed with my original production line team leader I think I would have stayed there very much longer. The term anal-retentive summed up my new team leader quite adequately. I know Toyota have their own efficient ways of doings things as outlined by the Toyota Production System method but some team leaders and supervisors just didn't allow for any deviation from this. I totally understood the need to remove overburden and inconsistency and therefore elimination of waste, but it was an absolute pain for me to be told to do things that actually slowed me down. According to my team leader, I had to do things by the book even though I was managing to complete my particular job quicker having done it in my own more efficient way. It began to get really silly when I was warned that I was going too fast and needed to slow down. This team leader was just one of those people in life who pay so much attention to the little details that their obsession becomes an annoyance to others. He just couldn't get on with me. He just couldn't control me. Unfortunately, I have come across a few people like him in my life. They just refuse to bend to adapt. It's a shame because if you can't be flexible in matters like this then there is a strong possibility that you will break.*

Toyota was driving me crazy with the constant noise and the inability to engage in conversation with anyone but the voices in my head. I wanted to start talking with people again. I needed to start talking with people again. The long hours and constant pain in my fingers and joints was also causing me great discomfort too. It was such a relief when I finally made the decision to leave and then began covertly planning my great escape. As I did this I also informed some of the team members of my intention to leave. Many of them thought I was quite mad for wanting to leave as they felt I wouldn't find anything better paid or even close to what I was earning at Toyota. I took the risk though because, fortunately, I had my university education to fall back on when trying to find something new and different. I could totally understand their point of view, but I needed to get out of there for my own sanity. Money was not the be-all and end-all. Job satisfaction and happiness was all I cared for.

My leaving day finally arrived, but it didn't fall on the day that I'd initially circled. Enough was enough; I just didn't want to be there any longer. So, I told a few members of my team that I would be leaving during the shift. A couple of them even suggested that I should just walk out whilst the production line was moving. However, I decided against this because I didn't want my actions to have any consequences on those left behind. Having come in knowing that this particular day would be my last, I decided to leave during my lunch break. As I bid my team members goodbye, I heard their cheers behind me as I left our little team area to make my way to the car park outside. However, as I was leaving I bumped into my team leader who was on his way back. 'Where are you going?' he asked. 'I'm going home,' I smiled. 'You can't do that,' he said. 'I am and I'm not coming back,' I said. 'But what will you do?' he asked. 'I'm going to become a teacher, goodbye.'

I didn't like leaving this way, but I had no choice. The life I had found myself in within the last couple of months or so was just not the life I had dreamt of. I was being treated like a sheep that just followed the crowd and the instructions given to it. I wanted no part in it. I had to get out. I had to sort my life out, the personal side as well as the work side. I wanted to live again and not just exist. I also needed to find myself a wife. At no point after leaving Toyota did they ever get back in touch with me, or ask why I had walked away. It just summed up my whole miserable experience with them, in a nutshell.

I decided not to go straight into teaching after initially leaving the University of Leicester in 2001 because I felt I first needed more life experience before I entered the classroom. So, for the next four years after leaving university I studied for a part-time MSc Science with the Open University. During this time, I also worked at the National Railway Enquiry Service call centre on London Road, Toyota in Burnaston and then later at Pektron on Alfreton Road, Derby. I began my PGCE Secondary Physics course at the University of Leicester in late September 2004, whilst still in the process of completing my MSc.

On the night before March 1st 2006 I remember lying in bed when I suddenly had an urge to check my mobile to see if I had Mohan's youngest son's phone number in my contacts list. The reason I wanted to call him was so that I could find out if he was ok. Having got out of bed I unplugged my mobile from its charger then began to scan for his number in my contacts list. I scrolled all the way down until I eventually found him. A couple of contacts further below, I spotted M. Dhindsa's home number, my father.

I didn't get the chance to call Mohan's son the next day as he ended up making his own way to my house.

That day was Wednesday, March 1st 2006.

Chapter 5: Derby – England
Pear Tree

1967 was a monumental year in the lives of ordinary Derby folk and my future self in particular. Not only was it the year that brought the arrival of my father to Derby, but it was also the year that brought the arrival of the greatest managerial football partnership the world was to ever witness. In May 1967, Brian Howard Clough was interviewed for the vacant post of Derby County Manager. In July 1967, two months later he was appointed alongside Peter Thomas Taylor, as the new joint managerial partnership at the Baseball Ground, home of Derby County Football Club, in Pear Tree, Derby.

The UK musical Number 1's either side of my father's arrival in England were Scott McKenzie's 'San Francisco (Be Sure to Wear Flowers in Your Hair)' and Engelbert Humperdinck's 'The Last Waltz'. The Beatles were also climbing high in the charts with their Album 'Sgt. Pepper's Lonely Hearts Club Band' and Patrick Troughton was playing the role of the second incarnate of the Doctor in Doctor Who.

My father first arrived in England during the first week of September 1967. Accompanying him were his mother, Mohan, Major and his youngest sister, Seece. His two other sisters, Simoh and Rivaloh remained behind in India knowing that their parents and younger sister would eventually return to Punjab. Prior to this arrival, Sohan Singh Dhindsa, my father's eldest brother had already settled in England having made the same journey alone a couple of years earlier. Once Sohan had managed to sort himself out with some accommodation and work, his father then subsequently joined him. Having settled down, my grandfather and Sohan then decided to bring over the rest of their family as part of the voucher scheme, which allowed work permits to be allocated to family members who could then also come to England to earn a living.

My thiah, Sohan, once told me a story, which, if true, would have effectively decided the whole future of my entire Dhindsa family tree in England. When my thiah first landed in England he had one final obstacle to overcome before he could leave the airport. This obstacle was in the form of the customs officer. On showing his passport and travel documents, the customs officer didn't believe that Sohan was the age that was indicated on his passport. It was only after he was given no other alternative than to show the hairs on his right armpit that the customs officer was finally convinced that he was telling the truth. I never found out if the story was completely true, but I remember my thiah telling it me with a smile.

My father was born in the village of Ram Rai Pur, Nawanshahr in the Punjab region of North West India on the 15th December 1954. He was only twelve years and eight months old when he made his life-changing journey across, to England. All three of his elder brothers, including himself, eventually settled down in Derby. His parents and his youngest sister later returned to India to join his two other sisters and that is where they all remained for many years after. One by one all the brothers married in England after their wives-to-be also made the journey across to England to meet their new husbands and then marry them. The exception to this was Mohan, who returned to India to get married and then later brought his wife back home to England with him.

My mother initially arrived in England in February 1977 and then settled down with her two brothers and their families at 34 Pear Tree Crescent. Within ten years of first arriving in England, my father and mother were married at the Derby registration office in the company of a few close family members. Their actual traditional Indian, Sikh wedding took place a few weeks later in July 1977 in the company of many more family and friends at the original Guru Arjan Dev Gurdwara on Shaftsbury Street. The post wedding party was held in the Chestnut Pub on Portland Street, which was attended only by the menfolk. My mother didn't have very far to move once she got married to my father, in fact it was only across the road. A displacement of less than 30m from 34 Pear Tree Crescent to 160 Portland Street. I say displacement because the actual distance she covered to move over to her new home was actually a bit further.

As is customary with Punjabi weddings the bride leaves from outside her old family home in the back of the wedding car with her new husband sat beside her. Just before departing and closing the back door of the car, family and friends of the bride will cry uncontrollably as they say their final goodbyes to her and the life she is about to leave behind. Parting gifts of money, hugs, snot and tears are then offered to the new happily married couple. Only after all the goodbyes and well wishes have been performed is the back door of the wedding car steadfastly slammed shut in the bride's face. The car is then ready to be 'pushed' away by the men who are now gathered in a flock within a cloud of exhaust fumes behind the wedding car. A mighty push is then re-enacted as a symbolic gesture of letting go as coins are then thrown in front of the car as a blessing for the newly married couple and the journey they will now share together into their new happy, hopeful future. Like any Punjabi wedding, the sight of these glinting coins results in vast numbers of young children throwing themselves into the path of the moving car in search of the elusive silver coins and the even more elusive gold one. It must be quite a peculiar sight for any non-Punjabi to look upon; watching children diving in front of the car whilst, simultaneously, grown men fall behind the car, trying to regain their balance and composure having put so much effort into the great push. Some of these men would no doubt have completely lost their balance anyway, having still been drunk from their previous excesses in the pub earlier in the day.

By the time the last of the copper coins were all collected up and the drunken men had all returned to their feet, my father and mother would have returned to their initial starting point having done a half circuit of Pear Tree Crescent and passed by the Chestnut Pub on their way back to my mother's new home at 160 Portland Street.

Not only did my father and mother live very close to each other when they first arrived in England, they also lived very close to each other in Punjab too. My father's village, Ram Rai Pur, and my mother's village, Sahabpur, are only less than 2.5km's apart. Both of my parents' fathers would therefore have known of each other and my parents themselves may have even met during their younger days, never knowing that one day they would get married to each other in the not so distant future.

Once my father's parents and his younger sister had made the journey back to Punjab after a short period of stay, all that my father had left, in terms of family in England, were his three brothers. Sohan would then become the head of his family in England. It was quite a responsibility to take on, but fortunately over the next few years a network of new friends, fellow Ram Rai Purians and new relatives would settle in Pear Tree bringing back the sense of community that they all once had back in their homeland of Punjab.

My eldest thiee, Chindar, arrived in England in late September 1967, not long after my father. She would initially stay with her chacha, Chuhar Singh Mander, his wife and their two sons at a house near Rose Hill Street. After living with Chuhar and his family for about six months she married my thiah, Sohan, in March 1968 and moved into 49 Fleet Street with all his brothers. Their English wedding had taken place a few months previously in December 1967.

Chuhar and my eldest Mamma, Avtar Singh Thiara, initially came over to England on the same plane in the late 1950s. Once my thiah and thiee were married, this association no doubt led to the eventual marriage of my father and my mother through their friendship.

*

This part of my story would have been so much easier to write with my father by my side. The time to the second of just about anything and everything in relation to where it occurred, what he was wearing and what he had in his pocket at that point would not have been overlooked.

The following dates and places detailing my father's education and employment history are all taken from an old address book he once used to write in.

Pear Tree School, Pear Tree Street, Derby.
25/09/1967–21/12/1970.

This school building later became a primary school by the name of Pear Tree Community Junior School, which I myself attended from 1987 to 1991.

During the three years that my father attended Pear Tree School he lived at 49 Fleet Street. Next door to them, at 48 Fleet Street lived the Meehan family which consisted of Morris, Christie and their two daughters and son. Throughout this whole time the Meehan's treated my family like their own. My family were forever grateful for the compassion and love the Meehan's showed toward them during those early formative years in Derby.

Many years later I would go on to teach science to Morris Meehan's grandson at John Port School, not realising who he was until after the events of March 1st 2006.

Most of the early economic migrants into England initially planned to only stay for a brief period of time. The plan was to make as much money as possible and then return back to their homeland at a later date in a much healthier and wealthier position than they had originally arrived in. However, many decided to remain and create new lives for themselves in England, as commonwealth immigrants.

Whilst attending Pear Tree School my father managed to get himself a job working at a grocery shop a stone's throw away from the Baseball Ground. A man called Gurmail Singh, affectionately known as Tiger, owned the shop. It was located on the corner of a street that no longer exists, which eventually made way for the Shaftsbury Leisure Centre close to the site of Ley's Malleable Casting Foundry on Columbo Street. My father would work in this shop, assisting with deliveries, stacking shelves and occasionally working on the till when required.

My father made many friends during these days. Most of these friendships came about due to the shared connections he had with fellow migrants, who like him had also made the journey over from Punjab. All the Punjabi settlers knew each other very well back then and a close tight-knit community developed that would look after each other. One of his best friends during this period of his life was Major Singh, who was also from the village of Ram Rai Pur. They were both around the same age and Major Singh also shared our family name, Dhindsa. Growing up together they would have spent a lot of time in each other's company as they walked and cycled around the streets of Normanton together.

In later years, Major Singh who was a baptized Sikh, would be referred to as just 'Singh' so that we could differentiate him from my father's brother, Major Singh (Dhinsa).

Not long after my father finished attending Pear Tree School he left his job at the grocery shop and then managed to get another job at the Reckitt & Colman 'shampoo' factory.

Reckitt & Colman – Toiletries Division LTD, Sinfin Lane, Derby
Storekeeper No 2
04/01/1971–25/07/1975
Changed Work

During my own Pear Tree School days, I used to walk to school along Portland Street, cross over Harrington Street then wait for the lollipop lady to guide me across Portland Street. From there on I would walk further down the other side of Harrington Street into either Pear Tree Infant's or

Junior's depending on which school I was attending at the time. In the early days this was with an adult, but as I grew older I would be allowed to walk alone.

Whilst my father was working at the 'shampoo' factory, as he called it, he worked alongside a lady who would go on to become my school lollipop lady. Her name was Mrs Varty and she would patrol at the cross-section of Portland Street and Harrington Street; making sure that the children from Harrington Street Nursery, Pear Tree Infant's and Pear Tree Junior's could safely cross over Portland Street.

She was a lovely lady who would always greet me with a knowing smile. As I would take my position on the opposite side of the road, she would walk into the middle of the road, stop and then stand firm as she raised her lollipop upright. All oncoming traffic would then immediately stop for this Gandalf with a lollipop. I would then await her beckoning hand so I could then, and only then, cross the road safely. 'Thank you, Mrs Varty,' I would say with a smile as I passed her to reach the other side. She was always smiling but the only time I ever recall her being cross was the one time she gave me an absolute roasting because I had crossed her crossing point without her signal to guide me over. I remember the throbbing beat of her words striking my ears as she began shouting at me just as I was about to reach the other side. I looked up at her angry face and only then did I realize what I had done. On that particular day, as I was waiting to cross I became distracted by a man who was standing next to me and who was also waiting to cross. Momentarily, I looked down at my feet perched on the edge of the pavement and then I glanced at his next to mine. I then saw his feet step into the road so I automatically followed suit, assuming, with mistaken belief, that it was safe to do so and that Mrs Varty had beckoned us both to step forward. As I began to cross with him I had assumed she was already in the middle of the road; stopping traffic. She was not though. I had foolishly not been looking up, as I had been too busy looking down. I had crossed without her assistance. Just as I was about to reach the other side of the road I realized what I had done as Miss Varty's agitated face came bearing down towards me. As her eyes pierced into me I realized what a silly boy I had been. Fortunately, for us both, I didn't get physically hurt. My feelings however, were very much hurt. 'Sorry, Miss Varty,' I whimpered as I walked away, upset that I had unintentionally caused her such great alarm and concern. It might also have been the case that she was genuinely worried about my welfare, knowing full well whose *son I was. I believe she later left England, to set up a new life in America. She really was a very lovely lady.*

In 1974, Sohan, his wife Chindar, my father and Mohan along with his wife, Reshmo, moved to 160 Portland Street. Major and his wife, Pajo, had already previously moved out of 49 Fleet Street and bought their own house at number 50 Fleet Street.

Major would later move to 26 Willn Street and then make his final move to 159 Portland Street.

Whilst my father was living at number 49 Fleet Street, the house had no plumbing for a bath throughout the whole duration of their stay. What they did have, though, was one of the first telephones owned by any Punjabi family in the street. My thiah, Mohan, with assistance from his brothers also managed to buy a family car that he would drive everybody around in. Chuhar, who had previously been living with his two young sons near Rose Hill Street had also moved to 30 Fleet Street, which was closer to his niece. It was Mohan who later sorted out their plumbing so they could afford the luxury of a fully installed, working bath.

Prior to my parents' wedding in 1977, Mohan and his family would move out of 160 Portland Street to a new house of their own at 54 Portland Street. He would then make his final move to 52 Cromwell Street. Sohan would also eventually move out of 160 Portland Street too, first to 72 Cameron Road and then finally to 5 Pear Tree Crescent.

After four years at Reckitt & Colman, my father decided to look for another job.

Derby and Burton Co Operative Society LTD, Peak Bakery, Osmaston Park Road, Derby
Machinists Operator. Sliced Bread
27/12/1975–13/10/1979
Changed Work – Sacked

He worked at the Bakery with Mohan for nearly four years until the incident with the cup of hot tea and a stool, which resulted in the termination of their employment.

Richard Lees LTD, Weston Underwood, Derbyshire
Machinists Operator
15/10/1979 – 18/12/1992
Redundant

My father was sacked from the bakery exactly a month after I was born. Fortunately for us all he began his new job a couple of days later, with Mohan once again at his side. He then happily worked at Richard Lees for thirteen years until three days after his thirty-eighth birthday, when he was forced to take redundancy due to the early 1990s recession.

Jobseeker Allowance
18/12/1992–19/10/2000

After his brush with death in February 1993, he didn't work for a long while, during this lengthy period of not being able to work he also began to claim invalidity benefit and then Incapacity benefit. However, as time went on he began to get very bored and restless at home.

Chaucer Food Group, Uppermoor Road, Allenton, Derby
19/10/2000–01/03/2006

In late 2000, he managed to once again get another job at a bakery, which was close to the Spider Bridge in the Allenton area of Derby. This would become his final place of work.

*

I was born in Derby in 1979 and the first home I ever lived in was at 160 Portland Street. At the time, this house on the corner of Portland Street and Pear Tree Crescent was inhabited by my parents as well as Sohan's family.

During these early years, I managed to pick up an awkward habit of not addressing my father as 'Dad'. This mix-up came about when I began to copy Sohan's children in the way they would address, not only my father, but their own father too. This resulted in me calling my father, Chacha and my thiah, Sohan, as Dad. In Punjabi, a chacha is a father's younger brother. But oddly I still called my own mother mum and my thiee as big mum. However, as muddled as I was about how to address people, deep down I always knew who my real father was. When Sohan and his family moved out of Portland Street in 1986, I slowly began to feel more comfortable in calling my father Dad for the first time. It initially did feel a little embarrassing having to acknowledge him in this way because I just wasn't used to it. I guess it was a strange mixed feeling of embarrassment and pride that I must have felt at the time. I finally had a dad I could call my own.

My earliest memories of my father are of him raising me high into the air and holding me in his arms. He was a tall man – a giant in my eyes – and he would take me everywhere with him. He was a good man; a gentle man. Over the years he would share many stories about our early escapades together.

The very earliest of these stories occurred on the day I was born at the Derby City Hospital on the 13th September 1979. Very soon after I was born, I was placed on a paediatric scale to be given a health check by a nurse who had assisted in my mother's delivery. As this nurse peered over me to check my weight, I unintentionally peed into her face.

A couple of years later, my father momentarily left his Ford Cortina unattended with me still inside. As soon as he stepped out of the car and slammed the door behind him I had immediately pressed down on a manual door lock. For the next half an hour or so he had to coax and bribe me with sweets, until I eventually released a door lock to allow him back in. I can imagine this to be quite true because I've always loved exploring how things work.

Another incident occurred at our house on Portland Street, which we shared with my thiah, Sohan, at the time. My father and Sohan had invited some close friends and family around for a small get together. On occasions like this, my cousins and myself would always be barred from entering the front room. My cousin, Jasbinder, and I would not be deterred though. We were always very inquisitive as to what the menfolk might be up to, so we entered the old living room then climbed up onto the back of the sofa that leant against a partition wall. We then began to peer through a little rectangular window, into the front room. As we jumped up and down trying to see what they were all up to we quickly worked out that they were drinking whilst playing cards. As soon as our little topknots were spotted bobbing through the window, we quickly jumped off the sofa and ran, giggling into the kitchen,

About an hour or so later, the little get together in the front room had come to an end and everyone began making their way out of the front door, followed closely by my father and thiah. My cousin and I then decided to enter the unattended front room and have a game of snap. Once again my father failed to foresee another possible blunder in the making; on his return to the front room my cousin and I had already gulped down a glass of whiskey between us. I can't actually recall the latter part of this story myself, but then again, under the circumstances would any toddler? Apparently we were rushed to the hospital, but I have no memory of it other than my cousin led me to believe it was medicine we were drinking.

Not long after my first encounter with alcohol, I began attending Harrington Street Nursery. Every weekday morning before I went to nursery, my mother would comb my hair, tie it into a topknot and then cover it with a clean circular cloth, called a ramaal. A homemade polyester-braided elastic band would then be slid over it to keep it from unravelling. Having eaten breakfast, my mother or my father would then drop me off at the nursery, which was only a short walk around the corner from our home. I loved my time at Harrington Street Nursery and particularly enjoyed morning breaks when I would drink milk from my own little mug. My mother had told me how important milk was for my bones and muscles so I would gulp it down quickly and then flex my biceps to see if I could feel any change. It never seemed to have any noticeable effect, but I guess it was better than drinking whiskey any day of the week.

After a couple of years at Harrington Street Nursery I moved on to Pear Tree Infants. The school itself was across the road from the nursery and next door to Pear Tree Junior Community School.

I remember my first day at Pear Tree Infants quite clearly. On this particular day, my father and I walked hand in hand from our home on Portland Street, all the way to the main gate on Harrington Street. We then walked through the playground, entered the school and then made our way into a large, almost empty hall. It was only then that my father let go of my hand. I was then beckoned by a teacher and told to sit down on the dark brown parquet wood floor with a small group of four other children who were already sat waiting patiently. I followed the instructions without hesitation, but as soon as my bottom touched the floor I quickly realized that I was no longer a small child any more. It dawned on me that I was in the process of making the next step up to big school. Another teacher then stepped forward to talk to us all. At this point I knew that my father was going to leave me behind. As soon as he saw the teacher in conversation with us, from the corner of my eye, I noticed him turn around and make his way out of the hall. I turned my head and immediately wanted to follow him back home, in my mind I had already stood up and rushed towards him, but I remained seated. I knew I had to stay and be brave. So I remained silent and sat there pretending I was unaffected by the whole occasion. Inside however, my stomach was doing cartwheels and there seemed to be a swarm of butterflies also trying their best to follow my father home too. Once the teacher had introduced herself she led my little group out of the hall and took us to our new classrooms. As soon as I was taken away from the hall and put into my new class everything felt better. I quickly became easily distracted and the feeling of being abandoned evaporated from within me. Anyway in my mind, I had already reassured myself that if I really didn't want to be there I could have quite easily managed to make my way back home unaccompanied. Home was only a three-minute walk away and if I did get lost all I had to do was listen out for the sound of the cooing pigeon that would guide me home.

When I was younger I used to always hear a cooing pigeon, which nested in the pear tree in our neighbour's back garden. To this day, whenever I hear that sound, it reminds me of home; Pear Tree.

I loved my time at Pear Tree Infants; it was a beautiful little school. I remember the day I learned how to read, or should that be, told I could read. During my first year I used to be given words that were individually printed on card strips and then kept in a little tin box with my name on top. At the end of every school day I would have to take these words home to learn. On one particular day I had to be tested on my new set of words. On that day I knew full well that if I had been able to read and recall all these words I would be given my first ever reading book. On the day of my test my teacher became a little busy and distracted by another child who was struggling with his own box of words. So an older pupil in my class who could read was asked to test me instead. He was very patient with me and I remember reading the words to him but then began to struggle to recall one or two of the longer ones. So this older boy helped me out by telling me what they were and how they were pronounced. He then informed our teacher that I had got them all right. My teacher then tested me again, but this time I was able to remember them all. I was so happy. I had passed my first great test in life and gained the ability to read. After thanking my new friend with a smile and a mutual thumbs-up, I was able to pick and choose my reading book from the bookshelf and take it home. The memory of taking home my first ever

'Peter and Jane' Ladybird book is something that I have never forgotten. On that afternoon I hurriedly made my way home and then entered through the back door with a big smile on my face. My mother was waiting for me as she sat at her sewing machine. 'What are you hiding behind your back?' she asked in Punjabi. 'Are they your new words?' 'No,' I said smiling. 'I don't have any.' 'Where are they then? You better not have lost them?' she said as a little bit of annoyance flashed across her face. 'I don't need them any more,' I told her. 'Why?!' I then whipped out my new book from behind my back and showed it to her as I laughed. 'I can read now!' My parents were very proud of me, knowing that I could now do something that both of them had very much struggled with; to read, write and speak English.

I remember a time before this when I was once flicking through the Derby Evening Telegraph and I stumbled across something that was very appealing to me in the TV Guide section. I couldn't read at the time, otherwise I would have known what was coming on, but in my mind I had convinced myself that the film that was to be televised later that evening would be a Rocky film. I even told my cousins about it. That night, even though I wasn't feeling very well, my father stayed up with me as I was adamant that I wanted to watch the film. However, after a while we both realized that it wouldn't be coming on, so we went to bed. The next day my cousins began teasing me by asking if I'd enjoyed the film, knowing full well that I had misread the TV guide. From that day on I tried very hard to improve my reading, not only to make sure I could understand what was going on but also to assist my parents.

In January 1986, when I was six years old, my mother decided to take all of my family to India; all except my father, and myself that is. It was my father's youngest sister's wedding. Around the same time that my mother, sister and brother departed for India so did nearly all of my cousins and relatives. It seemed that just about everybody I knew would be leaving for India sooner or later whilst my father and myself would be left at home, alone at 160 Portland Street.

During this period I stayed mainly at two houses, one was my mother's brothers' house across the road at 34 Pear Tree Crescent and the other was my thiah, Sohan's, house on 72 Cameron Road. Sohan and his family eventually left for India a few days after my family, but before they did so I was able to stay in their company for a short time. I had grown up with them all on Portland Street before they moved to their new home on Cameron Road, so I fit like a mitten. Their house was located opposite the back of the White's Brothers soft drinks factory. Fortunately for me their home was not too far from my home on Portland Street either. Even more fortunately for them, especially my thiee, they also lived on the same road as the Bajwa Food & Video store, which they frequently visited, not only to do some of their food shopping but also rent out the latest Bollywood blockbuster.

On the day that my father and I dropped my mother, sister and brother off at Heathrow Airport I was not worried at all. It just seemed like any other normal day for me, there was no reason to be worried or even upset. They would be leaving my father and I for a short while but would be returning within a couple of weeks. However, it was only when my mother had hugged me goodbye that I truly began to realize how much I would miss them. As my father and I waved them through the final point-of-no-return I became overwhelmed with emotion. It hit me like one of my mother's slaps as my tears streamed down my cheeks. Suddenly my mother was gone, followed by my three-year-old sister and two-year-old brother. I looked at my father; five had become two. I then began to sob uncontrollably. I just could not hold back my tears as I began to snort like a pig with a runny nose. Then a thunderbolt struck me. Who was going to tie my topknot!? The long drive back home didn't help matters at all as I spent most of it crying. After a while I nodded off with the sound of my father's voice in my ears telling me what a great time we would have at home by ourselves, together. My ears were burning. I missed my mother. It was a terrible feeling knowing that we were not all together.

When we finally arrived back, the streets of Pear Tree and especially the area around my house just seemed vacated and grey. After parking the car, we made our way into our, now silent, empty house. It then struck me how quiet it all was without all the normal sounds and voices of our home. We were now well and truly alone. After a brief little stay my father then had to leave me with my big mammi at 34 Pear Tree Crescent, as he needed to get to work.

A few years later my masser, Darbara, and his family would move into 34 Pear Tree Crescent from their previous house at 83 Harrington Street.

That afternoon when I was left alone with my big mammi, Harbans, we were the only two people in the house. As the feeling of abandonment rose within me again, I began to cry again and I just couldn't stop myself from doing so. Fortunately, my big mammi managed to get me to stop crying by hugging me tight and then telling me in Punjabi, 'If you don't stop crying then I'm going to start crying too.' I believed her and immediately stopped crying because I didn't want to upset her.

At the time, two families were living at 34 Pear Tree Crescent. My little mamma Sucha's family consisted of him, my little mammi, Shamindro, Suki, Juewy, Mani and Mandeep. My big mamma Avtar's family consisted of him, big mammi, Jasbir, Pam, Kully and Jazz. The eldest daughter, Pam, had moved out by then as she had gotten married and the eldest son, Jasbir, was at the University of Sheffield and living in halls of residence at the time.

I didn't mind staying around their house during the day because my little mamma's young children would always keep me entertained. However, during the night the only place where I really wanted to be was in my own home across the road, watching my own TV in my father's company. At the time, I also got the impression from some of my older cousins that I wasn't always welcome around their house, but by the end of my little hobo period they all seemed to have warmed towards me.

As well as the house, they also shared a blue VW T3 Box Van. This van would be used for many years, transporting all our families from place to place, until a fire finally destroyed it. Within it there used to be a sofa and a collection of small round pouffes that we would all sit on. At the rear of the van was a raised section above the back wheels. Above this a thin piece of rope was stretched from one side of the van to the other and tied at both ends so that you could grab hold of it should the van come to a sudden stop. On one occasion Jasbir was driving the big blue van and I was sitting in the back. Obviously with a sofa and a collection of pouffes in the back there was very little chance of any of us actually wearing a seat belt. As Jasbir set off from a stationary start he suddenly slammed down on the breaks and came to a sudden stop. This resulted in me flying face forward. It was just my luck that my topknot caught on the rope as I shot towards it and then my face crashed into people's feet below as my topknot unravelled into a plait. Jasbir then turned around and chuckled as I rummaged in the dark for my ramaal and polyester-braided elastic band, which moments earlier was holding my topknot together. I used to hate it when my topknot would unravel like that. Unfortunately, this was not the first time and it would not be the last.

For about half a month I was sent from pillar to post around the Pear Tree area and my topknot had never had it so bad. My biggest issue was that nobody could tie it quite like my mother could. When my aunties would try to construct a topknot on my head they would fail miserably when I compared their attempts to my mother's high standards. They would either do it too tight, resulting in Spock-like eyebrows and severe headaches or they would tie it too loose and the simplest action of looking left and right when crossing the road would unravel it. The other major thing about the topknot would be the position of it on my head when it's construction had been completed. Too far forward and it would look very silly and too far back and you could be mistaken for a girl. On one occasion my little mammi even experimented with two crossed plaits on my head, a type of hairstyle referred to as a telephone in my day. I did not like it at all and quickly unravelled them after I ran home and looked in the first mirror I could catch my face in.

My little mindy would also be missing during this hair-raising time too. A mindy is a thinner and shorter secondary plait, which is drawn together from all the loose mullet hair and then fed back into the main branch of the primary thicker and longer plait, which is then twisted to form a knot on the top of the head. No one knew how to construct a mindy apart from my mother.

On the first day back at school after my mother and siblings had departed for India, I had already decided what I was going to tell my teacher. I was going to tell her that my mother, sister and brother had gone on a trip to India. As I skipped into my classroom that day, eager to share my news, I excitedly called out 'My mum's gone to India…,' but then I almost instantly choked up and then quietly whimpered to myself, '…and left me,' as my smile turned upside down. Fortunately, I managed to quickly compose myself before I became too upset by distracting myself with some books that had caught my eye as I made my way to my table.

This trip to India is probably the main reason why I always felt a close connection to my father and the neighbourhood of Pear Tree. A powerful tug that always pulled me back home whenever I felt abandoned. Whenever I was sent away to stay the night at other people's houses, I would always be reluctant to leave my home on Portland Street. However, as the days went on my refusals intensified. I just didn't want to leave my home, whether my father was there with me or not. Sometimes I would run away from a cousin's house and make my own way home, even if I knew my father wouldn't be there. I would then play in the back garden on my own until somebody came along to find me. Eventually my father relented and allowed me to stay at home whilst he was working on night shift, but only if my cousin, Jasbir, would sleep over at our house.

At the time I could tell Jasbir was a little annoyed at my act of defiance. He could have quite easily spent the night in his own bed across the road, but I wouldn't be budged. I wanted to remain at home and I absolutely refused to have it any other way. Jasbir and his heavy-footed braking would eventually get the last laugh, though.

When staying at my thiah Sohan's house on Cameron Road my cousins and I would have regular tea-drinking competitions. In the evening just before bedtime my thiee would make us all some hot milk or tea and serve them in steel cups. Once the signal to commence drinking would be given we would then all try to finish our drink as quickly as possible. Jastinder would nearly always win no matter how hard Jasbinder and I tried to beat her. Although Manjit would never take part because by then she was almost ten and a little too old to play our childish games. We would then all make our way upstairs to bed A few minutes later my thiah would then come around and lift up the duvets at the foot of our beds and then gently warm our feet with his little electric heater and then snuggly tuck us all in.

On one occasion my thiah, Sohan, had to drop me off at home very early one morning. On that day we both got up long before everyone else and I quickly got dressed so that he could get to work on time. As we made our way to my house in the darkness of a very cold winter morning, the pavements were covered in ice. So my thiah decided to carry me on his back and then walk along the middle of the roads instead, where the ice had melted due to the passing of cars. A few minutes later we reached my home on Portland Street where my father was waiting for my arrival having returned from his night shift. My thiah then continued his walk to his place of work at the Qualcast Foundry on Victory Road and my father was able to drop me off at school a few hours later.

One of the best memories I have of this period was the brand new toaster my father bought. I had never seen one before and after the first two slices of toast popped out I was hooked. It was great. Put bread in and toast comes out. That is until one day, when the toast refused to pop out so I foolishly stuck a knife into the toaster whilst it was still connected to the mains, in the hope of dislodging it. I immediately realized that this was not the best of ideas when the knife made contact with one of the heating elements and a little flash of light emerged, followed by a bang and a puff of smoke. I had broken it. I was lucky. Fortunately, my father quickly replaced it, without ever knowing the real reason as to why it had suddenly become faulty. Whilst replacing the toaster he also bought a brand new microwave that still works, to this day. To cap it all off he decided to get the whole house rewired by his good friend Mr Dani, the electrician, but that was not because I had short circuited the toaster. The house was in need of rewiring due to its age.

Another thing that I used to absolutely love during this period of apparent abandonment was watching the television. Watching TV was a happy distraction. Some of my best TV moments, ever, were when I used to watch programmes like 'Boon', with Michael Elphick. I particularly loved the theme tune 'Hi Ho Silver', which was performed by Jim Diamond. It still reminds me of my father, whenever I hear it again.

I also loved watching 'Tomorrow's World' and becoming lost in the beautiful haunting theme tune at the start and end of every episode. Like my father I was also big fan of 'Auf Wiedersehen, Pet'. The Jimmy Nail character, Oz, always used to make my father smile and for this reason I always connected the pair of them in my thoughts. A similar connection also applied to 'Minder' which starred Dennis Waterman, as my father's nickname was M(h)inder. I also loved watching 'Only fools and Horses' and following the hilarious exploits of the Trotter family. This might have also been the case because I always felt that my thiah Sohan looked very much like Delboy, and his younger brother, Rodney, reminded me of my father. My cousins and I were also obsessed by a new soap at the time called 'Eastenders', which was still in its first year of broadcast. Fortunately, on most occasions we all tended to watch the same type of thing and my older cousins didn't have to be subjected to me sulking if I failed to get my way.

During this time I also have a sad memory of an incident that occurred on January 28th 1986 during one late evening at 34 Pear Tree Crescent. It was actually on the same day that my mother, sister and brother had departed for Punjab.

My little mamma had just come back from work and his two youngest daughters and I were playing around him whilst he was eating his roti and daal at the table. As my little mamma now had control over the remote, he decided to change the channel. A breaking news report then flashed onto the TV screen and I stopped to watch what was happening. I noticed a shuttle taking off and then a few seconds later a great big explosion occurred that filled the sky with a smoke plume that split into two at first, then many more branches.

I had just witnessed the Challenger Space Shuttle disaster. Seventy-three seconds into its flight it had suddenly broken apart leading to the deaths of its seven crew members, which included five NASA astronauts and two payload specialists, which included an engineer and a teacher.

As I was already watching the TV, I quickly became aware that lives had been lost. However, one of my cousins was not paying attention and then made an ill-timed joke. My little mamma felt it was at the most inappropriate time, so he gave her a little slap but then immediately apologized. He then had to tell his other daughter off for laughing at what he had just done. It was not a time to laugh. Once my cousins had fully absorbed what we had all just witnessed we stopped playing and then made our way to bed.

On some days my big mammi would have to walk me to school when my father could not. On one particular day we left my house on Portland Street together then crossed the road at the point where Mrs Varty, the lollipop lady, was stationed. We then made our way through the large groups of screaming children and to the other side of the playground, closer to the main classrooms. My big mammi then stood beside me, holding my hand as we both waited for the bell, which would be the signal for all the children to start going into their classrooms. We had not been waiting very long when suddenly the playful screams in the playground turned to screams of great distress as children began running in terror in all directions. I then saw it. An enormous harlequin Great Dane was running wild through the playground having come off its lead. The children had by now become hysterical and I have to admit, I felt some fear too, but I had nowhere to run. There was no point in running, it would have had no problem catching up with me. So I held tightly on to my big mammi's hand, trying not to panic as she pulled me closer into her. 'There was no chance it would come after me anyway; it wasn't as if I had a secret stash of scooby snacks.'

Scooby snacks: as soon as I thought it the dog stopped, turned and then looked directly at me. Out of a whole playground of children it could have chased down it was just my luck that it's attention was now drawn to me. I remained rooted to the spot as this enormous white dog with black markings began trudging and then bobbing its way towards me. Within a few seconds it was a tongue's length in front. 'I hope it doesn't take a chunk out of my topknot,' was the last thought that crossed my mind before it then began to slowly sniff me up and down with its large, black, wet nose. I momentarily looked into its piercing green eyes then just as quickly looked away as it continued to sniff at me. There was really not much else I could do but to stand firm and look away. Then unexpectedly out of nowhere popped out an enormous, long, pink, fleshy, wet tongue that licked the back of my free hand leaving a lovely warm tingling feeling of comfort and a drool of saliva. In my peripheral vision I then noticed a few children pointing in my direction and shouting, 'Wow look he's not scared!' Then suddenly, it turned around and darted back into the playground leaving a puff of vapour from its panting mouth in its trail. I looked down at my hand. It was still there. I grinned with relief that it was all over. The dog had now returned to its master and had been put back on its lead. A few moments later the bell rang. My big mammi then let go of my hand. After saying goodbye to me she made her way home having not once flinched throughout my whole ordeal.

The incident with the Great Dane remained a topic of great conversation for many weeks after, in the school playground. That is until another event occurred that scaled well above it. That was the day the perimeter wall on the Harrington Street side of the school was finally conquered. A small group of us had been egging-on the latest contender. After a couple of unsuccessful attempts, we watched in awe as he hauled himself to the summit and then began waving his arms in triumph as if he had straddled a mountain. Suddenly, the playground erupted with noise and all eyes looked up in his direction. Including those of a passing dinner lady who carefully brought him down to earth then seized him by the ear and marched him into the school hall through a sea of children engaged in a thunderous ovation.

The only other time children in the playground acted in such unison was when someone would spot an aeroplane flying overhead in the clear blue sky. This would result in every child in the playground freezing on the spot then thrusting their heads into the air as they raised a hand to their forehead, almost like a salute, to block out the sun's glare. They would then wave frantically with their other hand in the hope that the passengers above them might actually see them below. It was a regular occurrence during playtime. We all did it. I still do it to this day, with the exception of the waving.

After what seemed like an eternity, but probably only lasted a couple of weeks at the most, my mother and siblings eventually returned to England. I was glad to have them back and so was my topknot

*

Those somewhat traumatic couple of weeks in January 1986 would shape my character for the rest of my life. They would also allow me to experiment with food for the first time in my life too. At the time I really didn't like eating fruit or vegetables, although the potato has always been my favourite food. My main reason for disliking fruit and vegetables at the time was entirely down to one thing; the market. Every weekend, without fail, my father and I would visit either the Eagle Centre Market or Allenton Market. In the process of following my father in and around the stalls I would observe the bruised and soiled produce at very close proximity. It used to put me right off and was not at all appealing to me. I feel the same to this day whenever I walk through the fruit and veg aisles in supermarkets.

My first experiment with food began with a fruit. I remember peeling into my first ever orange at my masser's house on Harrington Street. I quite enjoyed the taste but didn't like the sticky juice it left on my hands and fingers.

My second experiment with food was introduced to me at 34 Pear Tree Crescent. I had never tasted bacon before so my little mammi fried me some for the first time ever. I've never forgotten the smell it emanated as it crackled in the frying pan.

In those days I rarely ate meat as my mother would only ever make meat dishes for special occasions. Although she would prepare and cook the meat she would never eat it herself. I also had a strong dislike of stripping chicken off the bone too so I didn't like to eat much of it. However, I did love soaking my chapattis in the masala it was cooked in, even though I bizarrely used to think it was made from the blood of chickens. I seemed to have picked up on an odd taste for blood because in the Infants we were once given some dragon's blood to drink to celebrate the Chinese New Year. It was blatantly Ribena though.

As well as eating every type of potato dish going, I also enjoyed eating fish fingers by the plateful. So, in a sense I guess I was a pescatarian who only ate fish fingers. Later on, sausages would also be introduced into my diet. However, beef was always a complete no-no in my house and I had never really tasted it until one day I had a sudden urge to taste the great celestial cow. So I decided to go to my mamma's shop on Balfour Road and bought a packet of beef and onion 'flavoured' crisps. My little mammi looked at me incredulously as I tried to pay for them. 'You sure about this?' she asked. 'Yes, that's the flavour I want.' I quite liked the taste too. A few years later I would eat my first McDonald's hamburger. However, the experience left me quite deflated just like its overall appearance. It was bland and tasteless and looked nothing like the pictures on the TV.

I loved my mother's cooking and the beautiful yogurt-based curry that she still continues to make, to this day.

My mother was always cooking in the kitchen when I was young. On one particular day, she decided to test out her new pressure cooker. I was watching the TV and she was also mopping the kitchen floor at the same time too. Having become distracted by cleaning up, her pressure cooker suddenly began to whistle furiously. She panicked and then shouted at me to get out of the kitchen. As she tried to depressurize it, I quickly ran out of the back door and then jumped headfirst into a little patch of grass in the back garden. Looking back into the kitchen, I heard a small explosion. My mother was still in the kitchen! 'Mum?!' I cried. There was no answer as I sheepishly set foot back into the kitchen not knowing what to expect. To my relief I saw her smiling back at me as she glanced around at the kitchen walls and ceiling which were now splattered in daal. She quickly cleared the mess up and then started all over again. I was mightily relieved that she hadn't been hurt. I still chuckle whenever I think about the pressure cooker incident as it takes me back to the words of an old school friend from Pear Tree Junior's, who used to sing 'shame steam pressure cooker' when she would laugh at other people's misfortunes.

I left Pear Tree Infants in 1987 and moved up to Pear Tree Juniors, which was the building next door. During my first year, Mrs Slater organized an art competition based on the theme of space. I loved anything to do with space at the time because I was already a big fan of science fiction and especially Doctor Who. So I decided to draw a pastel picture of two astronauts on a space-walk. A few days later, during an assembly in the lower hall we had a special visit from PC Pabla from Pear Tree police station. He had been invited down to hand out the prizes. I didn't think I had any chance. If anything I was hoping to catch the name of my friend, Suntokh. He was also a good friend of my cousin, Satnam, and they were both in their fourth year at school at the time. He was very good at art and had carved a space shuttle out of a block of polystyrene, and then painted it too. As I sat on the floor with my legs crossed, playing around with my shoelaces I heard a familiar name being called out. At first I thought I had misheard as another child called Kulwinder stood up thinking that it was her, but she too had misheard. As she quickly sat down I heard the name called out again. 'Kalwinder?' I remained seated. 'Go on Kally!' someone shouted out. As I looked up and to my right, I realized that the people shouting out my nickname were Satnam and Suntokh. It was me?! At this point I slowly got up still disbelieving as I began to make my way to the front of the hall whilst everyone around me cheered me on. After weaving my way through all the children, I shook PC Pabla's outstretched hand and accepted my prize. I had won my year group?! I then headed back to my little vacated spot on the floor and sat back down. Still embarrassed by all the attention I was receiving, I looked upon what I had won; a pack of felt tips, a sketchbook and box of wax crayons. As I made my way home from school that day, I passed Satnam in the playground who gave me a thumbs up and a smile. I then passed Mrs Varty at the crossing point and told her what I had won when she asked what I was holding. As soon as she had helped me cross the road, I quickly ran home as fast as I could to show my parents what I had won.

Whenever I achieved anything in life, I always made sure to tell my parents first. In 2001, a bunch of my friends from the University of Leicester played in a 5-a-side football tournament in Walsall. I was in the Leicester B team, and we were given no chance. I played as the goalkeeper; other members of our squad included, Aman, Jag, Ali, Danesh and Manj. We lost our first match, drew the second then won every other one, including the final. It was a great victory. There were so many better players than us on that day, but as a team we were the best. I phoned home that day after we received our trophies. My father picked up the phone and I told him we had won. It was just like winning at Pear Tree Juniors all those years previously.

As I was growing up I used to be very thin-skinned and I would always feel sorry for people who were suffering. I'm quite sure I got this side of my personality from my mother. I just hated suffering full stop.

One incident that springs to mind is when a small family of dormice occupied our house. Little mice used to terrify me as they scurried about, popping up unexpectedly from all places. Maybe my fear came from my mother's screams, or maybe I was genuinely scared that they really would run up my trouser leg as they had in Roald Dahl's story 'The Witches'. During this particular occupation, the little mice began giving me sleepless nights. So in the night time hours, whilst I was still awake and unable to sleep because I was listening out for every squeak and creak, I would think about ways of getting rid of them. That is until one morning, when I woke up to the sight of an almost decapitated mouse caught in a mousetrap that my father had put out the previous night. It left me quite heart broken and I couldn't get the image of it out of my mind for the rest of the day as I sulked around the junior school playground. As soon as I saw that poor dead mouse I was adamant that no more would die in my house. So I quickly convinced my father to remove all the mousetraps. We would catch them humanely instead and then set the whole family free. Eventually, my father managed to catch them and contained them all in a little shoebox. My own Rube Goldberg-inspired attempts to catch them with cheese, ramps and buckets had failed dismally. My father then released them all a few doors away on the corner of Harrington Street. I was so relieved when the rest of them had been saved, but I was still upset that one of them, who I imagined to be the father, had been killed in such a gruesome manner.

Another gut wrenching incident that occurred to me during my Pear Tree years was when my father and I attended a wedding at the Guru Tegh Bahadur Gurdwara on East Park Road, Leicester. This one incident made me realise the great importance a father plays in the life of his children.

A relative of mine, who was called Mandip, had lost his father a few months previously because of complications due to multiple sclerosis. Mandip was also at the wedding that day. He was older than me by about five years or so. Previous to this occasion we used to hang around together *quite a lot with other mutual relatives and friends around the Pear Tree area. However, on this day he decided he didn't want a small, scruffy, little kid like me following him around any more. At one point I got a bit too close to him and he suddenly snapped at me, 'You rabbit! Go back to your dad and hang around with him instead.' I quickly shot back with, 'No! You go back.' Immediately, I couldn't believe what I had said. As soon as I spoke I realized that I'd used the wrong choice of words. I definitely didn't mean, 'No! You go back to your dad.' It was like a poker had entered my stomach. 'How could I have said something so deeply hurtful to someone without meaning it?' I always knew there was a line you should never cross. Have fun, tease but never step over the line. I had done it unintentionally, but I had crossed the line and that hurt me more than any pain he might now want to dish out to me.*

Mandip's father, Chuhar Singh Mander, had come to England at the same time as my big mamma, Avtar Singh Thiara. The pair of them were like father figures to the younger generation that would follow in their footsteps from Punjab. Chuhar was diagnosed with multiple sclerosis in 1976, just prior to my parents' marriage. The condition had first materialized during a walk around Arboretum Park. At the time he was working at the Ley's Malleable Casting Foundry but had to give up his job when his health began to steadily deteriorate. In 1988, having lived with the condition for more than ten years, he finally passed away during his sleep. I remember when I first heard about his death and the responsibility that was placed on my father's shoulders when he had to disclose it to his two eldest sons. Chuhar's untimely death had an upsetting impact on us all.

I felt so saddened for Mandip and his siblings when their father passed away. I remember one occasion when we went around to pay our respects at their house on St Thomas Road. I had gone over with a handful of football stickers that I'd been collecting. Mandip asked if he could see them, so I handed them over to him. He then told me that he had also bought a couple of packets the previous day. As soon as he told me this I asked if he wanted mine to add to his collection. It was the only thing I could offer to try and make him feel just a little bit better.

Fortunately for me that day, Mandip hadn't heard what I had said. Although he did reply with a 'You what!?' With the hustle and bustle of people moving about, maybe he really didn't hear what I'd said. I then quickly replied, 'Nothing, I said nothing' as I sulked away absolutely deflated and upset. Seconds earlier he was not being very kind to me, but that didn't matter any more. I began to feel sorry for him and the loss he had experienced. I realized from that moment on that no child deserves to live without their loving father in their life. 'What if I was to ever find myself in his situation; I would be devastated if I lost my father'. Memories of my father began flooding my mind, and then I saw him looking at me from a short distance away. 'You ok?,' he asked. 'I'm ok, Dad.' 'You want some money?' 'No I'm fine.' I didn't tell him about what had just happened but he could sense I was not happy so to cheer me up he bought me a Punjabi alphabet poster from one of the stalls inside the langar hall.

The only thing that somewhat lifted my spirits that day was to spend time in my father's company. I remained distracted and upset for the rest of the day thinking about what I had said and done. But deep down, more than anything, I finally came to the realization that one day, I too would inevitably lose my own father and have to experience Mandip's loss.

Chapter 6: Nawanshahr – Punjab
Ram Rai Pur

On January 6th 1990, my father and I departed for our own voyage together, back to his homeland in Punjab. This time it would be my mother, brother and sister who would be left behind in Pear Tree.

A trip I had previously made with my father, mother and my sister on the 22nd November 1982. At the time of my first visit I was three years, two months and nine days old and my sister who was still a baby was one month and fifteen days old. The reason for the trip was so that we could attend Rivaloh's wedding. Growing up I only ever had vague memories of the two and a half months I spent there. However, one vivid memory that remains to this day, and which at the time left me quite confused and a little upset, was of a man who looked very much like my father glaring back at me in anger. I remember watching this man from a few feet away as he applied shaving foam to his face whilst looking into a mirror. Having seen my reflection, he then suddenly turned and began shouting in my direction. It was only years later that I realized that this man who had startled me wasn't my father at all but was in fact Mohan. It was only after seeing old photos of Mohan without his turban and beard, before his transformation into a Singh, that I finally saw the striking similarity between my father and his brother.

My second visit on January 6th 1990 would become the first trip that I would remember clearly and consciously. At the time I was ten years, three months and twenty-four days old. Therefore, it was the perfect age to fully absorb the experience and make connections with the people I met. This one trip gave me all the information I ever needed to know, in order to establish where my parents had originally come from before they made their life-changing move to England. Prior to this trip, my family knowledge was a little cloudy. Although I was aware of many of my relatives in Derby I didn't fully understand how they were all connected. I was also not very familiar with how I should address them all either. This is because in Punjabi culture titles given to relations are different depending on which side of the family the person in question is on and whether they are younger or older than your own father.

For example, a mother's sister is called a massi, her husband, a masser. A mother's brother is called a mamma, his wife a mammi. A father's younger brother is a chacha, his wife a chachi. However, an older brother is called a thiah, and his wife a thiee. A father's sister is called a phua, her husband a phuffhur.

The trip allowed me to discover more about my parents and their own families that remained in Punjab. My father's family consisted of his three sisters and his parents. My mother's family consisted of her eldest brother, another older sister and her parents.

One thing I never had any doubt in my mind over was knowing that my father had an older brother called Sohan, who I also referred to as 'Dad'.

The main reason for our trip in 1990 was because my father and his three brothers were led to believe that my grandfather was in a really bad state and that he was literally on his deathbed. As none of my father's brothers could make the journey, the responsibility fell on his shoulders to go in their place and once his decision had been made he immediately decided that I should go with him.

In September 1989, I began my penultimate year at Pear Tree Juniors, two months before the collapse of the Berlin wall. In the days prior to our departure I remember a feeling of great excitement as I happily revealed to Miss Koacher and my classmates that I would be leaving them for a few weeks. On the last school day before we departed I made a cross-stitch pattern on a piece of fabric during an arts and craft lesson that I was hoping to give to my grandmother as a present. However, it was so small that the only thing she could have really used it for was a doily. My mother doubted if it would ever get any use or if my grandmother would even appreciate it.

On the day we departed for Punjab my father and I brought together the luggage that we would take with us and placed it at the bottom of the stairs. It was early in the morning and coincided with the time that my brother and sister were getting ready for school. Unfortunately, when they both set their eyes upon our luggage they immediately realized that my father and I were going on a trip together. Both of them began to cry knowing that they wouldn't be coming with us. So my father had to tell a lie and make out we were not going anywhere. A few minutes later my father and I then tried to tip toe our way out of the house and towards the car with some luggage, but my brother and sister realized what was going on and came rushing towards us. Again they began to cry so this time my father bent down towards them both and planted a big kiss on each of their lips. This seemed to cheer them up and appease their suspicions that we were not actually leaving them behind. We then waved them goodbye and told them that we would see them when they got back. We would get back in four weeks.

Just as my father and I were about to leave the house for the last time, I remember my mother also getting a little upset too as we both made our way out through the front door with the last of our luggage. I wasn't at all upset, unlike when I had said goodbye to my mother and siblings back in 1986. She hugged me goodbye, but this time the roles were reversed.

*

Growing up in Pear Tree my mother always liked to think that she ruled our home with a rod of iron. Although my mother would thrash out the beatings to my siblings and I, it was never with an iron rod. In fact, it was with a burnt wooden spoon called a karchi, which always smelled of thurka. However, it soon reached the point that the karchi would not even have to come out of the kitchen drawer and strike our bottoms. All she had to do when she thought we were misbehaving was to rattle away at the closest kitchen drawer to hand and we would soon get the message inside the living room that a beating was on its way if we didn't immediately stop misbehaving. On hearing this death rattle, my siblings and I would instantly stop what we were doing and then fling ourselves horizontally towards the nearest sofa to make out that we were innocently watching the TV or asleep. Now this worked well for a while, but on some occasions the clattering from the drawers would fall silent and she would have already entered the living room and struck out at the first child who was not sat down and watching TV on the sofa or asleep. However, I soon put a stop to the threat of the karchi when I realized that to avoid any further beats with it, all we had to do was hide it. That worked for a good while. Until that is, she bought a new larger, yellow plastic karchi with extra flexibility and a sting in its tail when it smacked down on your bottom. Again, that soon went missing. When she finally realized that the beats with the karchi were not working she changed her method of discipline. Her next plan of action to keep us in order would be to threaten to burn our hands on the small wall mounted heater in the corner of the living room. The first time she ever used this approach on me was when she dragged me to the heater by my wrists and then forced my hands towards it as my sister and brother both looked on in terror. Obviously, I resisted with all my might and screamed my topknot off until she finally stopped forcing my hand towards the fire and after I had promised her that I would never misbehave again. However, after a short period of reflection following this particular incident, I quickly concluded that, deep down, I knew my mother would never really genuinely hurt any one of us deliberately. We all knew she was a big softie at heart. So the next time I was caught misbehaving and she tried to drag me towards the flames, I offered no resistance and smiled my way towards the heater as she pulled me along on my bottom. When my hands got close enough to the flames, it was in fact my mother who shrieked and not me as she pulled them quickly away from the danger. When she realized that I'd called her bluff, she let me go, gave me a short slap on the back of my head which knocked my topknot off and then went back into the kitchen to continue her cooking whilst muttering, 'Wait till your father gets home.' This was always her last resort and the final threat, when all other means had failed. However, even when my father would be told about our misbehaviour he would never really say anything or do anything about it unless we either damaged or broke something. We very rarely saw his blood pressure rise and we always knew my mother's bark was much worse than her bite.

For all of her life, my mother has been petrified of snakes and anything else that wriggles. She has ophidiophobia, which is the abnormal fear of snakes that she no doubt developed whilst growing up in Punjab. To this day she has an absolute fear of worms and snakes. Just a mention of them or the sight of them in a picture or on the TV makes her shriek and raise her hand to her face and shout out, 'hor passa la di,' which means 'put another channel on'.

My mother did love us and we always knew that to be the case, no matter how many times she tried to discipline us. I remember the day we all went in to the old Eagle Centre Market. My father was leading the way in front, followed by mother who was carrying my little brother in her arms. I was at the back of the line looking ahead making sure not to lose sight of my mother and father as well as also trying to keep an eye on my sister who was skipping along in front of me. As we walked through the bustling bazaar, a balloon distracted my sister and led her astray. I noticed that she was now walking away from us all, so I looked up towards my parents to see if they had also noticed. Unfortunately, they had not. I quickly looked back to the spot where I had last seen my sister but she wasn't there. I quickly alerted my parents as to what had happened. My father, mother and I then stood still and began to look around in all directions hoping that one of us might spot her. None of us did though. She was lost. My mother began to cry and then panic as my frantic father left us to wait in the main square of the Eagle Centre, underneath the waterfall clock so he could go and search for my sister alone. I looked up at the clock then looked around into the distance to see if I could spot my father and sister coming back. After a short while we heard my sister's name and description being called out over the Eagle Centre tannoy. After what I thought was a few minutes later, I looked at the clock again but the hands hadn't moved from the last time I had checked. Time seemed to drag, a couple of minutes later I looked at it again. Still no change, it was obviously not working. After what seemed like an age, my sister was eventually reunited with us. My father had found her and returned with her to our safe zone under the clock with her hand tightly held in his. For a few minutes, time literally stood still for all of us. My mother was very relieved, we all were.

On another happier visit to the old Eagle Centre Market, I remember my father taking my siblings and I into one of the passport photo booths. My mother was not with us that day. My father crammed us all into the little booth and we had our pictures taken together. One of those passport-sized photos remained in my father's wallet for the rest of his life. It now resides in my mother's purse.

A couple of years after the balloon scare, my mother, sister, brother and I went on a coach trip to Blackpool with some of our extended family and friends. This time, however, my brother and I got lost. I would have only been about eight at the time and my brother about four. I was hovering around the back of our little family group, keeping close tabs on my little brother as well as trying to follow my mother and relatives in front of us, when suddenly I realized my brother and I were completely on our own. I quickly grabbed him by the scruff of his neck and dragged him towards me. I then began looking around to see if I could see anybody that I recognized. After a few seconds I became a little unsettled and upset, but I decided not to show my panic to my brother. He was still very young so he wouldn't have fully comprehended the mess we had found ourselves in. He continued to hunt for shells in the sand, as well as picking up the odd bit of dry donkey poo. I then decided to take him away from the sand and lead us back on to the promenade in the hope it would be easier for people to spot us out in the open with our distinctive peculiar shaped white topknots. All we needed to do was to try and find someone, anyone who had made the same journey from Derby with us on the coach and then stick with them until we were reunited with our mother again. Fortunately, after a minute I spotted one of my mother's workmates and I explained to her what had happened. My brother and I then tagged along with her family until my mother finally noticed that we were missing and came smiling towards them to reclaim her short, lost sons.

*

On arrival in Delhi in January 1990, I remember the prickly heat and humidity striking me immediately as my father and I stepped off the plane at the Indira Gandhi International Airport. I also remember an instant sharp prick of a feeling in my right buttock too. That was my welcome to India: a mosquito bite. The fact that my father and I were still wearing our cold weather clothing from England didn't help either. My father continued to keep his blue 'Adrian Mole' parka on because of all the pockets it had; it came in very handy for gaining quick access to all our documents when required.

Once we had retrieved our luggage from the battered and broken carousel we waited in a long queue for our passports and documents to be checked so that we could leave the airport. Whilst my father and I waited in the queue, two white British men stood behind us. As I turned around and observed them I noticed that they were both having a very good laugh at someone's expense. My father then turned and smiled at them. One of the men then smirked and said something to my father, which made my father stop smiling and turn his head away. My father was quite obviously a little annoyed, judging by the look on his face. I then looked back at the two men as they continued laughing and smiling as one then tried to stop the other from making any more silly comments. As my father and I continued to wait in line, I began to get angry with the pair of them for laughing at my father. My father was only trying to be friendly. They were quite obviously drunk and were trying to take the mick. For a brief moment I pictured myself punching the one closest to me straight in his beer belly. Two things stopped me though. Firstly, I worried that he might then grab my topknot and pull it off. 'Who would tie it back again?' I thought to myself. Secondly, I worried that the Indian police might give my father a hard time if anything did kick off. To this day I wish

I had struck that man. I was the perfect height to hit him where it hurts.

Once we had finally cleared customs we both made our way out into the muggy darkness. My father eventually found a trolley with four wheels and then placed all our luggage on to it. I then began to push the trolley behind my father, avoiding all the potholes and cracks in the ground as he led the way ahead. However, it was so hot outside that even putting my hands on the metal handle of the trolley felt very warm, moist and sticky to the touch. In England it would have felt quite cold. My father now had to find a bus to take us on our first leg of the mammoth journey from Delhi all the way to our home village of Ram Rai Pur in Nawanshahr. Within a few minutes my father had managed to track down the right bus, heading in the right direction and at the right price. After placing our luggage within the storage compartment we settled down for a long and bumpy drive towards our final destination. As we travelled in the dark, the constant noise of vehicles hooting was absolutely deafening and was a stark difference to the relative silence of an English motorway.

Hooting is a very noisy Indian custom that allows other drivers around you to be aware that you are either behind them, beside them, or in some cases, on top of them.

The journey back to Ram Rai Pur took place on a series of buses through the night and into the next morning. On one occasion, I remember nodding off against a glass window as it shook me in and out of sleep. In the process of dozing, I would hear the voice of my thiee, Sohan's wife. But every time I was shaken out of my sleep I woke up and immediately realized that I was no longer in the comforts of Pear Tree. The sight of an elephant was a quick reminder to that fact. Thankfully though, every time I awoke, I also saw my father still by my side.

I remember, for some odd reason I also collected and saved all the bus stubs in a little telephone diary I had been carrying. I had written some addresses and phone numbers in there too as I planned to write home to my cousins in England. One letter that I did write on light blue airmail paper, was posted off immediately and arrived in England a week after my father and I had returned.

We eventually arrived in Ram Rai Pur in the dead of night after travelling for what seemed like days through the mud and rain, mostly on buses avoiding the many potholes and the roaming cows that owned the roads. The taxi dropped us off outside my father's old family home. My father then banged on the large iron gate, but no one answered. He then climbed to the top of the gate and shouted in Punjabi, 'Bibi meh aaghia, mehaa Mindy', which meant, 'Gran I'm here. It's me Mindy.' I thought it was a little odd that he called his mother Bibi as that normally meant grandmother or old lady.

He then climbed down from the gate and as soon as his feet touched the ground we heard the sound of doors opening and voices making their way towards us. A small door in the large iron gate then slowly opened and we were welcomed by my grandmother and my father's eldest sister, Simoh. They both then took it in turns to hug us and then welcomed us in. I was glad to be home. My father and I then spent the next half hour or so transferring all our luggage and belongings into one of the empty rooms that had been vacated and cleared out for us. As I walked out of this room after transferring the last of my belongings, I decided to have a good look around my home for the next four weeks. As I stood in the veranda, I looked to my left and saw the stairs leading to the kothi above. I then began to slowly pan right as I noticed the kitchen in the corner and then the lavatory next to it. My eyes then crossed over the large iron gate, onto a medium-sized tree and then towards a larger room to my extreme right. But before I could let my eyes settle on this larger room I had to make a quick double take. Having initially only glanced at the wall next to the tree, I was now looking straight at it, absolutely shaken and rooted to the spot. On the far wall to the right of the gate and to the left of the tree adjacent to the nalka (water pump), I had noticed a familiar shadowy figure. I had to blink a couple of times to force my eyes to open wider. I gaped into the distance. I had seen him before. I had seen him in my dreams. On a more focused examination it became clear to me that what I was actually looking at was a damp patch of water on the wall. This should have put me at ease, but it really spooked me because prior to this visit to Punjab, I once had a dream in which I was in this very same house in Ram Rai Pur and I had seen the same thing in front of me. However, in my dream this figure was wearing a stovepipe hat and smoking a pipe. The figure in my dream with a pipe, but now on the wall, without a pipe, was a silhouette of Abraham Lincoln.

I was only ten years old and I still had clouded memories from my previous visit a few years earlier but could I have really remembered the damp patch from my last visit when I was only three years old? Immediately after the encounter with Abraham's avatar I began to get genuinely freaked out. I had been spooked and this was the last place in the world I wanted to experience that feeling. It was then that I began thinking about my mother. I began to get upset as my ears spontaneously combusted with fright. I needed to calm down and cool down. Just before any tears could begin rolling down my cheeks I hurriedly rushed back into the room where all the luggage had been placed and I retrieved a magazine that I had taken from the plane many hours earlier. The magazine took my mind off Abraham. The rush to find something to occupy my mind also cooled my ears. Flicking through the magazine also made me realize how far I was away from my real home in Pear Tree, my sister, my brother and most of all, my mother. I didn't want my father to see me upset. Thankfully, the tears didn't flow.

An hour or so later, my father and I were tucked up in bed and I felt much safer having him by my side. However, as soon as the lights went out I began to get even more freaked out by the sound of things moving around outside beyond the walls. The sound of shrilling crickets throughout the creepy dark night was relentless so I decided to cover my face under the blanket we were sharing. It was even hotter underneath, but as I was so scared I had no choice but to have to endure the sticky heat and the occasional fart. I also took great care not to poke my feet out from under the blanket, in case they were bitten off during the night. After a few minutes, I quickly fell asleep only to be awoken by a piercing scream from beyond the iron gate. My father had also shot up out of bed but quickly put my mind at ease when he told me that it was only a bullock that had managed to free itself from its shackles. We then heard it galloping down the main road to Nawanshahr whilst screaming as it was chased by a pack of howling wild dogs biting at the poor cow's legs. It was still pitch black when we were both awoken by the noise, but once again I quickly fell asleep. The next thing I remember was a flash of intense bright sunlight as our blanket was stripped away. Still half asleep I snatched it back immediately and then pulled it over my head again. I then stretched out my hand underneath the blanket and felt for my father, but my father wasn't beside me. Again the blanket was stripped away from me. However, this time I was unable to claw it back. I had no choice but to sit up. I rubbed the sleep from my eyes and in front of me stood a bearded face with bushy black hair staring right back at me smiling. It was my cousin Amarjit, also known as Jeeta.

It was now morning and the light had completely extinguished all my fears from the night before. I looked out towards the iron gate in search of Abraham's damp patch but it was no more and I never saw him again. My father had already been up for quite a while by now. During that time, he made plans with Jeeta to visit the hospital as soon as possible. I therefore quickly got myself dressed and told my father I would also be going with them to see my grandfather. However, my father was very reluctant to let me go with them. I wasn't going to be left behind, though, and in the end he had no choice but to yield to my stubbornness. As soon as my topknot had been tied and my paratha were eaten, my father, Jeeta and I then set off for Nawanshahr.

The hospital was like no other that I had ever seen or smelled. I still had vague pleasant smelling memories of the time I visited my mother in the Derby City Hospital with my father and sister when my little brother was born. However, the one I now found myself in looked absolutely run down and the smell of disinfectant was non-existent. We followed closely behind Jeeta as he walked up a winding incline that eventually took us all to the floor my grandfather was on and then on to the room he was being treated in. At the entrance of the room Jeeta stopped, then pointed towards a bed in the corner of the room where an old man lay kicking out in pain. My father then stepped into the room and approached the old man who was screaming in excruciating pain as doctors and nurses rushed around him. My father hurried to the old man's side. I stood back and watched on from a few feet away. I didn't know what to do. My father grabbed the old man by his arm to restrain him and then called out, 'Father, I'm here. It's me Mindy!' I didn't say anything. I couldn't say anything. The old man that I didn't recognize was my grandfather. It had been seven years since I'd last seen him. At this point I began to get very upset as I realized that my grandfather was in a really bad state and there was nothing I could do for him, but watch him suffer. I kept looking on. 'Was this really his deathbed? We must get him away from here. Take him to England, the Derby City Hospital. The doctors and nurses in Derby would be take care of him. He might even have a chance of surviving.' My eyes began shooting in all directions as I tried to contain the tears welling up inside them. Looking down, I noticed the dirty floors and the broken tiles. I then noticed a power socket next to my grandfather's bed, which had blue flames flickering from within. My sight finally settled on the ceiling. My eyes were now filled with tears; I couldn't see. I didn't want to see. A few tears finally left my eyes and my sight cleared for me to witness my father's own pain.

After a couple of minutes, whatever the doctors and nurses had injected into my grandfather had thankfully settled him down. They then gradually began to step away from him as I slowly moved towards him and my father. A lady then lunged at me, smiling, and hugged me. It took me a couple of seconds to recognize who she was. It was my phua, Rivaloh, my father's middle sister. I hadn't noticed her sitting in the corner whilst my grandfather was striking out in pain.

Over the course of the next couple of days my father and I regularly visited my grandfather and to our great relief he progressively got better. After a few days he was eventually released to go home, but with the addition of a urinary catheter.

He would continue to use the catheter for the rest of his life, until he eventually passed away in Derby, in January 1997.

Once my grandfather was back home in Ram Rai Pur, the rest of our stay in Punjab was spent catching up with other extended family members. It was great spending time with my father's family in Ram Rai Pur and my mother's family in the neighbouring village of Sahabpur. My father's childhood home in Ram Rai Pur had been unoccupied for a while. However, during our stay my eldest phua, Simoh, and her husband, phuffhur Kashmir, along with their four children stayed over to accommodate us.

The only downside to my whole second visit to India was a recurring problem that once again reared its knotted head. Nobody could tie my topknot like my mother could. On many an occasion, I would have to take it apart and attempt the knot myself when others had failed so dismally. I got by though, only just.

In the village of Sahabpur lived my mother's side of the family. My nanna, my mother's father, had always been thought to be 100 years old. For as long as I can remember throughout any period of my life as I was growing up, this was always a matter of conjecture. Although his hair would be tied up in a little topknot under his loosely wrapped turban I always thought he looked very much like Gandalf the Grey from J.R.R. Tolkien's 'The Hobbit'. My nanny, in turn reminded me of Granny from the Sylvester and Tweety Looney Tunes cartoon series.

On one occasion my father and I slept over at Sahabpur. The next morning, I was awoken by the noise of people arguing outside. Having now risen, I quickly realized that my father was once again not beside me. I quickly got out of bed and tried opening the door to find my father. However, the door was locked from the outside. From beyond the locked door I heard my nanny and nanna having the loudest conversation ever, about trying not to wake me up. I then began shouting out for them to open the door, but all I heard on the other side was each of them blaming the other for waking me up. Eventually, the door was unlocked and opened. I stepped out of the room and looked around. I then noticed my father through the large iron gate, where he had been waiting on the side of the road for the next bus into Nawanshahr.

My youngest mamma also seems to have picked up this innate ability to talk very loudly for no apparent reason. I remember some of my cousins being quite afraid of his booming voice, as he would try to make conversation with them. He was always quite harmless though, and he used to make me chuckle as he would remind me of Zed from the Police Academy films.

A walking distance of less than 2.5kms separated the two family homes in Ram Rai Pur and Sahabpur. I enjoyed my frequent visits to Sahabpur and I would never fail to hear the name of a man my father and the whole village would refer to as 'Victoria'. Now my father had always had an embarrassing habit of getting his 'him' and 'hers' mixed up, but surely even he knew that Victoria was a female name? One day I finally asked my father as to who this feminine sounding Victoria was and why the villagers held him in such high esteem. My father revealed to me that the man they called Victoria was Gian Singh Sangha VC.

I am quite certain that I would have met Gian Singh VC during my early visits to Sahabpur. There is no doubt that my father would have spoken to him in my company as both of them would have been aware of each other, having lived so close together and because they knew of each other's families.

Many years later, I eventually carried out some research on Gian Singh to find out what deeds he would have performed to be awarded the Victoria Cross. On reading his citation I was left absolutely astonished and the hairs on my arms began to stand to attention.

My mother also had two siblings that remained and continued to live in Punjab. Her eldest brother, Joginder, had been widowed for some time since he lost his wife in tragic circumstances. From this marriage came three sons who were all a few years older than me. Two of whom were twins, Jeeta and Talwan and the third, Dalbir, who had married young and already had two very young sons of his own.

During my second visit to Punjab, I spent quite a bit of time with Jeeta, who many years later would begin a new life in the USA with his own family. Jeeta's twin, Talwan, was not in India during the time of this particular visit as he had been abroad.

Tragically, Talwan passed away in his sleep a couple of years after. Previous to this, he had visited England. In doing so he was able to meet my future wife; Rav had met him when she was younger when he spent some time in Middlesbrough. A short time before his death he'd sent my mother an A4-sized picture of himself. It was a sign to us all that he was now ready to settle down and get married. My mother was heartbroken when she heard the news of her nephew's death. A week or so after he passed away she received a letter that he'd posted from Germany a fortnight earlier. I remember crying when the news was broken to us all. I've never forgotten him.

In 2001, when I first visited Jeeta in the USA, I became very upset when I noticed that the only photo of Talwan that Jeeta possessed to remember his twin brother was a small photo taken of a photo. On my return to England I immediately collected all the photos of Talwan I could find and then scanned and printed them off. I then sent them all to him. One of the photos was a black and white picture of all three of the brothers sitting together with little white topknots on their heads.

The third and eldest of the brothers, Dalbir, was quite different to the other two. He had gone down the religious path and had grown a beard and wore a turban. He was also much more serious and strict in his ways, but he was always very caring.

My father once told me a story about Dalbir that happened during my first visit to Punjab. My mother and I were passengers on a scooter that Dalbir was riding. Dalbir somehow had a little mishap, which resulted in all three of us being thrown off. I don't think any of us were badly injured. Then again, I don't remember.

My mother had three sisters, Simar and Mindo, who were twins and then Surinder, the eldest. My little massi, Simar, and my eldest massi, Surinder, both lived in Derby too. My other twin little massi, Mindo lived in Punjab with her own family.

Before our visit, my father had told me how my Indian twin massi was identical to my little English massi. However, I didn't believe him until I saw her with my own eyes. On the day we went to see my Indian massi, I was absolutely amazed at how much they looked alike. The only major difference was that my massi in England could walk but my massi in India could not. At an early age, my Indian massi had been struck down with polio resulting in her legs becoming very frail. Therefore, she was unable to walk for the rest of her life. The only way she could get around was by crawling on her hands and then dragging her legs forward onto a small wooden block that she would be sat on. As I saw my Indian massi again that day, some memories of my earlier first visit in 1982 came flooding back as I remembered how she used to play with me on the floor. I still remembered her and became aware that I'd seen her before but my memory of her had become scrambled and amalgamated to make me think that I only had one little massi.

After visiting my Indian massi again in 2000, I was adamant that when I returned to England I would try and make her life a bit easier. I managed to find my grandfather's old wheelchair and quickly made plans to get it sent over to her. I couldn't do it entirely on my own so I asked for a little bit of help from my mother's side of the family. However, I became very frustrated and upset by their reluctance to assist me. I carried on regardless though and even had the wheelchair packed and ready to be sent off but at the last moment decided against it. Although my intentions were good I finally realized that if my massi had really needed a wheelchair, my family in Punjab and England would have got one for her years ago. My massi just didn't need it. She had become accustomed to living without one. If anything the wheelchair would probably have been a hindrance to her.

About three years later I was sleeping in my bed, at my home in Pear Tree when I was awoken by the sound of a phone ringing. My father answered it and then quickly passed it over to my mother. My mother then spoke in a faltering voice and asked the person on the other end if her sister Mindo was well. After a little pause, I heard my mother begin to cry softly and then wailed in pain, as the bad news was broken to her. My poor massi had passed away. All her sisters had married and lived comfortable lives in England but she remained in Punjab bringing up her own little family with my masser, Minder. She had bravely persevered with her disability for so long, until finally the day came that she could go on no longer.

On the last couple of days in India, before my father and I would return to England, I became quite upset at the prospect of having to leave my family. I had gotten to know everyone by now and became very saddened that we would have to leave them all behind. On the penultimate day, I was sitting on a makeshift swing in the barn area when I noticed the family dog approach. It stopped a few feet in front of me and began coughing something up. After a while it finally succeeded, then quickly trotted away. I jumped off the swing to see what it had regurgitated. It looked like a doily.

On the day my father and I left Ram Rai Pur, tears streamed down my cheeks as we all said our goodbyes. I was choked up with emotion and had a massive lump in my throat, leaving me unable to speak. But inside, I was also happy in the knowledge that I was going back home to Pear Tree. I just couldn't wait to tell all my family and friends about the things I had seen and discovered. Most importantly of all though, to let them all know that my grandfather was still alive and kicking.

Chapter 7: I

Steve Who?

Bloomer – Pear Tree

What's Your Beef?

In mid-March 1988 during a Pear Tree Junior School
assembly, I was thrust into a temporal state of confusion. It
began like any other assembly. My class had walked into the
lower school hall and were instructed by our teacher to sit
down on the floor, legs crossed and facing the front, in
silence. Once all the children had been assembled and seated,
we waited for the assembly to begin. A few moments later I
watched on as our deputy headmaster put the index finger of
his right hand to his lips and then curled his other fingers
under his thumb forming a fist. We all knew what that sign
meant; the whole hall suddenly fell silent. He spoke a few
words to greet us all and then asked if any of us had seen the
headlines in the morning papers. I looked at him curiously.
'Did I miss something?' I thought to myself as I drifted off
into a train of thought. As I continued to ponder on what he
might be alluding to he then hit me for six when he
unexpectedly began slating one of my great heroes. This
immediately regained my attention as I began to listen

carefully as to what he was about to reveal next. It turned out that the headline story in the national newspapers that day was about how Ian Botham of the England cricket team had become involved in an altercation on an aeroplane. We were told that Botham had physically and verbally abused a fellow passenger. As I listened on intently I became a little taken aback by the words my deputy head then used to describe my hero whilst also making sweeping hand gestures for exaggerated affect. In a booming but croaky voice he called Botham a buffoon. On hearing the word 'buffoon' a ripple of giggles swept through the hall and over my topknot. Still puzzled, confused and a little bit miffed, I just couldn't believe what I was hearing – I did not want to believe what I was hearing. Ian Botham was my hero and heroes never let you down, I assured myself.

Although I was still quite young, I was fully aware of what a legend Ian Botham was in relation to his cricketing exploits. I wouldn't have been clued up on every detail about his Headingley heroics a few years previously, as well as the significant contribution from other teammates. But I was certain of one thing, and that was that this man, known as 'Beefy', in my mind had once single-handedly destroyed the Australian cricket team during an Ashes series to claim victory for England from the jaws of certain defeat. He was a playground hero to us all who loved the game of cricket.

According to my deputy headmaster, Botham the 'buffoon' was acting like the 'big I am'. However, after hearing these words, I refused to accept that Botham was a bad man. I gently gazed from side to side to gauge the response in the faces of all the other children around me, hoping that, like myself, many of them would be frowning in disbelief at what they were hearing. However, the only reaction I detected was either disinterest or the occasional scrunched up face of those making guarded attempts to pick their nose without being seen. These responses didn't deter me though as I was adamant that there was no way I was going to judge Botham until I had found out more as to what had happened on the aeroplane that day. It seemed I was alone in my belief. 'So what!' I thought; I liked Botham and that was all that mattered to me.

I've always had great respect and admiration for people who have shown absolute defiance in the face of insurmountable odds. In my opinion, Botham was one of these people and he displayed this perfectly on the cricket field. Therefore, I found it very difficult to let him go having heard his reputation being tainted before me. I admired Botham and his unwillingness to never give in and never give up.

Botham was being made an example of. It was all to make a point and give every child a lesson in life. Never get too big for your boots and behave like a buffoon.

So what exactly did Ian Botham do on that eventful flight?

Many years later I read up about the incident in his own words and I realized that I was right not to have lost my faith in him. The story goes like this.

Having retained the Ashes with England in 1986–7, Botham returned to Australia a year later to play for Queensland in the hope that he would inspire his new team and win the Sheffield Shield for the first time. After reaching the final, Queensland needed to beat Western Australia in Perth. However, prior to the final, the tension rose on the flight when the captain of Queensland, Allan Border, began to argue with Greg Ritchie about why he hadn't selected him. Several other players then became involved as well as Botham. As the argument became more and more heated so did the language, which then led to some of the passengers around them becoming quite uncomfortable and upset. Ritchie then decided to go to the toilet so Botham used this opportunity to reason with his captain. However, a fellow passenger who was sitting close by then turned around and started complaining to Border about the language his team were using. Botham didn't take too kindly to this so decided to put his hands on the offended passenger's shoulders and redirected his attention to the front of the plane whilst also telling him to mind his own business. A short time later, Botham and his team mates disembarked the plane having landed in Perth. Botham used this opportunity to apologize to the offended passenger he had touched during the heated argument, knowing that he had clearly been in the wrong. That was the end of the incident until, that is, the police arrived at the team's hotel later in the day. Having heard a knock on his hotel room door, Botham opened it to see a duty officer standing before him presenting him with a cricket bat to sign. Once it was signed, the officer arrested and charged Botham for assaulting a passenger on the flight. Thinking it was only a minor incident, Botham had assumed that he would have no problem getting bail. His captain, Border, offered himself as a surety but the laws in Western Australia demanded that two people, who were both landowners of the state, were needed as witnesses. Fortunately, Dennis Lillee was at hand, arriving at the jail with a six-pack of beer. Botham was subsequently bailed and fined £400. To top off a miserable few days, Queensland lost in the final of the Sheffield Shield to in what would become Botham's last game before his contract was terminated.

Everybody makes mistakes and I've always found that as long as you learn from them and try to make amends, you will be a better person for it. I'm glad my opinion of Ian Botham was not swayed at the time.

Ian Botham will always be a great cricketing hero of mine, but outside of cricket he went on to do something even more breathtakingly remarkable and admirable. Whilst still playing the game, he once met a group of children at Taunton's Musgrove Park Hospital. During a period of treatment he was receiving for a broken toe, he inadvertently took a wrong turn into a children's ward that changed his life forever. In this ward he was devastated to learn that some of the children were suffering from child leukaemia and only had a few weeks to live. This particular visit was the driving force that inspired him to raise funds for leukaemia research. Ever since that day he has been a committed fundraiser and has raised more than £15 million. Since 1985, he has undertaken a total of sixteen long-distance charity walks, the first of which was a 900-mile trek from John O'Groats to Land's End. In that year only 20 per cent of sufferers survived the most common form of childhood leukaemia but these days the figure is now closer to 92 per cent. Ian Botham has said that his next great goal in life is to see that figure climb to 100 per cent and remain there. I am certain that one day he will achieve his century just like he did on his way to 149 not out, during the 2nd Innings of the 3rd Ashes Test at Headingley in 1981.

On the 10th October 2007, Ian Botham was knighted by Her Majesty, The Queen at Buckingham Palace in recognition of his cricket achievements and his sustained efforts in raising money for leukaemia research.

'I won't stop until we beat childhood leukaemia, but I can't do it without you'

Sir Ian Terrence Botham OBE, Knight Bachelor.

Not bad for a buffoon.

*

Say My Name!

It was during my days as a Pear Tree schoolboy that I first came across another one of my great heroes in life, a destroying angel that would never leave my side. Back then, a few cousins of mine and I would ramble all over Pear Tree in search of fun. Football was our main game of choice and when it came to finding a place to play, the Pear Tree Juniors playground was always our number one destination. The routine would always be the same; we would meet up on Pear Tree Crescent, walk up Portland Street and then take a right into Harrington Street and down towards the junior school gates. We would then climb over the large metal gate opposite the Pakistan Community Centre and descend into our own little Wembley.

On one occasion we decided to find an alternative venue with the added luxury of grass and a relatively flat playing field with full-sized goalposts. Having ruled out Balfour Park, we decided to walk down Shaftsbury Crescent past the Baseball Ground and beyond the Shaftsbury leisure centre onto Shaftsbury fields. As I was always prone to daydreaming I ended up walking alone and taking my time. When I reached the corner of Vulcan Street opposite the Baseball Hotel Pub I was then drawn to the exterior walls of the Baseball Ground. I then began to softly tap the knuckles of my right hand gently along these walls as I walked along the road singing to myself. However, a short distance later I suddenly stopped dead in my tracks, right outside the main entrance doors of the Baseball Ground. My open fist was now hovering above a very old weather-beaten brown metal plaque, which was screwed into the brickwork. On closer inspection I noticed the chipped, etched writing as an unfamiliar name caught my eye.

In Memory of Steve Bloomer
1874 – 1938
This tablet was erected by many of his friends and admirers as an appreciation of his services to Derby County Football Club and his country. Also as a tribute to one of the greatest players the game has ever produced.

I was dumbfounded. 'Who?' I read it again. 'Steve Bloomer, Steve Who?' Who was this guy?' I shouted out towards my cousins, 'Come here, look at this!' They all quickly gathered around the plaque with me. 'Who is he?' I asked. No one had a clue. 'Who cares, he's long-dead, keep walking,' someone retorted unkindly. 'Who is Steve Bloomer?' I asked again. Still there was no answer as they began to walk away. Not one of us had ever heard of him. Not one of us had ever stumbled across his plaque previously. I quickly calculated that he was sixty-four when he had died and then realized that had he still been alive he would have been about 115 years old.

Still rooted to the spot, I was suddenly struck by a football to the side of my head, which completely unravelled my topknot. However, I didn't mind one bit as it gave me a few more precious minutes to hang around the plaque and absorb all the information that was written on it. As I picked my ramaal and polyester-braided elastic band off the ground I stood mesmerized; I grabbed at my loose plait and slowly tied my topknot up again. I made sure not to forget his name by continuously repeating it. Steve Bloomer. Steve – Bloomer. I would not forget him. 'He must have been some player?' I thought to myself. 'One of the greatest players the game has ever produced.' That was something quite special to be said about a footballer I had previously never even heard of before.

During that period of my life, the greatest players that ever played the game in my own little blinkered world were Pele, Maradona and John Barnes. Even though Pele played long before my time, everyone I knew who loved football had heard of his name, especially, because of the film 'Escape to Victory' and his mesmerising bicycle kick. Diego Maradona was also in a league of his own having recently won the World Cup with Argentina, single-handedly, you could say. And lastly John Barnes; we had all heard about the sensational goal he had scored in the Maracana when Bobby Robson's England beat the mighty Brazil.

Steve Bloomer had now joined my elite little club. Steve Bloomer was now someone special indeed, especially in my book.

Unfortunately, as I stood fixed beside the plaque I began to experience a feeling of overwhelming sadness followed by a flood of thoughts. 'Why didn't any one of us know who he was? Did he have any children? Surely they would be dead now too? What about grandchildren? Would anybody alive now, still remember him?.' Then it struck me and I'm not talking about another football to the side of my head. 'What if the only piece of evidence that he had ever lived was this small neglected brown plaque?' My heart sank. 'What would happen to his memory if somebody stole it? Would that mean he would be forgotten forever? Was this plaque now the only solitary mark of his existence?' This plaque, which would have been quite easy to miss had you not been tapping your knuckles along the Baseball Ground walls.

I kept going over the sentence, 'A tribute to one of the greatest players the game has ever produced.' Surely, if this was the case then he would have had a more significant memorial and I would have definitely heard of him. 'A little weather-beaten brown metal plaque in the middle of Pear Tree, was that it?'

I turned away from the plaque having become overcome by a feeling of sorrow. I really felt for him. There he was, all alone, the forgotten man of English football. I then slowly turned and trudged my way towards the field to join the others. However, on seeing them having fun and laughing in the distance my spirits began to lift and I ran towards them as fast as I could. And as soon as I set foot upon the Shaftsbury fields I shouted at the top of my voice, 'Bloomer's here!'

From that day on Steve Bloomer's name was forever etched into my mind.

The very next day after my school day had finished, I rushed home and quickly grabbed myself something to eat and drink. I then retrieved the piece of scrap paper that I had hastily scribbled on the night before so that I wouldn't forget his name and then I dashed off to Pear Tree library. The Carnegie Library was on the top of Portland Street just past the Jolly Fagman newsagent and it was my only hope in finding out who Steve Bloomer really was. As I entered Pear Tree library I immediately made a beeline for the sport and football section. I then asked a member of staff if she knew who Steve Bloomer was, but she had no idea. After I mentioned to her that he had once played for Derby County F.C., she then picked a book off the shelf and passed it over to me, to have a look inside myself. The book was called 'Derby County: The Complete Record 1884–1984' by Gerald Mortimer and Mike Wilson, with further contributions from a man called Anton Rippon. I turned to the back of the book to find the letter B in the index. I then followed the B's down until my finger stopped on the first mention of Bloomer. He was there! I had found him! I quickly flicked to the first corresponding page and there he was. A ghostly, pale-faced nineteen-year-old boy with arms folded, wearing a black and white striped jersey, looking away from the camera, quite uninterested. I then turned over a few more pages and there he was again, but this time he was staring straight back at me, almost as if he was expecting me. Sitting on what seemed like a large tree stump, with a 1905 England International cap on his head, a white England jersey with rolled up sleeves, long, thick, black shorts that passed over his knees and finally wearing the most beautiful clean white pair of laced football boots that I had ever seen in my life. However, the manner of this photo was much more striking compared to the first. This Steve Bloomer was now a man that seemed to have been carved from a rock. The bulging veins in his forearms and hands showed what an industrious athlete he had become. His left fist was resting on his thigh and the thumb on his other hand was hooked into a loop in his shorts.

Stephen Bloomer was his full name, born in 1874 and died in 1938, just as the plaque had said.

I was so pleased with myself. I had rediscovered him. He was forgotten no more. I had remembered him. As I continued to read the snippets of information about him, one fact left me absolutely astounded. Steve Bloomer had scored twenty-eight goals for the England national football team in twenty-three international appearances. That was unbelievable. I also found out that he was also Derby County's all-time record goal scorer ahead of another man my father would often mention to me: Kevin Hector.

Up until that age, I didn't really know much about the history of Derby County F.C. other than the exploits of 'King' Arthur Cox and his squad. I also had no idea that Brian Clough had once managed Derby County. Although I did know that Brian Clough was the then manager of our local rivals Nottingham Forest F.C.

Twenty-eight goals in twenty-three England international appearances was the most essential piece of information that I needed so that I could tell the world about the greatness of Steve Bloomer. But what made me feel even more proud was knowing that this man once played for my club, Derby County F.C. Still smiling, I placed my scrap piece of paper inside the book and then took it to the helpdesk so that I could take it out of the library and bring it home. I couldn't wait to get home and read it in the comfort of my own living room.

Even though he had been dead for over 50 years, in a way I felt like I had brought him back to life by just remembering him. I previously thought his achievements and his memory may have died with him, but after visiting the library and finding out more about Steve Bloomer's amazing goal-scoring records, I began to share his feats over the next few days and weeks with anybody who listened. There were occasions when some people showed no interest at all, but that never dampened my enthusiasm and pride. I didn't care as I was happy enough to keep his legacy alive and to make sure he was not forgotten in death. From that day on, I always made sure to look out for the Steve Bloomer plaque whenever I passed by the Baseball Ground. With a gentle tap with my knuckles and a nod of my head I would remember him. I would remember his name.

However over the years, the thought of Bloomer's memory vanishing again returned and filled me up with my previous anxieties. Again I would think, 'What if someone stole his plaque? Would he disappear too?' At one point I even considered taking a screwdriver down to Shaftsbury Crescent to remove the plaque from the wall myself and then sneak it back home and keep it safe under my bed. The thought of it disappearing reinforced my belief that the plaque should really be kept in a place where it was safe from vandalism and theft: where people could see it and appreciate it in greater numbers knowing its significance. 'There was no doubt that thousands would have passed it on a Baseball Ground match day but how many would have actually stopped to read what it said?'. I always felt it belonged in a museum or inside the ground.

Steve Bloomer and his plaque touched my heart from the day I first came across it. I would reflect back on this day many years later when I reached a crossroads in my own life. Steve Bloomer never left my side. He was always there.

*

I have always had a strong connection to Derby County Football Club. Having been born in Derby it was in my DNA. But there was also another connection. My father's home village in Nawanshahr, Punjab was called Ram Rai Pur. The ram has always been a part of my existence. I was born a ram, you could say. Just like the English folk song about the legend of 'The Derby Ram'. For these reasons there was always only ever going to be one team that I was seriously going to support. Derby County F.C. – The Rams.

I've always been proud of my father's home village of Ram Rai Pur and the inner city suburb of Pear Tree where I was raised. These two places in particular defined my roots. Over the years I even considered having Ram Rai Pur printed on the back of my most recent Derby County jersey, but Ram Rai Pur sounds very much like ram raper when pronounced. Rape is a very evocative and nasty word so I didn't want people thinking I was making a joke out of it.

During these Pear Tree years, I really enjoyed my time at school. I loved it more than anything. I remember one moment in time where a big turning point occurred for me. I had made my mind up: I wanted to become knowledgeable. I wanted to understand and learn about everything. My journey of discovery had begun. So I asked my mother for some money and bought myself a pencil case from my mamma's shop. No longer would I waste my money on toys. Spending money on education was far more important. The pencil case would be the beginning of my new path in life.

One of my favourite topics at school was science. From an early age, science had always given me a feeling of great power and inner confidence that greatly assisted in my ability to express myself clearly and concisely. Science allowed me to be more confident in my abilities and my approach to life. How things worked fascinated me. Science was true. It provided answers and explanations. It was logical, systematic and pure in its explanations. Science intrigued me and captivated me and secondary school was the ideal environment for me to explore it further.

From Pear Tree Junior School, with very itchy feet and an absolute yearning to want to step up to a higher level, I moved on to my new secondary school. However, things did not go entirely to plan. My original first choice for secondary school had been the Village Community School, but at the last minute I decided I wanted to go to Littleover Community School instead, to follow a likeminded friend. I had already visited Village School earlier in the year and had been told that Mr Naylor would be my new form tutor. On hearing about my change of mind, my father quickly got on the case and rushed down to the Derby City Council secondary admissions office. Fortunately, he was able to get me a new school, unfortunately that school was not Littleover Community School but Bemrose Community School. My initial response when my father told me I was going to Bemrose was 'What?!' Then came, 'Where's Bemrose?' I had always been aware of Bemrose because of its unflattering nickname, 'Bumrose'. Yet I had no idea where in Derby it was actually located. I could not believe it. My father had decided that as I didn't want to go to Village and he couldn't get me into Littleover as it was oversubscribed, he would settle for the next closest undersubscribed school available. But what he didn't realize was that I would have been more than happy to remain at Village had I not got Littleover. But I had to be different, and look where it got me. I was stuck in a right mess of my own making. Nearly all of my extended family and friends were at Village and here I was, on my way to Bemrose, alone.

Chapter 7: II
Steve Who?
Jones – Village

September 1991 finally arrived. The six-week holidays were now behind me and a new adventure lay ahead, but not at the school I wanted it all to play out in. On my first day at Bemrose Community School my father could not drop me off as he was at work. So my thiah, Sohan, was asked to take me down with my eldest massi's daughter, Amarjit who would be driving us all to Bemrose. Once again the butterflies in my stomach were out in force. It was the most nerve-wracking moment in my life, up to that point. The journey to get to school was a short one: ten minutes at the most from where I was picked up in Pear Tree. In those ten minutes, I sat alone in the back of the car, ticking things off in my mind. Topknot – check, stationary – check, money for food – check, tie – check, topknot – tight. As we approached my new school and then entered the car park, I knew straightaway that I was in the wrong place. This was not the school I wanted to be at; I wanted us to all turn back immediately. Having got out of the car I was then led into the tennis courts around the back of the school. This was where all the Year 7 children were gathering and lined up in their new form groups. I had no idea where my class was being assembled, so Amarjit had a word with one of the teachers and I was then taken to the correct place and joined the end of the line. Looking up, I saw my thiah looking back at me with a worried expression on his face. So I smiled back at him to make him think that I was ok. I then waved the pair of them off, although I was hoping that I could still somehow manage to leave with them. It was not to be. Amongst a sea of children, I felt completely alone. I was not happy at all.

Standing in line with my fellow classmates, I looked around but didn't recognise a single person around me. After a couple of minutes, a register was taken and my new class was asked to follow our new form tutor into our new classroom. I sheepishly walked along with them, trying not to make eye contact with anyone. I was feeling a little insecure: I knew that as a Sikh with a topknot and a massive rucksack I was bound to get some unwanted attention. It then hit me that I seemed to be the only Sikh boy with a topknot in the whole school. It was not a good place to be. No offence to Bemrose but it was an awful experience; I wanted to cry at every turn, but I held it all in. When we finally reached our new classroom and we had all sat down, I looked around me to see if I could recognise anyone. I knew no one. Fortunately, though, I did recognize an old Punjabi school teacher from the past who was attached to my new form. She recognized me and must have been a little surprised at how quiet I was because I was never like that during afterschool Punjabi lessons with her at Pear Tree Juniors. As I sat on my own at the back of the classroom, all I could think about was: 'how I would get back home to Pear Tree.' I then began to plan my great escape as I stared down at my bulging, blue pencil case, deep in thought. There was no way I would be here tomorrow. There was no way I was coming back. My train of thought was then interrupted as I was asked to introduce myself. I slowly stood up, then nothing. I couldn't speak. My eyes glazed over; no words came out. I had a frog in my throat the size of my pencil case. After what seemed like an age my voice finally revealed itself. 'My name's erm…. My name's Kalwinder Singh Dhindsa and I'm from Pear Tree'. I noticed my old Punjabi school teacher looking at me as I was standing up, then quickly sat down. When the break bell rang she came up to me and had a chat. I asked her where the nearest pay phone was. She could see that I wasn't happy, but I told her I was ok.

It wasn't the place for me. I did not belong. Fortunately, during break I managed to hook up and mix in with some fellow Pear Tree old boys who were quite surprised to see me there and not at Village. I couldn't wait to hear the end of day school bell, but I still had the problem as to how I would get home. My father had suggested that I take the bus home with the other children that also lived in Pear Tree and if that was not possible, then I should phone home and let my mother know. Thankfully, during dinner break I had spoken to my friend Gilly who said I could go back home with him at the end of the day as his father was picking him up. What a relief. Eventually my long and unhappy day finally came to an end as I heard the school bell ring. All I had to do now was make my phone call home then meet Gilly in the car park. I managed to find the school pay phone and then dialled my home number. I was then able to tell my mother that my lift home was sorted and I'd be back soon. In the car park, Gilly and I were picked up by the 'Jolly Fagman'. Gilly's father owned the Jolly Fagman newsagents in the middle of Portland Street. The journey home in the back of their car was an absolute delight. As we exited the car park I looked back over my shoulder as I saw the huge Bemrose School towers becoming smaller and smaller the further away we went from them. I knew that I wouldn't see them again, up close and personal, for a long time, if ever again. It didn't take long to get home. I was dropped off in the middle of

Pear Tree, near Jolly Fagman's Newsagents, directly opposite 35 Portland Street.

I was home; I was back in Pear Tree where I belonged, with my people. After thanking Gilly and his father and telling them I wouldn't be going back to Bemrose in the morning, I waved them goodbye. I then ran down Portland Street with my eyes firmly fixed on Pear Tree Crescent. Past the Wallis clothing factory on my right, past both the Pear Tree schools on my left and then finally past Harrington Street Nursery. Home was now in sight, a minute later I was at my back door. 'How was it?' someone shouted, as I barged through the back door. 'It was rubbish!' I smiled in relief. I kicked off my shoes, threw down my bag and whipped off my tie. My mother then put on some tea for me whilst my siblings and a couple of cousins then laughed and teased me by calling me a 'Bummer'. I didn't care because all that mattered was that I was home – 160 Portland Street, Pear Tree, Derby. I then slouched down on the couch in front of the TV and then told them all. 'Tomorrow, I'm going back to Village. No way am I going back there.' More giggles followed and then came more taunting, 'Homo, Homo, Homo!' I smiled.

A few years earlier, Village Community School had been known as Homelands. Homelands Grammar School for Girls was originally opened in 1938. In 1972 it then amalgamated with the adjacent Normanton Secondary School to become Homelands Comprehensive School. In 1989, it was then renamed the Village Community School and then in September 2001 it became known as Village High School. Village High lasted less than a year before it was then finally closed down for good in June 2002. Not long after that, Charles Herbert Aslin's beautiful Hastings building was knocked down and lost forever. Village Primary School now stands in its place having opened in September 2008.

The very next day Manjit, the eldest daughter of my thiah, Sohan, accompanied me to Village Community School. The night before I had told my father I wouldn't be going back to Bemrose, he was a little puzzled and annoyed with me but quickly accepted that Bemrose was not meant to be. My father then asked Manjit to have a word with a member of staff to explain my situation and try to get me my original place back.

The next morning there were no butterflies in my stomach whatsoever. If anything, those butterflies were now lifting me up on shining wings. It was like a dream and I couldn't wait to start at my new school, again. However, there was still one final hurdle – whether Village Community School would accept me back or not.

After we walked to school together, Manjit and I both entered the school from the main entrance at the front of the Hastings building where upon a jolly, blue giant greeted us. As a WWF wrestling fan, the first thing that came to my mind was Hulk Hogan. However, this teacher didn't have the Hulk's blonde hair, nor a blonde moustache but what he did have was a brilliant bushy, black moustache, windswept black hair and what looked like a massive dent in his forehead. It was quite obvious he was a P.E. teacher. Manjit then explained to him the predicament I was in and how I was originally supposed to have started yesterday. He then immediately put me at ease by telling Manjit that he would take care of the matter. He then asked me for my name. 'Kalwinder Singh Dhindsa, Kal for short,' I answered. 'I'm Mr Jones, nice to meet you Kal.' He then told Manjit to leave me with him and that she could go back to her Year 11 form for registration.

At this point, I told him that I'd already been to a taster day, so I was already attached to Mr Naylor's form. Mr Jones then asked me to follow him towards the school staffroom and wait outside as he went in. A couple of minutes later out popped Mr Naylor, Mr Jones and a puff of smoke. 'Hello Kal, we were expecting you yesterday,' said Mr Naylor. 'I was at Bemrose, sir. It's a long story and I didn't like it.' Mr Jones then gave me the thumbs up and walked away. 'Follow me, Kal' said Mr Naylor as he briskly walked off in the direction of our form room. As I tried to keep up with his pace I asked, 'Have I missed anything, sir?' He looked at me, smiled and kept walking. A couple of minutes later Mr Naylor and I entered our 7PN form class. It was great to be back amongst my people again.

It was my first real day at Village Community School, the second for every other Year 7 child. The day before was probably the only complete day I ever missed in my whole five years at school. Gilly would also later join me having decided that Bemrose was not for him either.

Later on in the day, as I was climbing up the stairs of the Pear Tree building with my reacquainted friends from Pear Tree Juniors, I crossed paths with Mr Jones again. 'You all right Kal?' he asked. He had remembered my name. 'Yes, sir,' I smiled as he gave me another thumbs up on his way down. When I reached the top floor of the building I made my way into my new science classroom. A smartly dressed man then introduced himself as Mr Peel. He was the best science teacher I could have ever asked for.

I loved Village Community School. What more can I say? Yes, I knew it had a bad reputation for achievement and discipline before, during and after my time there. However, the people I associated myself with at school all just wanted to do well. My own little group of friends would compete against each other on friendly terms to outdo each other and that's what carried us all through. I didn't see it as a bad school. We just made the best of what we had there and I would like to think that those of us who really cared about our education gave it our all and always gave it our best. I definitely left the school feeling indebted to it and all the great teachers who had done so much for us all over the years. It was a great shame when it closed its doors forever.

A constant companion during my five years at Village Community School was my love of the British science fiction programme, Doctor Who. The original series itself had been taken off the air in 1989. However, during the early 90s pavements all over Pear Tree were dug up and then tarmacked again. Little brown boxes then began to materialise on the outside of people's homes. Nynex Cable had arrived.

After years of watching the same four channels, suddenly we had a hundred more, which included radio too. All these channels and so much to watch, yet there was only one channel I ever really watched on the Nynex Cable: UK Gold. The home of classic British television: the new home of Doctor Who. I loved waking up early on Sunday mornings and running down the stairs to catch up with the latest Doctor Who omnibus. Over the years, I watched all of Jon Pertwee's adventures, the vast majority of Tom Baker's too and then every single one of Peter Davison's, Colin Baker's and Sylvester McCoy's. As the BBC no longer aired the programme or even showed repeats, UK Gold was the only place to watch Doctor Who.

In 1996 there was even hope of the series returning off the back of the film co-production between BBC Worldwide, Universal Studios, 20th Century Fox and the American Fox Network. However, hopes were soon dashed when the plan did not come to fruition. We all thought Paul McGann would not be seen on our screens again, as Doctor Who. I was very disappointed.

As I began to watch more and more Doctor Who on UK Gold, I became enthralled in the Doctor's universe. I couldn't get enough and I wanted more and more. I even wrote to the BBC twice, asking if they would bring the series back. However, on both occasions I received replies telling me that it was not in their plans, but if I wanted to find out more about the show I should contact one of the many fan clubs that had been set up. It was nice of them to reply and send me a list of all the addresses of different fan clubs that I could join. Throughout the time I was watching Doctor Who, I also realized that there had been two Doctors before Jon Pertwee. The First Doctor, William Hartnell and the Second Doctor, Patrick Troughton. At the time I hadn't seen any of their adventures and it was looking increasingly likely that it would remain that way as UK Gold didn't show any of their repeats. I then later found out that many of Hartnell's and Troughton's original TV adventures had been destroyed by the BBC during the 1960s and 70s. I was gutted on learning this news. At the time more than a hundred episodes were still missing and thought to be destroyed. I would never be able to see any of them, I thought. On many occasions, I dreamed that I would one day recover all the missing episodes and return them back to UK Gold and not the BBC. But that dream of finding this Holy Grail seemed lost. I still kept watching though, and with my paper-round money I would order as many Doctor Who Target books as I could afford. In the end I must have had a collection of about fifty of them out of a possible 160 or so. Although I didn't actually read any of them. Maybe it was my own little way of trying to preserve the missing episode stories. I spent all my money on books and dinosaur magazines back then. I also ordered the DWB Compendium and the DWB Interview file both of which were edited by Gary Leigh; I read them from cover to cover. I initially had an issue purchasing these books because, at the time I had the money but didn't have the cheque required to make payment. So I had to ask my cousin Manjit to order them for me with her cheque book. They were crammed full of information and interviews, from the beginning of the series in 1963 all the way to its finish in 1989. I also tried to record as many of the serials as I could when they were shown on UK Gold. However, I soon ran out of video cassettes. Unfortunately for me, during my time at Village, not one student I knew shared my love of 'Doctor Who', the only people I spoke to about it with any great enthusiasm were the teachers who had also grown up watching it themselves, as children. Mr Browning the art teacher was my favourite teacher to talk to about all things 'Doctor Who' and on most occasions I knew more about the show than him, having watched all the repeats. I loved his art lessons for that reason: I could talk Doctor Who with him and draw all the Doctors and monsters I wanted. I also made a paper mache Zygon head. Having watched all these repeats, I took a real liking to both Jon Pertwee and Tom Baker, who played the roles of the Doctor before my time. Although Tom Baker was playing the role when I was born on the 13th September 1979 between the screenings of episode two and three of Destiny of the Daleks. During this serial the fourth Doctor's companion was Romana II, played by Lalla Ward.

I was heartbroken when Jon Pertwee passed away during my GCSE exams in May 1996 as I couldn't share my sadness with anyone, as no one knew who he was, or seemed to care quite frankly. I cared because I'd always wanted to meet him. The man who produced the wonderful voices for Worzel Gummidge, Spotty in 'Super Ted' and the narrator of 'The Little Green Man' was silenced forever.

Why did I have so much love for 'Doctor Who'? I think it's quite simple really because one of my earliest memories of watching TV with my father was when I was about four years old and I had caught the end of an episode from 'The Caves of Androzani'. Peter Davison was playing the role of the Fifth Doctor. It would be his last serial before Colin Baker took over. I remember looking up at the TV and seeing the villainous black and white face of Sharaz Jek. My mother didn't like me watching the show as she felt it was too scary and switched it off, but I wanted to keep watching. So I ran off into the front room. My father quickly followed and switched the other TV on for me. The Doctor was on his hands and knees dying. The stick of celery pinned to his lapel had turned purple and I was about to see my first ever regeneration and it seemed not a moment too soon. I don't think I saw many of Colin Baker's episodes during the original run and he was not the Doctor for very long. I did watch a lot more of Sylvester McCoy's episodes and I remember his appearance on 'Blue Peter' when it was first announced that he would play the seventh incarnation of the Doctor. 'Doctor Who' was just brilliant. Homemade science fiction on your own doorstep. That's what made it all the more appealing, all the more scarier and all the more beautiful. The Doctor felt so real, it was as if he could just walk into your life and just take you away in his TARDIS for the adventure of a lifetime. The theme music was also absolutely mesmerizing too, very much like the intro of 'Tomorrow's World' another BBC Science programme. The Doctor, in whatever form he was in was my hero. A man of science with morals, who was brave and courageous, was always there for you and never let you down.

Later on I stumbled across Sky One and 'Star Trek: The Next Generation', 'Deep Space Nine' and then 'Voyager'. All in all, it was heaven in space. There was also another channel that was always on in the background when I wasn't watching science fiction: VH-1. Most children I knew at school who had satellite television would fall in the MTV group. However, my music channel of choice was always VH-1. The songs were like my own little TARDIS that would whisk me back to years gone by. My favourite bands during this period of time were Fleetwood Mac and Queen.

I adored my years at Village Community School but the unhappiest memory I have of my time there occurred just after the incident on Tuesday, February 11th 1993.

It was a usual Tuesday night. It had just turned nine and my sister, brother and I were sitting around in our pyjamas watching the TV. 'Question of Sport' had just finished and my great hero Ian Botham had just beaten Bill Beaumont. It had been a bath night as my brother and I both had our long hair hung loose down our backs. My mother and my little massi from over the road were also in the living room. Earlier in the evening, my father had gone out to see his brother Major. News had made its way to England from Punjab that their youngest sister, Seece, was now not well and that one of the brothers should go and visit her. Once again the responsibility fell on the shoulders of my father and Sohan. As my father made his way home that night, he was walking back towards the house after he'd parked his car when he came across some youths who were walking past the front of our house. Some words were exchanged between them and my father and then one of boys pulled a panel of wood from our fence and struck my father on the back of his head and down the side of his neck. They then all ran off. My father quickly made his way into the house and then went straight to the mirror in the living room where we were all sitting, to check upon where he had been struck. I noticed a few red marks on his neck and some minor cuts and grazes to his skin but it didn't look particularly bad to me. However, I did sense his agitation and anger. My mother then began to pull back at his shirt collar to see how bad it was too. My father decided to drive himself to the hospital to get himself checked. Just as he was about to leave, my little massi asked if he would like to take her eldest son with him but he declined her suggestion and instead went alone. I could have gone, but my hair was not tied in a topknot and I still had my pyjamas on. Then again, I don't think I would have wanted to step foot out of the house. We were all quite frightened and we still didn't know if it was safe to go outside. My father left the living room saying he would be back in a couple of hours and went out through the back door. Having had this almighty fright, we all decided to go to bed. However, I found it very difficult to sleep. I stayed awake, waiting and hoping to hear the jangling of his keys in the door downstairs as he let himself in. After a couple of hours, I began to get really worried. It was nearly midnight and still, he hadn't returned. In the very early hours of the next morning, my mother received a phone call from the hospital that woke me up. I listened in and it didn't seem to be good news as I heard my mother's voice beginning to break then softly cry. I heard her say ok a couple of times then she put the phone down. She was accepting something but I wasn't quite sure what. 'Accepting that he was hurt? Or that he was now making his way back home? Maybe she was just crying because she had been so worried but now the phone call finally put her mind at rest that he was ok?' I fell asleep. The next morning, I came down the stairs in my pyjamas and I noticed somebody sleeping on our couch, their whole body was covered with a blanket, I was relieved: my father was home. 'Dad?!' I said as I pulled the blanket away. But to my dismay it was not my father. It was my cousin Cully, my little massi's youngest daughter. What was going on? Over the next hour or so I began hearing more and more about what had happened to my father during the early hours of Wednesday morning.

My father had arrived at the Derbyshire Royal Infirmary without any further issues. He parked his car close by and then made his way to the accident and emergency department. He spoke to the receptionist then waited for his name to be called so that he could be treated. As he was waiting he also met my cousin Amarjit who was a nurse. He explained to her what had happened and showed her the abrasions to his neck. My father who had been sitting, waiting patiently for his turn to be seen suddenly began to feel faint. As the night's events started to overpower him he began to lose all his bearings. In a moment of absolute weakness his upper torso alarmingly tipped forward and his head crashed into the solid waiting room floor.

Within the hour he was rushed to the Royal Hallamshire Hospital in Sheffield and was then put on a life support machine.

One of the most awful things that I ever had to experience as a child occurred at Village Community School during the week my father was in a coma and fighting for his life. A few days after the incident a special school assembly was arranged for all the students.

As I stood and waited for the lower school assembly to begin, a police officer from the Derbyshire Constabulary introduced himself. He then began to tell everyone in attendance about an incident that had taken place on the evening of Tuesday, 9th February in which a gentleman on Portland Street was attacked. My heart sank as I raised my head, and scanned the hall to see if anyone was watching me. I caught the eye of my cousin, Mandeep, my little mamma's daughter looking back at me. She was a year below me in Year 7 and we both knew that he was talking about my father. I quickly looked away.

Jastinder, Sohan's youngest daughter, who was in my form, had also been standing behind me.

The police officer then gave further details as to what had happened, what time it occurred and what the current state of this gentleman was. He added that this man had been beaten around the head with a piece of wood and that there was a high likelihood that he would die. He made it quite clear that the chances of him coming out of his coma were very slim and even if he did, there would be some degree of brain damage.

To end his appeal for information, he finished off by telling us all that the incident which had taken place on the previous Tuesday evening was such a serious crime that it was now being treated as a possible murder investigation.

I gritted my teeth as my eyes pierced into the tiled floor beneath me. I was angry. Not because I wasn't told beforehand that the police were coming into school to talk to us all, but because he had effectively told everyone that my father had been set upon and beaten up. Beaten into a coma! I knew full well that was not the case. I knew what had happened as my father had told me when he came into the living room that night. He hardly had a mark on him, but for the small abrasions on his neck and we had passed all that information onto the police. I was beyond angry. How dare they come into my school, into my assembly and tell me my father was going to die. 'He is not going to die!' I assured myself. Screw you.

I remained rooted to the spot. The police officer had finished talking by now. I then began to think, 'What if some children in school find out it was my father?' Children can be very cruel. It wasn't the finding out that it was my father that bothered me. It was the finding out that it was my father and then thinking that he actually did get beaten up. That was a lie and not one I was going to entertain or allow anyone to torment me with.

A couple of days later I heard some giggles in my science class and then caught a fellow student passing around a torn out picture from the Derby Evening Telegraph of the Derby County Squad. One of the players had a bandage drawn on his head, blacked out eyes and a piece of wood with nails sticking out of it, striking his head. Yes, I was angry and upset. I immediately got into a little confrontation with the person who was supposed to have drawn it. However, the

matter was settled in school. I no longer saw him as a friend.
A few years later, I approached him on my first day at
Mackworth College. We found ourselves in the same tutor
group and I didn't want the bad blood to continue. 'Let's
forget about it,' I said. He apologized and we shook hands.

On my way back to our form room, I felt I needed to talk to
someone. I needed to tell someone the truth before the lie
became a fact. I chose my classmates, Hardeep, Richard and
Randheer. I told them quite calmly and clearly 'the guy the
copper was talking about is my dad, but he was NOT beaten
up.' On my way back home from school that day I heard
people talking about the assembly and my father's chances of
survival. 'Was he really going to die?' It was a question I
needed answering. As I walked the last few steps to the back
door of my house I knew I had to share what happened in
assembly with my mother. I needed to get this horrible
thought off my mind. But I also knew that I needed to remain
calm and composed. As I opened the back door I went in
through the kitchen and straight into my living room where a
lot of people were now congregated.

I was upset but I had to share with them what the police
officer had told everyone in assembly about my father dying,

in the hope that, like myself, they would also dismiss his opinion. Standing close to the door with one foot in the kitchen and one foot in the living room I quickly said to all those gathered 'the police came to my school today in assembly and they said that Dad was going to die.' As soon as I had said the word 'die' I knew that I was on the verge of bursting into tears. I immediately turned away very upset and rushed towards the stairs. As I was doing so my mother stood up and called back at me in Punjabi with a laugh, 'Don't be silly. No he's not, he'll be fine.' My mother laughed off my concern to try and downplay what I had heard. By the time she had caught up with me and reassured me that my father would not die I had managed to hold back my tears.

Maybe my family and everyone else were also led to believe that things were not going to turn out well for my father, but they never let this pessimism show. Maybe that is why I also refused to believe he would die too.

Later on that day, all of my father's brothers as well as my masser, Darbara, were gathered in the front room. My thiah, Sohan, had given me some money to buy some chips. He knew I loved chips so I went down to the Holcombe Street fish and chip shop and returned with a few bags. All my cousins were in the front room playing together as usual, being our boisterous selves when Mohan suddenly snapped and shouted at us all. In his anger and frustration, he commented on the noise we were making. He then said in Punjabi, 'You probably had your TV blasting like this the day it happened too and because of that you didn't hear your father's screams as he was being beaten up.' I was furious. 'What a horrible thing to say!' I thought. I was a thirteen-year-old boy, my sister was eleven and my brother was nine. Upset or not he should not have been saying things like that to young children like us. I had no words to fight my corner. I was seething inside as my ears burned. I raged within, 'My father did not get beaten up!' My thiah, Sohan, immediately saw that I was angry and upset. As I left the room to go into the kitchen I heard him admonish his brother. I had completely lost my appetite at this point and threw my bag of chips into the microwave.

Many years later as Sohan Singh Dhindsa breathed his final breaths at the Derbyshire Royal Infirmary, a similar thing occurred again with Mohan. However, this time I would not let it go.

My thiah, Sohan, was a good man. In 1992 he had a double heart by-pass at the Groby Hospital in Leicester. My father and I visited him regularly during the time he was at the hospital. Thankfully, his operation was a success and he was able to live another ten years before he finally passed away in 2002. The day before he died I was supposed to go around to his house to see him. It was only a short distance up the road. I had last seen him earlier that day having picked him up from the hospital. When I went to collect him I made sure to collect his walking stick. However, it wasn't required. I had originally bought him the walking stick a few months previously from a mobility shop in the centre of town. I remember the day I presented it to him. I took it over to his house and as soon as he saw it his face lit up. He then asked that I follow him into the back garden and into his little shed. He then put the walking stick into a vice and used a hacksaw to cut it down to the correct length.

When I met my thiah at the hospital he was still very weak and unable to walk even the shortest of distances. So we had to use a wheelchair to take him to my car, which was parked outside the entrance doors. It was a bit of a struggle manoeuvring the wheelchair and at one point I pushed him straight into a wall. We both found this quite funny, though and had a good laugh on the drive home about it. I then dropped him off at his house on Pear Tree Crescent and stayed in his company for a bit. It was good to have him back. However, in my naivety I assumed that because the hospital had let him come home he was now getting better, and his angina was not as bad as it had been. After an hour or so I decided to give him some time alone to rest. So I left the back room and began to slip my shoes on when he suddenly shouted at me. Telling me off for no particular reason at all, I thought. It was an odd moment. It was almost as if he wanted to make me turn around so he could see my face one last time before I left him. I wasn't offended. I just smiled at him and told him that I would see him soon. I never saw him alive again. Later that day I ended up watching a special one-hour episode of Eastenders and by the time it had finished I thought it would be too late to go and visit him. 'I would visit him tomorrow morning' I thought to myself, 'straight after I returned from the gym.' However, the next day after coming back from the gym I ended up going to my friend's house instead to help my big mamma out with some paperwork. When I finally returned home I was told my thiah was in hospital again. Mohan was also at home with my grandmother. My father was already at the hospital by his brother's side. As I did not have the car, I asked Mohan if he wanted to go to the hospital to see his eldest brother, in the hope that he would take me too. Mohan said he didn't want to go. Fair enough I thought. I don't think either of us ever believed that day that Sohan would pass away. That refusal denied me my last chance to see my thiah alive. A bit later on, I got a phone call to say I had to get down to the hospital as quickly as possible, as things were not looking good for him. I managed to get a lift down to the Derbyshire Royal Infirmary. As we got closer and closer I began to well up and as I stepped out of the car tears streamed down my face; deep down I realized his end was near. I managed to make my way to the main corridor where he was located, but it was too late, I was too late. I met my poor father who had been looking out for my arrival. He shook his head, 'he's gone,' he said. Although he wasn't crying I had noticed that just before he had spotted my arrival he had wiped a tear from his cheek. I had never seen my father cry in my entire life. I could always tell if he was upset, but I had never seen him actually cry.

In 1997, shortly after his own father passed away, I noticed him do exactly the same thing. I knew he had shed a tear for his father but he'd concealed it from me.

We stayed in the hospital room with my thiah's lifeless body for a short while after his death. My father was there, Major had also now arrived too, but Mohan was nowhere to be seen. I knew that the relationship between Sohan and Mohan was not great, but even so, I felt that somebody had to tell Mohan about his brother's passing. So I phoned him to let him know. He arrived a short time later, after my father and Major had left the room. Mohan came into the room and looked at the body of his dead brother then immediately began to have to have a go at Sohan's youngest daughter for not playing hymns. 'Hymns?! What would hymns have done for him? He was dying?!' I seethed under my breath. I looked at my cousin shaking with rage unable to speak. I was angry too but this time I had the words. He immediately left the room and I quickly followed him out. I admonished him, 'What are you playing at? Her father's just died and you're going on about hymns.' There was no response. He just walked away, helpless. The insensitivity of it all. I was not a thirteen-year-old boy any more; I was a twenty-two-year-old man. Boy or man, I knew what was appropriate and what was not. Maybe I should not have phoned him, I thought to myself. But at the end of the day I didn't want my thiah's good name to be tarnished in death by gossips commenting on how nobody had informed Mohan of his brother's death. My father wasn't in the room when this incident occurred but I'm quite certain that had he been he would have done exactly the same as me.

Over the next few days, news of the incident and pictures of my father's face were splashed all over the media, including the local East Midlands TV News and the Derby Evening Telegraph. The whole of Derby expected my father to die. Not me though.

The police continued to visit our house and always had questions to ask. On one occasion a couple of my cousins, my siblings and I were sitting in the front room playing on the Super Nintendo Entertainment System.

The SNES was bought a few months earlier. I had saved about £70 from my paper round and my father then contributed the rest of the money. I had initially bought it without any games as they were far too expensive to buy. However, when it came to playing on the console my cousins and I just borrowed the games from friends or hired them from Cavendish Video.

Two uniformed officers stood inside the front room door watching on. One of them asked me what we were playing on, so I told him that we were playing Super Mario World and that my father had bought me the console. I then told him, 'When my father comes out of hospital he's going to get Sky installed too.' He looked down at me with a smile then turned his head and caught the eye of the other officer. I knew exactly what they were thinking. I turned my back on them and continued playing on my SNES. 'My father was NOT going to die. Screw them.'

More days passed. Family and friends continued to come around to my house after visiting my father at the Royal Hallamshire Hospital. Initially, my siblings and I weren't allowed to see my father during the first couple of days. However, my mother eventually relented and allowed me to visit him.

On my first visit, I hesitantly approached my father and stood beside him. 'Dad, I'm here, it's me. Kally.' He did not react. He was completely still. No movement at all but for his chest and lungs moving up and down slowly in time with the ventilator machine next to him. I noticed a needle inserted through his veiny hand, a tube coming out through his nose and another into his mouth all connected back to his life support machine. It did upset me that he wasn't moving, but I was glad that he was still alive. His blood was still pumping around his body and his heart was still beating so I knew there was still a possibility that he could hear me. I didn't stay for long during that first visit. On my way out I touched his hand. I was pleased to see him again.

Over the next few days my family continued to talk to him, hoping that he would respond to their voices, but there was no response. They held his hand hoping for his fingers to move just a fraction, but there was no response. For almost a week nothing happened and then one day the news that we had all hoped for finally arrived. My father was beginning to show signs of recovery. He had begun to respond to voices and grasp at people's fingers as they held his hand. He was out of his coma. Life was returning to my father. He was back. Back to life. Back to reality.

I was over the moon. I wanted to see him with my own eyes. I wanted to see my father awake from his deep sleep. My father originally had reservations about seeing his children. Maybe he didn't want us to see him in such a vulnerable state so soon after his trauma, but I needed to see him and nobody was going stop me. The very next day I would finally see him awake. I remember the short journey towards Sheffield; it was a happier journey than the previous few and my smile didn't leave my face for a second for the entire journey.

A week or so earlier the England rugby team had lost against Wales in the Five Nations, ruining their chances of winning the Tri Nations and a possible back-to-back Grand Slam. It all started off so well for England having initially beaten France but then it all fell apart. Since those early matches though, I hadn't really thought about anything else other than my father and the coma he was in.

As I walked towards his bed, he was sat upright with a few pillows propped up behind him. He then turned to look at me and I spotted his bottom lip quiver. I walked towards him joyfully and smiled at him as we touched hands, making sure I didn't disconnect any of the tubes. I was so proud of him. He'd beaten all the odds. He'd beaten death. He had come out of the darkness and into the light. He was really back.

I then stepped away from him and sat down on a chair close by his side and listened as others members of my family talked to him. I looked around the room knowing I would never have to visit this ward or this room ever again. Beside me, I spotted a rugby stadium cushion with the French logo on it. When the time came to say goodbye to him. I smiled and nodded at him. 'See you later Dad,' I said, a little embarrassed as I made my way out. Over the next couple of days, he was moved out of his Intensive Care Unit and placed in a room of his own, to recuperate. I visited him a couple more times again, this time with my mother, sister and brother. Not long after, he was finally discharged and able to return home to Pear Tree. Many family and friends awaited his arrival that day. How pleased we all were to see him home again.

About a month later France went on to win the Five Nations. Having initially lost their first game to England, they then won their remaining three and were crowned champions. Victoire indeed.

I had always found the feeling of pride and embarrassment very closely linked, and during my younger days almost impossible to differentiate. My history teacher at Village Community School, Mr Montgomery, once noticed me absorbed in a particular page from a history book. The page I was reading from was from a book my father had bought me called 'The World at Arms' which I had brought into class. On this page was a picture of a turbaned Sikh soldier in uniform. Underneath the picture, it explained how more than two-thirds of the troops fighting the Japanese at Imphal and Kohima were Indian. With the vast majority of these soldiers being Punjabi Sikhs who wore turbans during battle. As soon as Mr Montgomery spotted what I was looking at, he raised his voice so that the whole of the class would listen and then said, 'Ah Kalwinder, the Sikhs played an important role for the British Empire during World War I and II. Thousands fought and died with great courage on the battlefield.' The hairs on the back of my neck stood up. I looked around, I didn't know what to say or do. I felt embarrassed. Why did he say that to me, I thought? There were other Sikhs around me he could have looked in the direction of. Why was he just directing it at me? After some reflection I realized that it wasn't embarrassment that I'd felt. It was pride. Yes, there were other Sikhs in my class, but I was the only one with a topknot and to Mr Montgomery topknots were synonymous with Sikh men and what they wore under their turbans. The feeling I had experienced was not embarrassment. It was actually a feeling of prickly pride. I felt this same prickly pride when I first heard that my father had awoken from his coma a couple of years earlier. It was also the same prickly pride I felt when I finally called my father Dad for the first time.

My happiest memory of Village Community School was when my old English teacher, Mr Singh, invited both my parents to the end of year GCSE presentation evening. I couldn't believe it when they both showed up out of the blue. Mr Singh had invited them without telling me. Only a small number of parents had actually shown up and there in front of me was my mother in her bright pink coat and my father sitting beside her in his grey blazer. They watched on together as the certificates were handed out; smiling proudly.

We never did get Sky TV installed. However, not long after my father's first brush with death another regeneration quickly followed. Nynex Cable and the little brown box brought the upright Doctor back into our lives and back onto my TV screen once again.

Chapter 8:

Into The Storm

The incident on February 9th 1993 forever changed my father's life. As the years went by, I gradually noticed a change from the good man that he always was to a man who still had a good heart but was now increasingly prone to periods of bitterness and depression. The darkness still lingered.

*

A few months before Mohan's death, I graduated from the Open University with a MSc in Science. The graduation ceremony itself was held at the Derby Assembly Rooms and my father and mother accompanied me. To have the ceremony in the centre of Derby made me feel even more proud of my achievement. It was an occasion that I was very much looking forward to, so I wanted to make sure that it became a day that I would never forget. Therefore, I paid particular attention to what I would be wearing. On the previous day I visited my thiee's house and borrowed my late thiah, Sohan's, favourite tie. The Qualcast foundry in Derby had presented him this tie for 30 years of continuous service.

I also made sure to attach a Derby County pin badge to my suit jacket, which I had purchased very soon after the death of Brian Clough in September 2004.

This pin badge had BRIAN CLOUGH O.B.E written along the top and 1935–2004 underneath. Below this was DERBY CO. In the centre of the badge was the old Derby County DCFC logo with a ram's head within it. To the left of the logo was CHAMPIONS 1st DIVISION and to the right CHAMPIONS 2nd Division. Finally, underneath the logo was MANAGER 1967 ~ 1973.

I decided to wear the pin badge on the day of my graduation because I felt that it perfectly reflected who I was and where I came from. The little ram's head also paid homage to my father's village of Ram Rai Pur, Nawanshahr. I was a very proud Derby man that day. The tie and the pin badge were my own special way of honouring my roots and I knew full well that without this attachment and connection to my people, I was nothing. For that reason, I made sure I paid my respects to my family, Ram Rai Pur and my beloved City of Derby.

The Brian Clough pin badge was also a nod to both Peter Taylor and Dave Mackay too, who between them had won two 1st Division League Championships as Managers of Derby County Football Club in 1971–2 and 1974–5 respectively. The fact that a provincial town club like Derby County won the League Championship not once but twice has forever filled me with immense civic pride. What an incredible and remarkable achievement it will always be. It could even be said that these three men went on to play a significant role in the town of Derby being awarded city status by Queen Elizabeth II on the 7th June 1977.

Once inside the Derby Assembly Rooms, my father decided to have a couple of drinks and then almost missed my big moment when he went in search of a toilet. Fortunately, he made his way back to his seat next to my mother just in time to see my entry onto the stage. As my name was called out I walked towards the presiding officer who shook my hand and then commented on my thiah's tie as he had noticed the Queen's Award to Industry logo on it.

A lot of Punjabis who originally came to England, settled in the Midlands having headed north from London and other southern cities. Many of these men then managed to make

their way to Derby to take up jobs in places like Reckitt &
Colman and Qualcast.

When my thiah, Sohan, passed away two years previously, I
did contemplate taking a break from my MSc or even putting
a stop to it all together. I was completely heartbroken by his
death as he was someone I could always turn to and we
would spend a lot of time in each other's company.
Sometimes we didn't even have to speak, yet we still
communicated.

The graduation day was such a happy day for me and I felt
immense pride at graduating in the city I was born in. I was
also glad that I saw it all through, having completed the part-
time MSc over a four-year period. These four years also gave
me the time to seriously consider whether I wanted to go into
teaching or not.

I now found myself with two degrees yet I felt greater
satisfaction completing my MSc than I did with my BSc.
During the BSc years in Leicester, I just became a little too
distracted with all the things that were occurring in my
personal life at the time. Most of these things on my mind
back then revolved around my father. I just wanted to be one

less thing for him to worry about. I just wanted to show him that I was a responsible person who wanted to settle down and that I could make a good life for myself. I lost much enthusiasm for my course after my first year, but I persevered to see it through to the end. On completion I still managed to get an Honours in Physics with Astrophysics, but not the grade I had hoped for. I was disappointed, but I was not gutted. I could have done better but my mind was just not on it. It was a shame because during my younger days I had spent many hours gazing into the night sky with my binoculars pondering the existence of life outside our solar system. Being a massive fan of Doctor Who and Star Trek, my mind would effortlessly be taken away to galaxies far, far away. But all that seemed to fade away at university when I realized it wasn't all about looking through telescopes and the search for extraterrestrial life. But I genuinely did enjoy my time at the University of Leicester and the biggest thing I took away from it all was lessons in life. I learned a lot about what people were like. Who you could trust and who you could not. Best of all I made a handful of very good friends, and detached myself from others that I could do without. I learnt a lot about loyalty and that it is better to have a couple of close friends that you can trust absolutely than many who might not always be there for you when you need them most.

My mother also taught me a very valuable lesson in life. She taught me that I must always address my own mistakes by looking within myself and being accountable to myself. But when seeing others make mistakes, if they can't figure them out for themselves then let that be their weakness, do not let it be yours. Be good and treat others, as you would expect to be treated yourself. For that, I must show empathy to others at all times.

I will always be grateful that I attended the University of Leicester, even though the degree I studied may not have completely lived up to my expectations. Living there also left me with a great fondness for the City of Leicester and it's ground-breaking university. For this reason, there was never any other place I wanted to return but the University of Leicester when I decided to apply for a teacher training course.

I was overjoyed that I had finally completed and passed my MSc (Science) with the Open University as well as nearing the end of my PGCE Secondary (Physics) with the University of Leicester. My life and my future career finally all seemed to be coming together just at the right moment for me, and to top it off, within a couple of months I would also be getting married to Rav.

*

I began my PGCE at the University of Leicester, School of Education in late September 2004. A couple of weeks after the death of Brian Clough and a day after taking part in the Great North Run. You could say that it was a very painful start to my teaching career. I had managed to run, walk and sometimes crawl my way through and beyond the half marathon, then spent the next couple of days in severe pain, unable to walk at all. If anything, it was actually easier to manage the cramp when I jogged. I was glad that I completed the half marathon though. I did it in the memory of my thiah, Sohan, as well as to collect funds on behalf of the British Heart Foundation. During this time, Rav and I were engaged and our wedding was to take place in August 2005. Time was ticking and the pressure on me to complete and pass my PGCE intensified. My life depended on it. Our future together depended on it. I had to pass.

My PGCE year was very tough. As passionate as I was to reclaim my love for science once again, the whole process of completing the course was increasingly fraught by the fear of failure that was drilled into all of the trainee teachers. Unfortunately, I found myself attached to a tutor who I really didn't get on with. There just didn't seem to be any constructive relationship between us at all. I wasn't alone in feeling this way.

Thankfully, I always had another PGCE tutor to turn to in times of need. He was a lovely man by the name of Dr Laurence Rogers, who was always willing to help anyone who required his assistance.

I also didn't like how nearly every question asked about the course would result in the same stock answer: we should refer back to the colour-coded PGCE course book as all the relevant information we needed would be located in there. In all honesty, I found it all quite shambolic. Through gritted teeth, after a lot of tongue biting and jumping through many paper hoops, I passed my PGCE year. It was difficult, but it need not have been. Even a week before we found out whether we passed or failed, many of us on the course still did not know if we were going to be successful. And then in the end only about six people were chosen to be group assessed. We still had our main course folders checked to see if we had jumped through all of their hoops and that everything was signed off, but the actual inspection of all our course material wasn't even done. It was madness; many of us had piles of paperwork about three feet off the ground that had been wheeled in using suitcases, yet none of it was even touched or inspected. Throughout the whole year we were constantly alarmed into thinking that we may not pass, then suddenly, 'Oh well done, but be aware next year the NQT year will be even harder'. Mercifully I had a good companion during my whole PGCE year and it just so worked out, after a bit of manipulation, that Tom Martin and I were sent to the same Leicestershire schools for our first and second placements. Ashby School in Ashby-de-la-Zouch and then Shepshed High School in Shepshed, where I had the great fortune of working alongside my old history teacher at Village Community School, Mr Montgomery. It was good to see him again.

My next year, the NQT year, would indeed be the hardest year of my life.

*

My father was a loyal man. There was no doubt about that. He looked after his people. However, I would sometimes get very angry and frustrated with some people and their attitude towards him. During one incident, I remember I became extremely annoyed with the behaviour of a cousin from whom I expected better. He didn't agree with something that my father was doing, but that didn't mean he should desert him or speak rudely about him. I would still have my father's back and support him, even if I felt he was in the wrong. I might not always have liked how certain family members conducted themselves, but I would always have their best interests at heart. I could never truly walk away from anyone. I would have to help. I always backed my people and looked after my own.

My father's eldest brother, Sohan, always backed my father. Even if he didn't agree with some of the things my father did, he was always on his side. It used to really get my father down when people wouldn't stand by him when he needed their support. Even though he would go to the end of the Earth for those who required his help. I think, in later life this is what really used to get him down more than anything.

When it came to favours and helping people out, my father just couldn't say no to anyone. It was his great mantra in life, whenever assistance was required people used to seek my father. I was well aware of his place in our community and I think deep down he knew his place too and he was more than willing to help, because at the end of the day it reflected positively on his family name and his parents.

As soon as my father and I returned from our visit to Punjab in 1990, my father made immediate plans for his own father and mother to visit us in England. My father was instrumental in bringing them over. Once they arrived they then stayed with us for a while, then returned just before their visas expired. A couple of years later he managed to bring them over permanently when my grandfather's health began to deteriorate further. He never forgot about his family back home in Punjab, nor the people he left behind. In all the years that my grandparents lived in England, they lived with us at 160 Portland Street in Pear Tree, Derby. It was his duty to look after everybody.

With Sohan's passing I felt my father handled the responsibility that came with being the main head of the family as well as could be. But he missed his brother's input.

He would also feel very hurt if the loyalty he had shown to others was not reciprocated. Unfortunately, my own family would bear the brunt of the moaning and whinging that would stem from these knockbacks the most as he would try to explain to us all how he had been done wrong. We heard these grumbles more and more as the years went on and they would come out repeatedly after periods of drinking. No longer would he be funny and cheerful when he was inebriated, only bitter and disappointed.

With Mohan's passing, life became unbearable for my father and he became consumed with grief. He could no longer put others first. Nor could he now put himself first. His mantra in life was broken. All his life he had been one step behind his beloved brother, Mohan. Little did we imagine, that he would follow Mohan all the way to his own tragic death.

Chapter 9: The Silence
The Worst Chapter of My Life

On Wednesday, March 1st 2006 I set off for work at John Port School in Etwall, Derbyshire, leaving behind, at home, my father, my grandmother and my brother who was still asleep upstairs.

Not a day has gone by since I haven't wished that I could have taken that Wednesday off. I only had three lessons to teach on my reduced timetable as an NQT so this meant I was actually looking forward to the early finish. Year 8 for Period 1, Year 11 for Period 2 and then finally Year 9 for Period 4. Leaving Period 3 and 5 free for planning, preparation and assessment.

Period 1 and 2 went as well as could be expected. As Period 3 was free another science teacher, Sue Stokes, chatted to me during break and then invited me into her lesson so that I could observe a lung and heart dissection. I had never seen a pluck dissection before so I said I would be happy to observe and take part if need be. A few minutes into the lesson I watched on as Sue placed a tube down through the larynx and then the trachea of what was left of a poor, little lamb.

She then used a pump to fill the lungs with air. I squeamishly watched on as I observed the lungs begin to rise and inflate. It wasn't a very pleasant sight. To add to this, the raw flesh and blood made my stomach feel quite queasy. The tube and pump were then removed and the lungs began to deflate and expire for the last time, then nothing. Nothing but the stale scent of pre-decomposition that lingered around and then settled on my nose hairs and on to my beard. This smell of death would stalk me throughout the remainder of the day.

Once Period 4 was over, my school day was effectively finished. I used the last period to prepare for lessons on the following day. In the process of doing so I went into the reprographics room during Period 5. Whilst in there I became a little distracted and then began showing a couple of the technicians some pin badge designs that I had asked a badge company to create for me. These designs had the John Port School logo on them and I had planned to show them to the senior leadership team in the hope that they would give the go ahead for them to be produced and then be presented to hard-working students. However, just as I was about to put the designs back into my rucksack, my friend and fellow science teacher, Dave Sankey entered the reprographics room. 'Kal, there's a call for you. It's your brother,' he said. I was puzzled. 'Why would my brother call me? What would he need to call me about? How did he even find the number to call?' I left what I was doing and made the short journey to the staffroom and picked up the phone.

'Hello? What's up?' I asked.

'Come Home. Dad's….Dad's hanged himself,' he said.

'Ok…..I'm coming' I said, as I put down the phone.

Dave had been standing close by next to the open door, he knew immediately that it was bad news. He looked at me quite concerned. 'You Ok Kal?' 'No' I said. 'I've got to go home.' 'I've….' I switched off as I began looking ahead into nothingness. Whilst trying to collect my thoughts together, I was then suddenly whisked away into my own little world as I desperately tried to make sense of what I'd just heard. 'My Dad's hanged himself. I've got to get home, nothing else matters. Go home. Nothing else matters. Home'

Dave snapped me out of it. 'Go home Kal, I'll sort it out with the office. Go home.' I went back to the reprographics room, put my pin badge designs back into my rucksack then made my way towards my car.

Silence.

I stayed calm. I didn't panic. What else could I do? I didn't know if my father was still alive or not. 'Dad's hanged himself.' What did that even mean? I had to get home. A minute or so later I was at my car. I quickly got into the Ford Mondeo, turned the key in the ignition and I was gone. There was no need to speed, I needed to be in control. After a couple of minutes of driving I finally registered that there was music playing in my car. I hadn't realized until a particular song came on. 'The first cut is the deepest.....' It was Cat Stevens. I immediately switched it off.

Silence.

The tips of my ears began to burn as the silence pierced right through them. He'll be ok. I pictured him in the corner of the living room in his navy blue jacket sitting on a stool next to the fire grabbing at his neck in a distressed and upset state but he would be ok. I would enter the living room and I would rush towards him and grab him by his lapels and draw him closer. I would not leave his side ever again. He'll be ok. I would be home in Pear Tree. I would be home soon.

Silence.

'Dad's hanged himself.' Where? Why? With What?

'Dad's hanged himself.' My tie?!

Silence.

A couple of weeks previously I had bid on some clip-on ties on eBay and won. From then on, I began wearing them all the time instead of my usual standard necktie. On occasions when I would conveniently snap them off during hot spells in the classroom, the students would laugh and ask. 'Can't you tie a tie, sir?' 'Of course I can tie a tie.' 'Are you afraid of being attacked, sir?' 'Yes, I am afraid of being attacked, by teachers!' As I no longer required my standard necktie I left it on a pile of books next to the TV.

Silence.

I was now driving past the City Hospital, a right on to Manor Road then Warwick Avenue, down Kenilworth Avenue and then a left into Village Street. Another right and then a left onto St Thomas Road at the bottom of Village Street. I was moments away from home. A final right into the top of Pear

Tree Crescent and then a left. I could now see my home on the corner of Portland Street. As I approached to park up I noticed that the parking area in front of our garage had now been sealed off with police crime scene tape. I parked my car on the opposite side of the road and then slowly and calmly got out of the car. My cousin, Jasbinder, then stepped towards me as I made my way to the back gate. I can't remember what he said, but all I heard was 'he's gone'. What did that mean? Gone? Gone where? Dead? What did that mean? He leant towards me and began to cry as he gave me a hug. I didn't react. I approached the cordoned off area in the hope that I could pass through the gate and into my house. A police officer then stopped me going through. 'He's his son!' my cousin shouted at her. I wasn't going to argue. I walked off towards the front of the house to make my way around the side and then through the back door.

As I walked into the house I heard female members of my extended family wailing in pain. My mother saw me enter and then immediately grabbed at my hands forcing them together. 'Turn around and pray that he lives!' she cried hysterically. I wasn't one for praying but I turned around for her sake and bowed my head in almost dejection as I raised and pushed my hands towards the pictures of the gurus above the TV. There was nothing more I could do. I looked down and noticed my necktie still on the pile of books I had placed it on a few days earlier. Where was my father? That is all I wanted to know. He's either dead or alive? I was then told that my mother had found him in the garage and that an ambulance was immediately called for. He had been cut down but he wasn't breathing and had to be revived by a police officer. He was then rushed to the Derbyshire Royal Infirmary. My father was still alive! A lift was quickly arranged for my cousin, Jasbinder, and myself so we could visit him at the hospital. As I was driven through the streets of Pear Tree I didn't cry, there was no thought of doing so at the time. I just wanted to see my father; he was the only thing on my mind. He was still alive and while his heart still beated, while his blood still flowed, while his body still respired I knew he would still be able to hear me. I needed to see my father. The traffic was bad on the journey there; there was no way we would be able to drive into the hospital as quickly as we'd hoped. So my cousin and I had to get out of the car a hundred metres or so from the accident and emergency department. We then ran as fast as we could. I was a few feet behind my cousin as he kept turning around and shouting at me to hurry up. With every stride the realization then dawned on me that this was probably the end and no matter how fast I ran the inevitable had been written in the stars.

As I entered the waiting area I saw many of my male extended-family members, and my brother gathered around. I was quickly directed towards a side door and pointed in the direction of where my father now lay. I strode in purposely, without hesitation, the curtains around my father's bed were enclosed around him but for a little crack in the corner where I had entered. I stood over him, 'Dad I'm here. It's me Kally,' I said. There was no response. No movement at all but for his chest and lungs moving up and down slowly in time with the ventilator machine next to him. His neck was swollen, tubes were shooting out from his arms, hands, nose and mouth and were all connected back to his life support machine. There would be no more chances. I knew it was the end. My tears could not be contained any longer so I looked beyond the crack in the curtains and towards the light. I noticed a nurse looking back at me. My eyes were filled with tears. I released them. They streamed down my cheeks. The nurse could see I was crying now, she looked away. I didn't care. It did not matter. Nothing mattered any more. I just wanted my father to stay with me. I was a twenty-six-year-old man with a full grown beard, crying for my father. I bowed my head and grabbed for my lapels. 'It's ok Dad, don't worry. It's ok. I'm here.' I told him that I loved him and that I always had. 'Everything would be ok. It's ok, Dad. Everything will be ok from now on.' 'I'm sorry I couldn't help you.' I knew his pain would be over soon and that his end was near. He had suffered too much this was the way it had to be. This was his end. I had to let him go. I had to accept that he would die. There would be no more chances. I thought back to the last time he was in the same situation twelve years previously. He had beaten death back then, but this time it would be different.

Before entering the room he was in I still had hopes that there was a possibility that he could still be saved. Even if it meant he had to spend the rest of his life in a wheelchair with a degree of brain damage. I would have given up everything to care for him but it wasn't to be. I had to accept his end. There was no coming back

Over the next few minutes more of my extended family came in to see him whilst he was still alive. I was then called into a waiting room by a doctor to tell me of his diagnosis and severe predicament. As other family members also sat around, the doctor informed me that there was really nothing they could do for him. Scans had revealed that his brain activity was all but dead. He had been deprived of oxygen for too long. The game was over. I had to accept the doctor's diagnosis. His life support machine would have to be switched off. It was my decision to make. There was only one thing to do. Accept it. It would have been selfish for me to prolong his suffering any further in hoping for a miracle.

It was all too much to take in. I needed to get out of the hospital for some fresh air. My sister had already been informed but my wife had still not. So I texted Rav and told her that I would meet her at the Derby train station. I then walked the short distance down to the train station. As I was doing so I also texted my good friend Ather and phoned Sohan's eldest daughter, Manjit, to tell her what had happened. She began to cry immediately, unable to take in what I was telling her so matter-of-factly. 'Say it isn't so?' 'I'm sorry, but he will die,' there was nothing more I could say. I waited outside the train station and a few minutes later we then made our way back to the hospital.

My father was transferred into another ward after his life support machine had been switched off. About two hours later after we had all began saying our last goodbyes to him, I sat down next to him on his deathbed. His body was still warm and the blood still flowed. I cracked a smile. 'I'll see you soon dad, it might be another fifty years but I'll see you again' I said. My mother, sister, brother and myself remained by his side as he expired his last few breaths. His body was shutting down, we could see it and smell it from his last breaths. A few moments later he began making some gargling noises. Almost as if he was snoring, just like he used to at home during the nights. We smiled. How we would miss his snores. His lungs inflated and deflated for the last time. My father died on Wednesday, March 1st 2006.

Eventually we all returned home, leaving my father's body behind. Later in the evening, I called my head of department and let him know what had happened and that I would need to take Thursday and Friday off.

That night I went to bed and cried and cried. My poor father, I couldn't save him. I eventually drifted off and began to dream. In my dream my father and I were at home in Pear Tree and some bad people were after him. They tried to force their way into our home to attack him. I led my father into the shower room so that they couldn't touch him. I would protect him. I saw his smiling face for the last time as I closed the door on him. There would be no more pain.

Suddenly I was awake and choking. My hands were wrapped around my neck as I was choked by an enormous lump of emotion inside my throat. Even in my dreams I felt a compulsion to cry.

Chapter 10: DeAD
The Milk of Human Kindness

On the day of his suicide, my father seemed to be in a better mood. I had instantly sensed something different about him but I just couldn't quite put my finger on it. Yet, I knew that some kind of change was looming. It was this perceived rejuvenated attitude that was the mask behind which he concealed his plans to end his life. The change within him was the relief that he had finally accepted and chosen his only way out.

The day after my father took his own life, my immediate family and I began to make preparations so that extended family and friends could begin to start gathering at our house to offer their condolences. As is customary for Sikhs, the Sri Guru Granth Sahib Ji was therefore arranged to be brought into our home so that the Holy Scriptures could be recited.

This ceremony is known as a Sehaj Paath and is conducted over a period of a week. The recital of the Guru Granth Sahib from beginning to end helps to bring peace into the home and give a family the strength to accept God's will.

In preparation for the Guru Granth Sahib, the larger contents within the upstairs front room were the first things to be removed and cleared out. A canopy was then raised and installed, which our holy book would be later placed under. Finally, white sheets were laid out on the floor so that people would be able to sit on them just like they do in a Gurdwara's Diwan Hall. Only when the room was completely cleared of its contents did I then decide to go through all his clothes and possessions that still remained in the wardrobes. A day previously this had been my parents' bedroom but now it was just an empty shell. It then struck me that he was really dead. Gone. As soon as I opened the first wardrobe door I saw before me many of the clothes that he had accumulated and worn over the years and each item brought back its own unique memory. It was too overwhelming, so I turned around to look away. It was then that I noticed his favourite jacket still hanging from the hook on the bedroom door where he had left it the day before. I decided to take it off the hook and search the pockets. In the inner pockets of his jacket I found a coin purse, his wallet, a white handkerchief, and his glasses case. Within the purse I found some money. It wasn't much, a few pounds in change and a £5 note. I then placed his coin purse in my trouser pocket knowing that its contents would never ever be spent. I then opened his glasses case to find his gold-rimmed glasses inside. On the inside cover of the case, written in pen in his own unique handwriting, was his name, address and phone number as well as a couple of crossed out attempts to write his name 'Mohinder Singh.' Tears immediately began to well up in my eyes upon seeing his writing again. I then noticed a piece of card underneath his glasses and through the tears I just about managed to read what was written on it. It was the names of Jaz and Ajaib Singh Rai, who were the two sons of my eldest massi, Surinder, and her late husband, Karnail. Along with the names were their addresses and phone numbers. At that instant I immediately realized why he had written their details and not my own. Their details were written as a definite notice of next of kin. 'Why else would they be in there. He must have known what he was going to do?' He had planned it all along. He clearly knew that he would one day take his own life. If his body had been found in any place other than home, then the first numbers the police would have called were those of his nephews. On finding that piece of card my mind became flooded with many thoughts. 'Maybe he had initially decided to take his own life away from the house? Maybe he didn't have my details written down because he didn't want to put me through the heartache of having to identify his body? Maybe that is why he decided to try and take his life at that time so that I wouldn't be the first person to find him?'

I looked at the clock on the wall. It was a few minutes past two. This time yesterday, I thought. This time yesterday he was about to carry out the act. If I had been here this time yesterday I could have rushed out and saved my father's life. As it happened it was my mother who found him first and then raised the alarm to my brother. Another cousin, Rajinder, from across the road then heard my mother's screams and quickly rushed over to help my brother cut my father's noose. Rajinder had seen my father earlier in the day from his front room window. My father had been in our back garden fiddling around with the clothes pegs on the rotating washing line, whilst looking a little distracted.

In June 1991, a group of us Pear Tree boys went to watch the film 'Robin Hood, Prince of Thieves' at the Showcase Cinema when it was first released. One scene that always stuck in my mind was the part in which Little John hysterically tried to save his young son from being hanged by single-handedly bringing down the gallows. I wish that I could have done that for my father that day, I would have brought the whole garage down, but it was not to be.

The day after my father's death I accompanied my sister, Rav, Jasbinder and his sister, Jastinder, to the morgue at the Derbyshire Royal Infirmary to see my father's body before he was transferred to the funeral parlour. On this day we were all driven in a police car through the streets of Pear Tree. It was exactly the same journey I had taken the previous day in the hope that my father would still be alive as I rushed to be by his side. It was a strange journey in a police car through the streets of Pear Tree whilst staring out the window and seeing past memories flashing through my mind. It was a journey I had made hundreds of times, with my father by my side. When we reached the Derbyshire Royal Infirmary we were then all led into the morgue and were asked to wait in a little side room. I then entered another small room as the others watched on through a glass window. My father was laid out on a table, wrapped in a white blanket, dark, lifeless and dead. I kissed him on his forehead for the final time. He was at peace. We left the morgue very soon after. The police car then took us back home to Pear Tree.

It is there that I remained for the next few days, just like my father had done at Mohan's house when his brother had passed away a few months earlier. It was the time for grieving and I knew that many people would visit my house to pay their respects.

The subsequent days after my father passed away became the most difficult of my life. I was now the man of the house. How I did not want that title. Hour after hour and day after day, people kept coming around to pay their respects. Each and every one of them, were absolutely devastated by my father's death. At times it was good to hear them talk so fondly about him. On many occasions I would begin to smile as I heard some of the stories they would share amongst themselves. It filled me with great pride and happiness when I would hear people talk about what such a nice man he was and how he would do anything to help the community he so dearly loved. However, the most painful thing about the whole experience was having to sit and hear the same story being told over and over again to all those who would come over, sit down and then ask in disbelief: 'What happened?'

What happened? After having had to sit and listen to the same question being asked time and time again, I finally began to piece together what had happened.

After I had departed for work on that Wednesday morning, my father went to visit his mental health therapist. After his appointment had finished it seems he took a detour to a DIY shop to buy a new padlock for the garage door. A friend of his then saw him wondering around Fleet Street, near his old childhood home which was close to Arboretum Park. On his way home to Pear Tree he then met an elderly neighbour from up the road who'd seen him and noticed that he kept looking over his shoulder. 'Are you all right?' she asked. 'I think so,' he replied. Once he had reached home, my cousin's grandmother had by now also popped over to keep my own grandmother company. He asked if they were both ok then made them some tea and offered them some Indian sweets. After a while he closed the living room blinds and went into the front room to chat to my brother. Having chatted with my brother he then left the house through the back door and into the garden, closing the door behind him. He pulled a wheelie bin towards the garage and left it in front of the open garage door as he placed the new padlock on the latch. With the living room blinds now closed, no one could see what he was up to. He then stepped into the garage.

In these conversations I also heard that on the Sunday before his passing, he had also visited Hounslow with my mother to see my cousin, Jazz. Jazz later told me that on the day he had visited he hadn't been his normal self and was in a hurry to get back home to Derby. At one point he even held Jazz's new-born son and for a brief moment a little joy had returned into his world. It was obvious to Jazz that he wasn't his normal self, when she later tried to speak to him alone. As he was leaving her home for the final time he looked back one last time to see the newest addition to their family. His eyes lingered on the child for a moment and then he looked away. 'Are you ok?' Jazz asked again. He was in a different world. Maybe in the end he really did begin to start thinking about the beginning. Or maybe in the end he was just not thinking straight at all as the depression had completely distorted his mind; the darkness prevailed.

Sometimes during these long periods of sitting down in the company of all the people who would come over to offer their condolences, a memory would flash into my mind and I would begin to well up with tears thinking about the good old days and the things we used to get up to, the happy events and places we had all visited. Tears would then begin to stream down my cheeks and I would begin to miss him terribly. In many cases the thoughts that brought the tears to my eyes most often tended not to be in relation to how he died but how he had lived. It was good to share these memories with everyone who knew him so well. But it was also difficult for me to talk to others as to how I felt because it was all so impossible to comprehend. There were just too many questions in my mind and nobody to answer them.

As Rav would be sitting with the women in the living room, I was left alone with the men in the front room so it was always difficult for us to talk during the day. On one particular occasion while sitting in the front room, I just couldn't take it any more and had to leave the house to get away from it all. As I became more and more upset, the lump in my throat just wouldn't shift as I tried to swallow hard and dislodge it. I needed to get out for some fresh air and take a few deep breaths. I just needed to get out, but where? I didn't know. I asked my cousin Jaz to follow me outside. It was only when I got outside and sat in his car that I said, 'Let's go and find Brian Clough.'

The lump in my throat had become unbearable. I had never felt such emotion before in my life. The closest I had come to this previously was when my thiah, Sohan, had passed away. But my father's passing was off the scale. In my mind the lump in my throat became synonymous with hurt and death. I needed to take control of it before it choked me and squeezed the life right out of me.

It had to be displaced so I tried to think back to a time when I had last experienced the same feeling of being choked, but not for reasons of hurt and pain. Within moments I was taken back to Thursday 21st October 2004 – Pride Park Stadium, Derby.

On this day a memorial service to celebrate the life of Brian Howard Clough had been arranged. Thousands of rival football fans came together to sit side by side to honour the memory of a man who led both Derby County and Nottingham Forest F.C. to unprecedented glory. I'd already managed to get myself a ticket for the event, which was originally supposed to be held at Derby Cathedral. However, due to a massive demand the venue had to be changed at the last minute to Pride Park. On that day I attended the service alone, to pay my respects to a great man who I had admired immensely and especially for having made Derby his adopted home when he first arrived in 1967.

A few weeks before, I had been looking forward to meeting Brian Clough at a book signing he was due to attend with

Archie Gemmill at Waterstones, Derby. The event had been advertised in the Derby Evening Telegraph. However, on September 20th 2004 Brian Clough passed away. On that day my sister came rushing into my bedroom to tell me of his passing. 'Your hero's dead.' I knew immediately who she meant. 'No! Never! I was going to meet him next week,' I said. I opened up the BBC homepage on my PC. My great hero Brian Howard Clough had indeed passed away. I never got to meet him in life.

My father knew how much I idolized Clough. I would talk about him, glowingly, at every opportunity. So on the day of the memorial service he dropped me off outside Pride Park Stadium. I then told him that I would make my own way home to Pear Tree after the service finished and that he didn't have to worry about picking me up. It would be a long walk home but I didn't mind.

Nigel Clough's words about his beloved father that day left a deep impression on me.

'For all the kind and generous tributes that have been paid in the last few weeks and especially this evening, we will remember him most, just for being our Dad.'

On hearing these words, I swallowed hard as a tear rolled down my cheek. The stadium erupted into applause and cheers. Pride consumed me and I couldn't speak.

The way Nigel spoke about his father that day made me appreciate my own father and the city of Derby even more. The lump of emotion that I'd felt in my throat was a feeling of immense pride and happiness and not one of hurt and pain. Never in my life before that point had I ever been as proud to be a citizen of Derby, the place of my birth. When the memorial service finished I walked all the way home back to Pear Tree in the cold and rain, soaked in pride.

'Take me to Elton Road, I want to see Brian Clough. There's a Derby mural painted on the side of the Brian Clough Business Centre,' I said to Jaz. It was a mural that I was well aware of; I'd come across it many times over the years having crossed the Pear Tree Train Station Bridge to take shortcuts into Allenton and beyond. The mural was only around the corner on the other side of Pear Tree. As we made our way there it began to get darker. During the course of the short journey, I began thinking about the items that were found in my father's possession on the day he died.

When his clothes were returned to us not long after his death we found an A6 plastic wallet inside his shirt pocket. Inside the wallet were two pictures. One was a photo of a portrait of Guru Nanak, which was originally painted by Sobha Singh.

I had bought this with my own money when my father and I visited Punjab together in 1990. On the other side of the plastic wallet was a picture of Guru Nanak and Guru Gobind Singh standing shoulder to shoulder, with the Guru Granth Sahib below them under a canopy. Squeezed in between these two pictures was a small brown envelope folded in half. The front of the envelope was addressed to my father:

Mr M. Singh
160 Portland St
Derby
DE23 8PJ

On the corner of the envelope was a 2005 1st Class Christmas Stamp of 'Madonna and Child' by Marianne Stokes. On the other side of the envelope he had written:

GURDEV. KAUR . 3-9-58

I began to speak but then immediately broke down. 'Why didn't he write our names, on that envelope?' I asked Jaz. 'Did he not love us?' The envelope only had my mother's name on it. 'Why did he not have our names on it? Did he not love us? Why had he not written our names and birth dates? His children. Had he stopped loving us?' I asked. 'Of course he loved you all,' Jaz said. Deep down I knew that he must have loved us, but I just needed someone to give me an answer to an insufferable question. Again the name on the envelope would have been another message he left behind for someone to contact my mother had she not found him first. Another note for the police if need be. But still the question remained, tormenting me. Did he not love us? Was it true that in the end he just started thinking about the beginning? A time before he had his children and only had my mother? Were myself, my sister and brother not on his mind when he decided to take his own life? 'Had he had enough of us? Me? Is that why he decided to end his life?' I asked. I had no answers. There were no answers. I began to get very upset as the tears streamed down my cheeks. Once again I began choking up and was unable to speak. Then I began to think that maybe if he had written our names, he could have prevented himself from doing what he did. Maybe he deliberately didn't write our names because he knew it might make him change his mind. The questions kept coming but they could never be answered. I would never see my father alive again and only he had the answers.

I then looked up and through the tears I saw the Derby Mural in front of us. 'Park up here' I said, falteringly. We remained in the car as I tried to compose myself. As soon as my vision cleared I looked to my left then, slowly panning right I began to see some words emerge from the wall in front of me, Spirit – Community – Pride – Vision – Derby. In between these words were also painted pictures related to Derby's rich heritage and history. A black silhouette of a man playing keepie uppie with a football. Another man holding a ladle filled with molten metal as flames leapt from within. Two large hands engaged in a handshake. Another silhouette, in white this time, of a man playing keepie uppie and then finally the face of Brian Clough smiling back at me through the darkness. Below him was the Ram logo of Derby County Football Club. Clough's smile immediately lifted my spirits. It was good to see him again. I hadn't been down this part of Derby in a long while, but Clough's smiling face still remained on the wall after all this time. Untarnished and untouched by vandalism.

Recollecting the last time I was standing in the same spot, I began reconnecting with my roots. Once again I was taken back to that day at Pride Park. Recalling and feeling the immense sense of pride I felt when I attended Brian Clough's memorial service. Hearing all the good things being said about him and how much he had contributed to my city. I felt absolute pride knowing that he had chosen to bring his young family to Derby and made it is home. In the process of achieving such great success with Derby County Football Club he also brought so much joy and happiness to ordinary Derby folk like my father. Another wave of pride then hit me again. My father, like Brian Clough, had made the same journey to Derby in 1967. It was the year Brian Clough and my father made Derby their home. It was a good year for my people.

After that visit to see Brian Clough I just knew I had to do something for him. To help recognize and commemorate his contribution to the town that became the city of Derby. It was only right.

The very next day I was sitting in the front room again, when I began to experience the same feelings of sadness I had felt the night before. Seeing Brian Clough on the mural had raised my spirits and temporarily cleared my throat. So I knew I had to get out of the house and somehow experience the same feeling again. This time however, I told Jaz I wanted to go to Arboretum Park. 'I want to see the Florentine Boar,' I said. 'Why?' he asked.

When my father first settled in Derby. He lived in a house on Fleet Street, not far from The Arboretum Park. It is for this reason that I wanted to go back to the park. I wanted to believe that my father had spent many happy days playing in that park when he was growing up in Derby. I wanted to somehow connect to places where my father would have been happier in times gone by. Maybe this was also the same reason why my father was seen near Arboretum Park on the day he died.

My father would never have seen the Florentine Boar in Arboretum Park when he was living there, though. The original earthenware Florentine Boar had been placed in the park in 1806. However, it was decapitated during a German air raid on Derby on 15th January 1941. Although, it was later reported that a Derby resident had, as a child, accidently broken off the boar's head while climbing on the statue. Either way, the statue was taken down until a bronze replacement was erected and unveiled in November 2005 by Councillor Hardyal Dhindsa (no relation).

The new Florentine Boar had been in place for only a few months but I had not been able to get down to see it due to my heavy workload at school so I used this opportunity to go down and have a look for the first time. A Derby historian by the name of Christopher Harris had long fought for the return of the much-loved sculpture to Arboretum Park. Chris and his friends at the Derby Heritage Forum had argued that it was a part of the city's heritage and that there was a general consensus in the community for the boar to be returned. It was a battle they won, although it nearly didn't happen after the politically correct council, at the time, thought that having a statue of a pig would be offensive to the local Muslim community. Chris and his friends were not deterred, though, and fought boar tooth and claw to get what they felt the people of Derby deserved. I was reminded of this happy story when I told Jaz I wanted to visit Arboretum Park. It was nice seeing the Florentine Boar for the first time; I touched the cold bronze and then read the plaque next to it that explained its history. I then took a few photos of it just as I had done with the Derby Mural on the previous night.

It was only a statue, but it had a beautiful story behind it that refused to be forgotten. I realized then that objects such as this are good things, especially when you can attach memories of happiness to them.

Over time I began to get very distracted by these memories, places, people and objects. It was all good though because every now and then it would make me forget about the hurt and heartache. Thinking about these things cheered me up and lifted my spirits during these dark, dark days and if that meant rambling around Derby searching for murals or Florentine boars to raise a smile, then so be it.

The more and more I thought about why he decided to take his own life, the more I began to realize that if he hadn't done it on that day, he would have tried to do it another. Had my mother come home from work earlier that day, he would have just tried it another time. It was something he would have gone ahead with regardless; his mind was made up. The only thing that may have prevented his death was if he had shared his thoughts of suicide with those closest to him.

'Maybe we could have asked more questions? Maybe we could have tried to get him better medication and care?'

Feeling that he was not getting any better and constantly being told there was nothing outwardly wrong with him, there is no doubt this would have only pushed him further into the darkness. I feel that on Wednesday, March 1st 2006 my father had just had enough and wanted no more of life. It had become too unbearable for him to live. There was only one way out. After seeing his mental health therapist earlier in the day, he must have realized that he was being prescribed more of the same medicine that had done nothing to lift his spirits previously. Is this what tipped him over? Enough is enough? No more? Lights out? The bottom line. My father was ill. Depression due to mental illness took his life.

But still the questions came: 'Was it our fault? Was it my fault? We knew he had depression, right? Why did I believe him so readily when he said he would never take the path to suicide? Why did I not just take a few days off work. I could have spent more time in his company. I could have asked him more questions to try and understand his pain. I could have done more to try and help him, but I failed. I should have been there that morning with him. If only. If only I had a TARDIS'. So many questions, but the one that was always at the forefront of my mind was: did he not love us?

My school life during this period was seriously getting me down, yet I kept going back for more, trying to make amends. Trying to become a better teacher, I ignored the needs of my father. 'Was my life that important? Was my job that important?' Maybe I just didn't want to keep confronting his cloak of darkness. I was caught between a rock and a hard place. I just wanted him to be happy, but I was failing to succeed on all fronts. 'Did he think we didn't need him any more? As I was now a teacher and a so-called pillar of society, did he think that I didn't need him any more? Did he think that I'd outgrown him? Did he think I was set? Was that an extra reason for him to let go? Why did I not see the signs?' I honestly believed that he would not take this route. 'Not my Dad'. 'Suicide is not the way to go,' he once said to me. I had too easily accepted his words, without doubt.

On one occasion, not long after his brother had taken his own life, we were watching TV together. He was eating at the table and a man being hanged flashed up on the screen. I

quickly switched over the channel in the hope that he hadn't
seen it.

'In those last few days when his whole outlook on life changed so drastically from what it used to be, was he really trying to deliberately create a wedge between us and him to give him the justification he needed to go ahead with his plans? Did he seriously want us to dislike him? Did he not love us?' Surely the signs were there, yet I wasn't able to act. My mind cast back to a clash about not replacing the toilet roll. 'Nobody's going to die, if it doesn't get replaced,' I said with a sarcastic smile. 'You'll find out when I'm gone.'
He knew his time had come. 'Was he trying to tell me his end was near? Was he trying to prepare me for the worst?'

I began to wish that he'd told me that he'd been contemplating suicide. I would have immediately shot back with: 'Well if you try to hang yourself, then I'll be following right behind you.' Just to scare him into not contemplating the thought any further. Just to put that doubt in his mind, that if he ever was to go down that road, then so would I. Not that I ever would. If only he'd let his guard slip. Something? Anything? Was it not obvious that he was trying to prepare me for something after the event? Maybe buying the padlock in the last few hours of his life was his last effort to try and prevent himself from going ahead with his final and desperate plan. Maybe the padlock was to close the garage door and resist the temptation to end it all; keeping the garage locked so he wouldn't be drawn inside to end his life. Then again, maybe the padlock was so that once he had carried out his act we would have a new lock to keep the door locked for good. No further invitation to anyone else. I wouldn't have been at all surprised if that was the reason. I feel that he would have tried to make sure he had left us in good hands after his death. The bizarre questions about knowing where certain keys were and the alarm code, if it went off, were all to make sure we would survive without him. He had fulfilled his role in life, but could do no more due to his illness. He was preparing us for life without him.

All his life, my father looked after his family. Always putting himself forward if anything needed to be done. Always putting the needs of others first. 'I will do it' he would say without hesitation. Maybe in the end, he also saw what he was doing to his family? Maybe he felt that not only did he have to ease *his* pain, but the pain he felt he was putting us through? He was a man of pride who never liked to let anybody down. Yet he found himself in a position where he could no longer function as he used to. My father made the ultimate sacrifice for his family; he gave up his life so we could live without him being a shadow of the man he used to be. Well, maybe that's the way he justified it to himself in the end? He never let us down. Maybe he thought he was doing the right thing for us?

'Why did he do it? Would there ever be any closure? Could there ever be any closure?' I would be tormented with the question for the rest of my life. There would be no closure.

The black poison cloud had finally overcome him. The darkness had consumed him. His brave and private battle with depression, which he was so determined to overcome, ultimately took him away from us all. Leaving behind an everlasting gaping hole in our lives that could never be filled again. His last act of duty was to offer his loved ones tea and milk. His final act of human kindness was to make sure that we were all catered for. He had battled on till the bitter end, to do the right thing.

Chapter 11: Bury your Head
Bury your DeAD

As a Sikh the preferred method for the disposal of a body was for it to be cremated. In the Sikh homeland, Punjab, this would normally have happened within three days after death. However, away from Punjab it could take longer due to the processing of cremation forms in order to receive authorisation. Therefore, the date of my father's funeral fell on Thursday, March 9th 2006 at 09:15am at Markeaton Crematorium, Derby.

It would be a long, drawn out eight days from the day he died to the day of his funeral. During this period of bereavement, I knew that I needed to keep myself busy. So I decided to do something productive and positive that would also, in the process, lift my own spirits. I knew that I had to somehow honour his contribution to our little community: I had to try and express to everyone the man I believed he truly was before the mental illness took him away from us all. It was my own personal way of trying to reclaim my father's legacy.

I loved my father, I never told him that but I would like to think he knew. As I was growing up I was always very aware that he didn't always find it easy to express himself. I also had similar problems when I was younger, especially when my emotions got the better of me. But as I matured I found it easier to express myself more clearly. This was now my opportunity to do the right thing and I was not prepared to let my father down again. My words would not fail me.

It all began with a small piece in my local newspaper, the Derby Evening Telegraph.

The day after my father passed away I started thinking about all the things I wanted and needed to say before he was to be cremated. I considered my words very carefully, and I redrafted them many times on my PDA before I finally settled on what it was that I wanted to be published. I also attached a picture of a khanda and a photo of my father.

Originally printed on Tuesday 7th March 2006, in the Derby Evening Telegraph.

DHINDSA

MOHINDER SINGH Passed away – Wednesday, March 1st 2006. Aged 51 years. Dear husband of Gurdev Kaur and father of Kalwinder Singh, Daljinder Kaur and Manjinder

Singh. A loving son, husband, father, relation and true friend. A like never to be seen again. He may have gone but he will never be forgotten and as long as he lives in the hearts and minds of those that loved and cared for him he will never die. God bless you, Dad.

'Never reject your own community no matter what faults you find within it'

Funeral service at Markeaton Crematorium on Thursday March 9th at 09:15am. Flowers may be sent to K.S. Dhindsa and family, Portland Street, Derby. Telephone: 07940 575321.

The quote is something I had always thought that the character Atticus Finch had said in 'To Kill a Mockingbird' which was written by Harper Lee. The message had remained with me ever since I first read the novel in Mrs Dancer's English class at Village Community School. It would stay with me for the rest of my life and especially the next few years thereafter.

Having reread the book and seen the film again, I realized that Atticus Finch never said it himself. However, I did later find a similar message in a study guide. The passage revealed that Atticus Finch had warned his children not to reject their own community, irrelevant of whatever faults they might find within it. Likewise, it suggested that Harper Lee had also used the novel to criticize Alabama society, yet she still retained some attachment towards it.

My original quote in the Derby Evening Telegraph was not far off from what I had rediscovered in the study guide. It summed up perfectly Atticus Finch's conduct and character in 'To Kill a Mockingbird'. Fundamentally, that he was an upstanding member of his community and a great father to his children.

Around the same time, I also asked that my big mamma have something written up in the Punjab Times newspaper too. It was a great honour to see and read the obituary in the local Pear Tree based newspaper a few days later.

A couple of days after my father passed away, I also received a card and bouquet of flowers from the Science department at John Port School. I felt very grateful that they had been so kind to care.

On the Monday and Tuesday after my father passed away, I decided to go back to work. Returning to school, if anything, was a bit of a blessing as it enabled me to take my mind off the things that were so obviously upsetting me at home. Being at school kept me distracted, regardless of whether the distractions were good or bad. This was a real reversal in feelings as only a week before I wanted to escape from school altogether to spend more time at home. Now it was the complete opposite.

Possessions can stir a lot of emotions and memories. The day after my father passed away I made sure to collect together some of his belongings, which I felt he was in some way attached to, so that they would never be lost in time. The fear of forgetting was a deep concern for me even then, so soon after his death.

- Peg – From the rotating washing line that he had been fiddling with on the day he died.
- Credit card – With his name on it.
- Membership card – Labour Party.
- Polling card – With his name and address on it.
- Coin purse – Containing £5.40.
- Glasses and case.

- Parker pen.
- White ramaal (handkerchief).

In the days before my father's funeral I also had to give great thought to what he would be wearing for his final corporeal appearance on Earth as well as the items he would have in his possession during his cremation. I needed to give him an honourable send-off but also forever remind myself of what he meant to me by attaching these items to his body and preserve my memories of him. It was also my way of trying to put one particular tormented thought to rest: 'Did he not love us?'

- Derby County F.C. pin badge.
- Parker pen.
- Comb.
- Yellow Livestrong wristband.
- Doctor Who notepad.
- Clip-on tie.

Derby County F.C. pin badge – It represented the city where we lived and the town my father first planted his roots and made his home when he arrived in England in 1967. The gold badge also had a Ram logo on it, which was a connection to our village of Ram Rai Pur in Nawanshahr, Punjab.

Parker pen – My father would always carry a pen in his top breast pocket. I kept his original one but replaced it with my own silver one that I had used for many years during my time at Village Community School.

Comb – Like the pen, he was never without a comb.

Yellow Livestrong wristband – I had been wearing one ever since I had first seen the, then legendary, Lance Armstrong wearing one during the 2004 Tour De France. I had initially ordered my original one from eBay. However, I managed to buy many more during our honeymoon in California. I felt it was only right that my father should wear one on his wrist too. In my opinion, back then and still now, the wristband represented triumph and the desire to never give in. It would also be a reminder to me; to live strong. The message was still good.

Doctor Who notebook – A few weeks before my father passed away I had been at a Year 10 Parents' Evening at John Port School. Whilst talking to a parent, I noticed the younger brother of the student, playing around with a Doctor Who Sonic Screwdriver. I commented on the child's toy pen and told him, 'I'm a big Doctor Who fan too and I'll be ordering one of them as soon as I get home.' When the oversized sonic screwdriver arrived a couple of days later I noticed that it also had an extra UV pen attachment and a UV light to reveal any secret writing. It also came with a little blank Doctor Who themed notebook. I would use this notebook to leave a final message to my father.

With the standard pen I wrote the names and dates of birth of my father and mother on the first page. Below this I used the UV pen to write the names and dates of birth of my sister, brother and myself. Finally, I added a little message that read, 'We loved you.' I then took the sonic screwdriver in hand and slid the button on it to activate the UV light; it began to produce a high-pitched whirring sound. I waved it over the notepad to make sure that the secret writing had materialized.

'Did he not love us?' This was my way of saying goodbye and letting him know that we had always loved him and always will.

Clip-on tie – My father had tried to take his own life with a noose, there was no way I was going to send him off with another one tied around his neck.

On Wednesday, the day before the funeral, I managed to do a half-day of teaching in the morning. Just before lunchtime I made my way to the Co-operative Funeral Care building on Normanton Road. I parked my car close by and was met by some close family members who were already waiting outside for me, as well as my eldest phuffhur who had by now hurriedly managed to return to England for the funeral. Again, as is custom with Sikh funerals, a yoghurt bath was prepared to cleanse the body and in the process of bathing and dressing my father, prayers were also recited. This was the first bathing of a dead body I had ever taken part in. I didn't go to my thiah Sohan's, nor Mohan's.

As we entered the small room, I saw my father laid out naked before me, with a cloth covering his pelvic region. I didn't really know where to look. Eventually my eyes settled upon his left forearm and the tattoo of a little swallow. It brought back memories of the day he had first showed it to us all. I began to choke up, so I quickly looked up at a clock on the wall. It was just before two, 'This time last week,' I thought.

'This time last week he was about to carry out the act. If I had been off like I was today, this time last week I could have saved his life. Instead, here he was in front of me, darker, lifeless and dead; stretchered out on a cold stainless steel trolley on wheels.' It just wasn't real. 'What was I doing here?' With small pieces of cloth in hand, a couple of my relatives who had done this before, immediately got on with the process of cleansing his dead body. I tried to involve myself too but every now and again I would just stop and then take a step back, then begin to look over and past his body, as my eyes would stare into nothingness beyond the walls. My father was dead and all that was left of him now was the shell of his former self. I did the best I could, as we all took it in turns to gently lift and lower him when need be. As rigor mortis had already set in, the process of cleansing and handling was made more manageable.

The smell of embalming fluid in the air was quite nauseating and made my stomach feel queasy. It also lingered around my face and nostrils since it had been absorbed by my, now, bushy beard. It reminded of the same queasy feeling I had a week earlier when I was partaking in the lung and heart dissection at school. As I had come straight from school I was still dressed in my work clothes, it was a horrible reminder of the week before.

A funny thing then happened. As my father's upper body and head was being lifted to allow us to wash his back someone shouted, 'Grab the legs!' in Punjabi. Another relative of mine then immediately grabbed the table legs. I began to chuckle as we all leapt forward to make sure my father would not slide off the table and onto the floor. I'm sure my father would have also laughed had he been in the same position as me. Instead, he was somewhere above looking down on us all, probably biting his bottom lip, desperately trying to suppress a laugh.

What a time to laugh. But it made me feel better. In that moment of slapstick, I had released a suppressed laugh, and in my mind also pictured my father smiling with me.

Dark humour can sometimes be a blessing and it's amazing how a good chuckle can make you feel better. Straight after this moment the nausea in my belly quickly left me and a chuckle had filled its place. But it still could not entirely hide the fact that my father lay dead before me. It was my father's body, but his soul had long since left. It was so sad. During the process of cleansing I also noticed a long incision on the back of his head, which had been crudely stitched up after the post mortem.

Only when his body had been completely dressed in his newly bought clothes, was I then able to place the various items I had brought with me, onto him. The pin badge was attached to his lapel. The Parker pen and comb were placed in his breast pocket along with another handkerchief. The yellow wristband was rolled over his right hand. The top button of his shirt was fastened and the clip-on tie attached. Finally, the Doctor Who notebook was placed into my father's inside jacket pocket.

The final thing we did was to put a pre-tied turban around his head. That was that. As we began making our way out of the room to leave, I noticed my brother fumbling about with his mobile phone to take a photo of my father's tattoo. I guess he wanted a picture so he could get a similar one tattooed onto his own arm in the future. I walked over to him and told him there was no need to take the photo as we already had a picture of my father and his tattoo at home. He accepted my reasoning and as we both walked out of the room together I made a mental note as I looked down at my own left forearm.

After I returned home from the Co-operative Funeral Care, the smell of embalming fluid had not left my thoughts nor my nostrils, so that night I decided to hack my beard off; I would be clean-shaven for the day of the funeral. My beard had been growing unperturbed for almost a week now and it was time for a change.

Thursday, March 9th 2006; the day of my father's funeral finally arrived. My father's body arrived outside our house just after 8:30am. There were by now already quite a few people waiting for his arrival. The hearse parked up, close to the garage on Pear Tree Crescent. As we all waited to take my father's coffin inside I noticed Daljit Singh Dhindsa standing close by but keeping his distance from the hearse. Daljit had been a fellow pupil at the Pear Tree Schools with me and then later the early years at the Village Community School. He was also the son of my father's childhood friend, Major Singh. I signalled for him to come forward and help slide the coffin out of the hearse and then carry it into my home with other family members beside us.

Major Singh and my father were very close. During their childhood years they used to do everything together. They shared the same surname and were also from the same village in Punjab; a fellow Ram Rai Purian. From the village of Ram Rai Pur to Normanton-by-Derby they had always been close and together. A couple of weeks before my father's death, Major Singh had come around to visit my father to see how he was, one last time before he visited Punjab with his wife. Major Singh was my father's best friend and they were like brothers. He was well aware that my father had recently been very unsettled and down in the dumps. At one point he even suggested that he would cancel his trip if my father didn't want him to go. But my father knew that he had not been back for many years and that he was very much looking forward to returning. 'Go, enjoy yourself and be happy' my father said to him. They shook hands for the last time as they bid each other goodbye. Major Singh was heartbroken on hearing my father's death. He had tried his best to make my father snap out of his darkness, but like myself he had also not been successful. On the day of my father's funeral, Major Singh was not present because he was unable to return to England in time for the occasion.

My father's coffin was carried past the garage, through the back garden and then taken into the house. It was then placed in the living room, where I had last seen him alive and well only eight days previously. The coffin lid was then unscrewed to reveal my father's face and the turban we had put on him the day before. The open casket then remained like this for about 20 minutes until everybody who had attended was able to pass by and see my father's face for the last time as well as pay their final respects. As prayers continued to be recited, close family and friends stood next to him, watching on. Some prayed, some wept and some remained silent. I stood by him, watching him in silence as the tears rolled freely down my cheeks; I made no effort whatsoever to contain them. Eventually the moment came when his coffin would be sealed forevermore. I observed my father's face for the final time as the coffin lid slowly passed over his body and the darkness consumed him for the final time. My eyes rested on the little plaque on top of the, now sealed, coffin.

Mohinder Singh

Dhindsa

Died 1st March 2006

Aged 51 years

As I looked around to see the faces of all the people who had thankfully attended. I caught the eye of another good friend, Nazim.

Nazim Hussain had visited earlier in the week to offer his condolences. On this previous visit to our house I made sure to follow him out of the front room as he was about to leave. Catching up with him, I put my arm around him and hugged him. 'Thanks for always being there for my father' I said. He didn't have the words to reply and shook his head in sorrow. He was visibly upset. I had never seen him not smiling. I thanked him again and then shook his hand, 'Thanks for being his friend.'

My father left our house in Pear Tree for the last time to make his final journey to Markeaton Crematorium where his body would be cremated. Outside our house his coffin was gently lowered then pushed into the waiting hearse by close family and friends. Another hearse was also allocated for my immediate family but I didn't take up my seat. Instead, I decided to ask my cousin, Satnam, if he would take me in his car. I needed some time on my own to think. As we made our way to the crematorium I knew that I had to stand up and speak up for my father. He deserved that. He had spent his whole life doing his utmost to help others. He was a good man and I wanted everyone to remember that. There was no way I was going to shy away from it now. I would regret it for the rest of my life if I did. I knew full well there would be no second chances if I had backed out. I would not fail him. I had to send my father off with honour. I had to say something. I had to stand up. As we snaked around the streets of Pear Tree then through Cavendish and beyond I began to think about what needed to say. 'I'm going to say a few words,' I said to Satnam. He agreed that I should and that it was only right. There was no doubt that there would be others who would speak about my father in Punjabi, my big mamma being one. But I needed to say what I wanted to, in English. There would be no fear. I would not be frightened. My only anxiety was that whatever I might say wouldn't do him justice. I knew full well that I would be leaving out so much more about him by not telling his whole story. But I also knew that it was better to say something than nothing at all. We reached Markeaton Crematorium a few minutes later and parked the car. As I stepped out of the car I took a long, deep breath then tied my ramaal around my head. We then walked the short distance towards the front of the crematorium and stood and waited for my father's hearse to arrive.

After a few minutes of waiting my father's coffin arrived. I stood close by as I looked at the pallbearers slowly remove all the flowers that had been surrounding my father, in preparation for removing his coffin from the hearse. These flowers were then placed on the ground in front of me, one by one. I noticed the one that I had asked to be created for my family. This arrangement simply said DHINDSA with the second D in the name in a different colour to the rest of the letters.

There were many Dhindsa's from the village of Ram Rai Pur and we all had our own way of spelling it; Dinas, Dhiensa, Dheansay, Dhinsa etc. Dhindsa was my father's way of spelling it. The distinctive D was also a nod to our city of Derby.

I then turned my attention to the other arrangements that had now been placed on the ground. As I panned right to carry on with my observations I came across one that almost gave me whiplash on a double-take. With a stifled chuckle I quickly took my hand away from my mouth then nudged my cousin, Jasbinder, whilst pointing out the word 'phuf' to him. He was not amused.

It was not a name that people would have used to refer to my father. I knew instantly what had happened though. This particular flower arrangement was made in two parts. The second part of the word had been misplaced. It should have read phuffhur. You had to laugh. I did.

I quickly recomposed myself, then walked around to the back of the hearse. A small group of us were able to slide out and lift my father's coffin out; we then walked slowly into the main chapel.

Written below is near enough what I said on the day. It was probably a good thing I had chosen not to write anything down on paper because I doubt I would have been able to see the words for the tears. There was no fear any more, just a duty to my father. A year of standing in front of large groups of children had given me all the courage and confidence I required to express what I needed to say. In the end I just said what I felt based on what I was feeling at that moment in time. It was off the cuff, but from the heart. When my time came to speak, I walked towards the microphone to speak up for my father:

Hello everyone my name is Kalwinder Singh Dhindsa, Mohinder Singh Dhindsa was my father. I thank you for all coming. I was a little bit worried this morning when I

watched everyone slowly arrive outside our house. At one point I thought that there would not be many of you here.

(By now the whole of the main chapel was full to capacity and the entrance doors couldn't be closed as there were people also standing in the foyer. Even before my father's death, I used to make sure that I attended as many funerals as I could. It was the last chance to show respect to the deceased and their family. Funerals were always proud occasions for me and the amount of people that would come along to pay their respects spoke volumes about the people who had sadly passed away. Therefore, these occasions would fill my heart with joy and take away some of the sadness. The day of my father's funeral will go down as the saddest day of my life, but it would also be one of my proudest. Thankfully, attending Brian Clough's memorial service at Pride Park enabled me to connect the loss of a father to the pride of having lived a good life. Today would be my father's day. Our Dad.)

I thank you all for coming it has made me feel very proud.

Many years ago, when I was very much younger, I used to refer to my father as Chacha, but I was always aware of who my true father really was. It was quite simple. An uncle gives with one hand and tickles you with the other. A father gives with one hand and slaps you with the other.

(I cracked a smile.)

Dad? Chacha? It didn't matter what I called him. I knew who my father was.

The last few weeks were not the best of his life. There was definitely something wrong with him that he just couldn't put across to us. In the end he wasn't the same man that we all knew and loved. He had become very negative in his thoughts and outlook and I think he just wanted the pain to be over.

My father never let me down. From the day I started nursery, he would drop me off and pick me up. As time went on and I made the step up to Pear Tree Infants and then the Juniors, he would always be there for me. Again when I needed him at college and university, he was

always there. He never let me down, he was always there and I know that one day when my time comes, when I too shall die, I know that he will be waiting for me on the other side, just like he always did in life.

(At this moment I paused. I was still quite composed, but I sensed that my voice might crack at any moment. It didn't. I then told the congregation that I would like to say one last thing before I finished. So in my best Punjabi I recited the Sikh National Anthem.)

Deh Shiva bar mohe-i-hai
(Grant me this boon O God)

Shubh karman te kabhu na taraun
(May I never refrain from the righteous acts)

Na daron arr siyoo jab jai laroon
(May I fight without fear all foes in life's battles)

Nischai kar apni jeet karaun
(With confident courage claiming the victory)

Ar Sikh hao apne hi mun-ko
(May thy glory be grained in my mind)

Eh laa-lch hau gun tau uchraun
(And my highest ambition be singing thy praises)

Jab aav ki audh nidhann banay
(When this mortal life comes to end)

Aut hee rann main tab joojh maraun
(May I die fighting with limitless courage on the battlefield)

When I had finished I simply said:

That is all I have to say. I'm finished.
Thank you.

I stepped back from the microphone. I had said what I needed to say. My brother then pressed the button that began to draw the curtains around the coffin. The coffin was then sent through a little hatch, which gently took my father's body away.

I had decided a long time before that I wouldn't press the button. I owed it to my brother. The guilt that I will always feel for not taking the day off on Wednesday, March 1st 2006 would never compare to how he would have felt, knowing that he was in the house when our whole world collapsed around us; oblivious to what was going to occur as my father closed the back door behind him and then made his way to the garage to end his life.

From Markeaton crematorium we then all made our way to the Guru Arjan Dev Gurdwara, on Stanhope Street. During the ceremony I was asked to come forward. I knelt before the Guru Granth Sahib and joined my hands together towards the Guru. A siropa (a length of cloth bestowed on someone as a mark of honour) was then placed over my shoulders by the head of the Gurdwara who was also my big mamma.

Throughout this whole time, I had decided to sit on my own at the front of the Diwan Hall. Although there were still many people sitting close by around me, I needed to be alone to gather my thoughts and contemplate life. It had been a day of great sadness but also immense pride and briefly broken by a chuckle.

The end of the funeral ceremony was approaching. I prepared myself for what was to come. Having been to many funerals and Gurdwara ceremonies in the past, I knew there would be one final thing to raise my spirits before we would all head towards the langar hall. I awaited the hymn. A hymn recited in times of happiness and also in times of sadness. The hymn would awaken my spirits.

'Anand Bhaiya Meri Maye, Sat Guru Main Paya'

'God is ANAND because there is no death or sorrow associated with God. The true Guru connects us to God. God is Anand.'

Anand means bliss, happiness, ecstasy, contentment and satisfaction.

I became alive. I released a smile through clenched teeth. I was happy and filled with emotion. Charhdi Kala as us Sikhs would say. 'Goodbye, Dad.'

When I finally got home that day, Rav said she was very proud of me for what I had said and done. I had achieved what I set out to do. Nothing would have stopped me. Not now. Not ever again. I believed it was the right thing to do and I pursued it determinedly.

A couple of days later, I also heard from an old university friend. He had brought his own father to my father's funeral. His father, like my big mamma, Master Avtar Singh Thiara, were prominent members of the Sikh communities that they lived in. Although they shared the same faith, their political views differed slightly. However, on that day they came together, united in my family's grief. My friend and I had also had a big chuckle at what his father had to say about my little speech. As well as commenting on my poor pronunciations of certain words he also described me in Punglish, as Burah Brave (Big Brave). It was a new one on me. 'That could be my new Indian name,' I said. 'American Native.'

My father had a simple mantra in life: be truthful, and be honest. Although he may not have looked like a true baptized Sikh I would like to think that he behaved like one was expected to, in his actions and in his core principles. If that was fine by him then it was fine by me. He would have known very well that if you can't be honest and true to yourself, then life had no purpose. Mental illness broke his mantra. When the one thing that kept him alive was destroyed, his reason for living went with it. What was the point of life? In the end his mind and body could take no more. Suicide became his only option and his ultimate act of control.

No child deserves to live without their loving parents in their life and no child deserves to see them die in front of them. I am glad of one thing, on the day my father died. I am glad that I was never in a position where I couldn't talk to him because he was lying on a cold slab. Stone dead. Gone. The police officer from the Derbyshire Constabulary had brought him back from the jaws of death one last time for us to all say our final goodbyes. When I saw him still alive that day for the last time, his heart was still beating, his blood still flowed, his body still respired and I knew there was a possibility, however small, that he could still hear me. Whether he was listening or not, I was able to tell him I that loved him and it was all going to be ok.

On Thursday, March 9th 2006 my father was cremated. There was no burial. There was no grave. There was no memorial or gravestone. There would never be one, his body was only a shell, the real essence of his soul had long since departed with his last breath. Only the memories of him remained now. Yet I felt that these memories were nothing if I couldn't attach them to anything physical. I wanted to make sure he would always be remembered, even if my own memories should one day fail me for whatever reason. The memories had to live on. I would never forget. I would not lose my father again.

Chapter 12: Back to School

The Black Dog at the School Gates

I returned to work the following Monday. In total, I had taken four and a half days off in the last two weeks. The main reason I took so little time off was because I was genuinely led to believe that my NQT status depended on it. Under this apparent impression I did everything I could to make sure that I didn't jeopardize the future that now lay ahead of me. From the moment I began my NQT year, my teacher training course leader made it quite clear that any time taken off wasn't a good thing and that it was totally frowned upon. However, in the course of the next month I had no choice but to take further days off, as my body just couldn't cope. Having picked up a chest infection that left me breathless and unable to speak, I then decided to take a couple more days off to get myself checked by a doctor. This enforced break allowed me to take some time; even if it was only a little time to pull myself together. Maybe my body was once again telling me that something was imminent? Preparing me for another big hit? I had been absolutely battered in the previous weeks yet my life was going to become even worse, before it had any chance of getting better.

Grief affects us all differently and we deal with it in our own particular way. There is no right or wrong way to manage it, other than to get busy living. I know it might seem odd that I took so little time off, but looking back, it undoubtedly helped me a great deal. Being at school and not at home kept me distracted. It was not that I was trying to forget the death of my father. I just needed to stop myself from thinking about how he had died all the time. But as much as I needed to distract myself from one death, the last thing I needed was to be hit by another.

On Monday, 20th March 2006, nineteen days after my father passed away there would be another death in the family.

Darbara's, mother had been in the living room with my own grandmother on the day my father left them both to make his way to the garage. This time I would be at home as she would be taken ill.

Just before midday on Saturday, 18th March 2006, she had come over to our house to see my grandmother; something she would do regularly. As I sat in the living room I noticed her through the blinds, opening the back gate, then walking slowly and carefully through the back garden with the assistance of her walking stick. A minute or so later she entered our house.

For as long as I can remember she had always required the use of a walking stick because her knees caused her so much pain. The walking stick that she was using on this particular day was one I had given to her as a gift; it had once belonged to my own grandfather. I had noticed that her previous walking stick was in need of replacing so I offered her a relatively new one that we no longer required. Her face lit up and she smiled when I passed it over to her, she even gave me a big hug to thank me.

As she walked into the living room that day she was greeted by Rav, my sister, my eldest thiee, grandmother, mother and me. She then sat on the sofa opposite me just as her rasping cough once again began to flare up. After a few minutes of talking amongst ourselves some guests from out of town then arrived so I left the living room and sat in the front room with the male guest; his elderly mother remained in the living room with everyone else. After a short while I noticed a commotion through the glazed windows that separated the front room from the living room. My first thought was that it might have been something to do with the guest's mother. As

I made my way into the living room I immediately became aware of what had happened. My masser's mother had suffered a serious stroke. As we all gathered around her we began to manoeuvre her into a more comfortable upright seating position on the sofa. Knowing that she may have had a stroke, we asked her to smile, but only the right side of her face was responding. The left side, was now drooping and she also seemed to have issues with the sight in her left eye too. We then lifted her arms; again the right side was fine and her arm remained raised but her left arm didn't respond at all and remained limp. It became obvious that she was unable to move or feel anything on the left side of her body; it was completely unresponsive. As this was going on she also made attempts to speak but her voice had become slurred and her words would come out all garbled. Although it was quite clear to those looking on what had occurred she herself seemed to be struggling to grasp what was happening to her. As all this was happening, Rav had already begun phoning for an ambulance thinking that it would arrive very soon after. At the same time my phuffhur had now also appeared on the scene and was able to remove her false teeth in case she choked on them.

During this period of waiting our guests decided to leave and my masser's youngest daughter, Cully, had now also arrived in Derby from Walsall with her two young children expecting to spend some time with her mother and grandmother over the weekend. As Cully came in through the back door into the living room her grandmother recognized her voice immediately and tried to twist her body to see with her good right eye. It was only then that Cully realized what had happened. Rav then made a further call to the emergency services but still nothing. All we could do as we waited was to stay by her side and assure her that she would be ok. She had now been propped up with pillows and my mother had begun to massage the side of her body that had been afflicted. My little massi, Cully's mother then entered the living room having made her way from over the road with her grandchildren. After a wait of nearly five hours since the first call was made and a few more after, an ambulance finally arrived.

At this point I finally left her side and went outside to meet the ambulance crew. I was not happy. 'My cousin's gran has had a serious stroke. We've been waiting for nearly five hours for you to arrive,' I snapped at one of them as he entered the back garden. I was angry and frustrated but there quickly realized that there was no point taking it out on the ambulance crew. They had an important job to do, now that they had finally arrived. The delay was not their fault. It was quite obviously the call handlers who made these priority decisions.

My mobile then began to ring and I answered it immediately. I was then told by my little massi to go over to her house across the road and expect a call from my masser in India. So I jogged over the road and as soon as I entered their house I picked up his call. My masser had been informed of what had happened and then began to question me about his mother's current state. I didn't want to hide the truth from him. 'She is not well, but hopefully she will get better,' I said. 'Shall I come home?' he asked. 'Yes, it's probably best to come home,' I replied.

My masser had travelled to Punjab on his own, not long after my father's funeral. He had originally tried to get my father to go with him when he had initially made plans for the trip. He had also been aware that my father had been unwell at the time so he had tried to get him to travel to Punjab with him, just like they had once done a few years previously when they had both taken a trip to Greece together. But this trip was not to be.

I remember my first memorable encounter with Satnam's grandmother, when my father and I visited her in her home village of Ramghar Chunghia, Hoshiarpur, in 1990. Her husband had passed away a few years earlier and she was now living on her own. We visited her twice during that particular trip. On the first occasion my father and I delivered some cream that she needed to apply to her knees. On our second visit my father had been in conversation with her in Punjabi, when I asked him in English, 'Ask her if she has been applying the cream to her knees and if the pain has stopped?' Thinking that my father would ask her on his own behalf, he then gave me a little wink and smiled as he turned towards her and said in Punjabi, 'Kulvinder is asking me if you are applying the cream to your knees.' Embarrassed, I then noticed her smiling back at me, having acknowledged my concern.

What was going on? Death at every turn and thoughts of death in every corner. It was beyond surreal. It just seemed like a bad dream. I wish it had been. Later on that evening, I went to visit her at the Derbyshire Royal Infirmary with my mother. My little massi had been seated next to her mother-in-law's hospital bed for the last few hours now. By now Satnam's grandmother was aware of her surroundings and had come to terms with what had happened to her. She had even asked my mother to pick up her coat from our house to bring it into the hospital the next time we came to visit her. All three of us therefore genuinely believed and hoped that her condition would improve with time.

As it was a weekend there were not many doctors on duty if any at all. So the only people that would be caring for her were the nurses. On a few occasions I tried to get more information out of them but it was to no avail. They really couldn't tell us very much, only that the doctor could if and when he or she ever showed up. Eventually we all left her to rest and returned home after we had said our goodbyes. It would be the last time she saw me. As I was leaving I once again tried to ask the nurses about her well-being having still been frustrated with the almost non-existent care that she was receiving. Again, I didn't get any helpful answers.

Earlier in the day, we had waited nearly five hours for an ambulance to take her to hospital and now that she was in her hospital bed very little care was seen to be provided. The nursing staff appeared to be doing very little for her and every question was met with the same answer, that they would keep an eye on her whilst they waited for a doctor to come back and check on her. On the whole, the care, or lack of it, was quite shocking. I was very frustrated but I decided to bite my tongue rather than lose my temper and say anything that I may have later regretted.

The next day was a Sunday and I decided to visit her again, but this time alone. I wasn't going to let my frustrations from the previous night stop me. Having spent many hours during the day thinking about her, I felt it was only right that I should be at the hospital with her. Later that night, unable to sleep, I drove down to the Derbyshire Royal Infirmary to see how she was doing. I was well aware that my father's death had hit her hard and I honestly believed that she would definitely not have had the stroke had my father still been alive. I therefore felt saddened and somewhat guilty at her predicament. When I arrived to see her, she was already asleep and Cully was sat on a chair by her side. Cully and I talked for a short while then I made my way back home. I'm not sure if her grandmother knew or was aware that I had visited that night.

A few hours later she would go on to have another major stroke. However, this time it would all but finish her off. Still alive, but now unconscious she had held on long enough. On the Monday afternoon, she finally breathed her last breath with many of her close family around her and by her side.

I met my masser at the entrance to the ward. He had only just arrived back into Derby having been picked up from the airport. As I pointed the way to her bed he rushed past me. I then raised my hand to get the attention of his son-in-law, Resh as I shook my head from side to side. It was too late. Two minutes too late.

The last time she had seen me, she was still aware and responsive even though she was half paralyzed. She probably picked up on my concern and frustration at her apparent lack of care too. Although I had said goodbye, I had no idea it would be the last time I would see her awake and conscious.

During her last few minutes of life, I stood by her side and told her not to worry as my father would be waiting for her on the other side. She shouldn't have died in this manner. Neither of them should have. The death of my father had hit her very hard, he was like another son to her; she missed him terribly and she could never get her head around what he had done and how he had gone about it. It was my father's name on her lips when her stroke struck and I believe it was my father's death that also brought it on.

My father and Satnam's grandmother would die nineteen days apart. She would be cremated on Wednesday 29th March 2006, twenty days after my father. What a horrible month of March.

About a year or so later an almost identical occurrence was reported in the Derby Evening Telegraph regarding another patient that had been treated in the same manner. This elderly patient also later passed away. Reading the article brought back a lot of unpleasant memories. We didn't make anything of Satnam's grandmother's death, at the time. We just accepted it. Maybe if I was in a better frame of mind during that period I would have followed it up. But my chance had gone, so for that reason I made sure to share our own experience this time by adding it in the comments section below the article. 'Who Cares?' I asked. Did the life of an elderly patient not matter any more? Is this how we will all be treated in old age? All life should be equally as important when care is provided.

Two members of my family had now passed away in the same month. It was awful and to add to that, their cremated ashes had to also be taken back to Punjab. There was no way I could take time off work as I still had my NQT year to pass and complete. I wanted to go, for my father but I also needed to stay and pass for him too.

At school I had only told a couple of science colleagues how my father had actually died. So most staff would have known that he had passed away, but not how. I just didn't want to talk about it, in the sense that I wanted my home life and school life to be quite separate from each other. Maybe other members of staff did eventually find out what really happened, but nobody ever pushed me for these details. It was ok by me, I preferred it that way and I guess maybe they did too; they may have felt they might upset me further.

If I had been a borderline introvert before my father's death, I definitely became a clear-cut introvert soon after. This pattern of behaviour emerged when I created my own little personal space in the corner of the science staff room. A place where I could be alone but still be part of the wider team. From this point I became an observer, always listening in on the conversations around me and every now and again joining in when I had something to add. But if I didn't want to join in, I could be left alone, quite comfortable in my own thoughts.

Many of teachers in the staffroom and the technicians were a bit older than me. So it was difficult for me to interact sometimes, but I enjoyed their company, especially the teachers hovering around their fifties who would have been about the same age as my father. They included Tim Fearn, Stu Marsh and Geoff Brown. Another teacher much older than me was my fellow physics teacher, Michael Vick. He reminded me of Spock from Star Trek because of the way he looked so it was always good to see him and have him sat around my little table in the corner of the science staffroom.

Sometimes I would just have too much on my mind, so I just didn't want to talk to people unless I felt I had something of substance to say. Small talk was something I struggled with a lot. However, when I did talk on a one-to-one basis it used to be about shared interests and things that really interested and fascinated me. Talking to the staff and technicians about upcoming events such as the Tour de France and the World Cup really helped me a lot. It cheered me up a great deal.

On the whole, school was a good place for me to get away from what was happening at home. It was a helpful distraction. But one thing that really concerned me during this period of my life was whether any of the school children might eventually find out just how my father had passed away. I knew one child definitely would have known; he was a relative of a cousin. I remember thinking: what if he has told the others?

Sometimes things were said in class and I would think to myself: 'Was that directed at me?' It was during moments like this when the paranoia would really begin to set in and have me on edge. These constant thoughts then led to self-doubt and much insecurity. During one particular lesson I was not impressed with the behaviour of a small group of boys. So I began to reprimand them, when one of them suddenly smiled and called out, 'Calm down, no one died.' I looked around to examine their reactions as I noticed one turning his gaze away from me. Was that aimed at me? Did he know something about me? Did *they* now know something about me? Did they know? Were they deliberately trying to get under my skin?

When my father and his family first settled in Derby, they took up residence at 49 Fleet Street in the Arboretum area of the town. Next door to them, at 48 Fleet Street, lived the Meehan family, which consisted of Morris, his wife Christie and their three young children. The Meehan's looked after my father and his brothers and treated them like their own. My father and his family were always eternally grateful to them for showing such compassion and love towards them during those early formative years in Derby.

There was another child I taught who may also have known about my father's passing.

Only after the death of my father did I learn that Morris and Christie Meehan had two grandsons who also attended John Port School.

Ben could be a bit of a silly student at times, and during my first year at John Port School he really tested me with his behaviour. But in all honesty he was one of many. On one particular occasion he had pushed me so far that I was actually looking forward to taking him out of the lesson to have a word and share with him our shared history. Once outside, I began asking him why he was behaving so badly, but he just brushed off my questions with a casual lack of concern. Until, that is, I mentioned to him that I actually knew his family and that they would be very disappointed with his attitude towards me. He smirked, thinking I was pulling his leg and didn't believe me in the slightest. I then began to rattle off the names of his father, auntie and then his late grandparents. On hearing their names his whole demeanour changed. Surprised, he quickly became attentive as he began asking me how I knew them all. So I told him that many years ago his grandparents and their children had looked after my father and his family when they had first arrived in Derby. At this point I was still not sure if Ben knew who my father was and what had happened to him. However, at the end of our conversation I asked him to pass on a message to his father and let him know that his science teacher, the son of Mohinder Singh Dhindsa had said 'Hello'. I knew his father, Thomas, would then make the connection from there, if he didn't know already.

It was a great shame that I only found out about this connection to my family after the events of Wednesday, March 1st 2006. It would have been good to discuss it all with my father. It may have even cheered him up a little.

A few weeks later at a Year 7 parents' evening I shook the hand of both Ben's father and mother as I was greeted with a knowing smile. Since our conversation Ben had changed his behaviour and attitude towards his learning as well as me. So I let it be known to his parents how well he was now doing, but also how much better he could do if and when he settled down and began taking his education even more seriously. At the end of Ben's appointment I then bid his parents goodbye. Later on in the evening I was sitting alone deep in thought, when Thomas Meehan, son of Morris, came over to my table to say goodbye again. However, this time he came alone to also offer his condolences. I quickly stood up and raised my hand to shake his. 'Thank you, that really means a lot' I said. I felt honoured and pleased that he had indeed remembered my father. I then sat back down and smiled.

Suicide was constantly on my mind, whether it be in school or at home. Did I think about suicide? Yes! Most definitely. Did I think about taking my own life? No! Most definitely not. I refused to go down the road that my father had taken. I would not choose that path. It would not be contemplated. The act of doing it would not be entertained. Never! No way! This was easier said than done though. In the dark days after my father passed away I began to regularly see things out of the corner of my eyes. What looked like shadowy figures hanging from heights above me in my peripheral vision. These phenomena would be fleeting when they occurred, but quickly vanished when I turned to look straight at them. On one occasion my eyes began to glance up at the high ceilings and then settled upon the steel girders and cross beams. I then began thinking about how easy it would be to tie a rope around them. 'But why would you do it? What could lead someone to want to do it? What would be the final straw? Was I now seeing that final straw? Was I reaching my point of no return?' I needed to snap out of it, and snap out of it fast. There was only one place to return, my own little personal space in the corner of the science staffroom.

Snap! Snap! Snap! 'Kal, you ok?' Tim stood over me clicking his fingers trying to get my attention. 'I think so' I said. It was break time and I had been sitting alone in the corner of the staffroom, but in another world. The bell was about to ring for the next period. The feelings of anxiety at having to hear that bell again rose within me. So I got up, grabbed my possessions and then began to make my way towards the classroom where I would be teaching next. 'I'll see you later, Tim,' I stuttered as I walked out of the staffroom. Immediately a dark cloud enveloped me overhead. Through my peripheral vision I once again began to sense the shadowy figures hanging down from the ceiling above me. I was just about to look up to vanquish the shadows but then had to avert my attention to the floor as I skipped down a step below. At this exact moment the entrance door to the science department on the left of me blew wide open with a deafening crash against the brick wall behind it. The rushing wind outside crackled through the bushes and then whistled past my ears like small projectiles as beams of light pierced through my eyes. I was gone.

I overlooked a battlefield.

It was Friday, March 2nd 1945 and the Japanese were in the process of retreat. Combined British and Indian forces had made the widest river-crossing of World War II when they crossed the Irrawaddy and advanced on to the port of Myingyan. The Japanese army was now defending and holding a strong position along the road between Kamye and Myingyan.

As I looked down from my elevated position above, I observed Naik Gian Singh of the 15th Punjab Regiment of the British Indian Army leading his platoon ahead of the rest of his battalion; advancing down the road between Kamye and Myinggyan. Although Gian Singh couldn't see what was ahead of him, from my bird's-eye view, I could see it all. It was me who saw his enemy first. I called out, but no words were spoken. A few more strides and Gian Singh too identified the enemy in front of him. In a hail of bullets and fire, Gian Singh's platoon were savagely assaulted. Hidden behind well-camouflaged positions and a number of foxholes along cactus hedges the enemy opened up with a fierce barrage of both artillery and intense machine-gun fire. My fellow Punjabis were like sitting ducks in the midst of hellfire. My heart was racing, I looked back at Gian Singh. Astonishingly, not a single bullet had touched him. Relieved, I scanned the battlefield again, but my heart sank as I saw the twisted bodies of Punjabi soldiers scattered all over the battlefield.

The 15th Punjab Regiment of the British Indian Army were about to be obliterated before my eyes. Gian Singh, having now taken cover, looked around to see the fallout from the ambush. His men, bloodied and battered, lay strewn around him as the casualties began to rise. Immediately recognizing the gravitas of the situation, Gian Singh knew that the attack had to be repulsed, knowing full well that any action he took would ultimately lead to his death. There was only one thing to do; to go out all guns blazing. It was a good day to die; fighting with limitless courage on the battlefield.

In May 1944 at the protracted and vital battle of Kohima in Assam, Gian Singh had already witnessed the kamikaze methods of the Japanese attack; soldiers prepared to fix grenades to their bodies and hurl themselves at their enemy to accomplish their devastating and divine deliverance of destruction.

With the words of Major Tony 'Raj' Fowler quoting in Urdu from Shakespeare's King John, still ringing through his ears.

Come the three corners of the world in arms,
And we shall shock them.
Nought shall make us rue.

Gian Singh of Sahabpur Village, Nawanshahr uttered 'Waheguru' then boldly leapt forward and fought back like a tiger.

Suddenly, my vision blurred and I lost sight of what was happening. After a few seconds it reappeared. I then witnessed something quite unbelievable as an immense feeling of pride washed over me. Gian Singh was attacking his enemy single-handed, engrossed in absolute defiance and Charhdi Kala.

I briefly closed my eyes, unable to believe what I was seeing but when I opened them again; the battle was over. Gian Singh was now standing in front of what remained of his platoon. The proudest Naik that ever lived, bloodied and battered but undefeated, bowed his head, overwhelmed. He looked down at his blood soaked arm which was now hanging limp beside him. Turning his head, he then looked upon his other hand as his fingertips began to dig deep into his palm forming a clenched fist. 'JO BOLE SO NIHAL!' he roared as he thrust it into the air. 'SAT SRI AKAAL' boomed back the jungles of Burma.

The battlefield before me disappeared and the green undergrowth beneath my feet turned red.

I watched on as Gian Singh of Sahabpur village, Nawanshahr was awarded the Victoria Cross by King George VI.

From the ceremony at Buckingham Palace, I leapt into my younger self, sitting under a tree in my mother's village of Sahabpur.

Turning around I could see my father and a smartly dressed elderly gentleman engaging in conversation in the middle of the road. They seemed to know each other quite well. So I decided to slowly approach my father and stand by his side. 'This must be your son? What's his name?' asked the elderly gentleman. 'My name's Kalwinder Singh Dhindsa,' I replied. 'Nice to meet you,' he said as he smiled and then placed a shiny silver coin in my shirt pocket. I quickly delved into my pocket and pulled it out to examine it. Eventually they finished talking and bid each other goodbye. 'Who was that, Dad?' I asked. 'That was Victoria' my father replied with a mischievous grin. 'But that's a girl's name' I chuckled. 'What's his real name?' My father pointed towards the end of the road. 'Go and have a read of what it says on his house.' We then walked down the road to have a closer look. I looked at the large painted letters on the exterior wall, 'It says Gian Singh VC of Sahabpur village, but VC stands for....' My father stopped me with a smile. 'Yes, VC stands for Victoria...Cross.' 'Oh boy' I mouthed back as a spark of electricity charged through my spine and out through my topknot.

'Kal, Kal, you ok,' asked Tim again, having caught up with me. 'I think so,' I said. 'I am now,' as I nodded back at him. The shadows in the corner of my eyes were banished forever.

Even in his darkest hour, when the prospect of death was all but an absolute certainty, Gian Singh never gave up. He refused to lose and lived to inspire. Courage was not a matter of being frightened for him, it was being afraid and still doing what he had to do anyway. Gian Singh VC knew he had to win his battle or die trying. Life was paramount.

I kept thinking back to the last words I ever said to my father in the Derbyshire Royal Infirmary as his life drew to an end. 'I'll see you soon, it might be another 50 years but I'll see you again.' I will live a long life! I had known too many people who had taken their own lives in my lifetime. I was fully aware of the heartache they all left behind. I wouldn't go down that path and I would try to help others along the way.

Although the shadows had been banished, the darkness still remained and this darkness would be a constant companion during my long drives home from school. On one occasion I parked my car outside our garage and switched off the engine; I just sat there, in a world of my own, alone and in deep thought. Staring but not looking at the door to the garage where my father had tried to end his life. Tap! Tap! Tap! My little massi stood by the car, knocking on my driver side window, trying to get my attention. I was startled. 'Are you ok?' she asked. 'Yes I am, I'll join you in a bit,' I replied. I had been snapped out of my oblivion. I pulled the keys out of the ignition then looked down and checked the handbrake again. As I did this I noticed a pad of purple Post-it notes. I raised a smile as I remembered who had given them to me and for what reason.

A week before my father passed away I was sat in my car outside Derby Train station waiting around for Rav. I parked up on double yellow lines and was nervously looking around in full meerkat mode trying to spot any car park attendants bounding towards me when, suddenly, out of nowhere Roy McFarland, the former Derby County and England Football Captain, walked straight past me. As I looked on like a buck caught in the headlights, Roy McFarland looked straight back at me with a smile that acknowledged that I had recognized him. He then nodded at me as he continued to walk on by. Open-mouthed and star struck I could not believe my eyes. 'Pen? Pen! Paper!' I began to mutter to myself, whilst desperately rummaging around for them. After what seemed like an age I eventually found a pen but by the time I had looked up again, Roy McFarland was gone. I was disappointed in myself. I had blown my chance to show my father that I had managed to obtain the autograph of the great Roy McFarland. My chance to cheer him up a little, but I had failed. The next day at school I told my story to the technicians, about how I had missed my great opportunity because I was too slow in finding a pen and paper. 'Keep these in the car, for the next time you see him, Pet,' Lilian said jokingly as she then handed me a pad of brand new purple Post-it notes.

I was fully aware that my first year as an NQT at John Port School was always going to be a difficult one. I was under no illusion at all that it wouldn't be. Having spent the previous PGCE year filled with much anxiety, it didn't help my emotional state when the NQT coordinator told me, even before the deaths of both Mohan and my father, that if I carried on the way I was going then I could find myself in a position where I may not pass. He never actually said that I would fail but just that I could fail.

The school knew I was having issues with misbehaving students, but I had hoped that the management would have helped me to overcome them so that they wouldn't become a bigger problem later on. After all, that is what you would expect them to do, right? I thought I was doing the right thing by referring students on with the school's blue referral report form system. In the end however, it was the number I was passing on that management took issue with. It was a real Catch-22 situation. I thought I was doing the right thing, by passing information on to help others down the line, but in the process I wasn't doing myself any favours whatsoever. I was then told that out of all the NQTs, I was referring the most students on. Later on I found out that other NQTs also shared my problems too but didn't take the route I did in terms of dealing with them. They were also told about the dangers of failing. From then on I just effectively stopped filling in the referral forms and tried to deal with the behaviour issues as best as I could, on my own without any outside management assistance.

The blue referral report forms would go through a chain of people, each person trying to deal with the issue before they would make their way to the top of the management tree. I could see that the people at the bottom of the tree, who were one level above me, didn't always take too kindly to them either when the forms were placed in their pigeonhole. Maybe they thought it would possibly reflect badly on them too. The high frequency of receiving them, having to deal with them and also the pressure from the top didn't appeal to them either. This no doubt made other teachers in the same position as myself think that you were just better off dealing with your own problems and not get anyone else involved. I was not alone in doing this. However, things didn't get any better for me by handling the issue in this way, on most occasions. My hands were tied and I felt I had no other option. I needed to pass my NQT year. The subsequent deaths of Mohan and my father obviously made things even more difficult to manage.

Prior to beginning my NQT at John Port School, maybe I just expected too much from the management? Maybe I also expected the same high standards from the students too? Expecting that they would all be well behaved and that they all wanted to do exceptionally well too. It didn't quite live up to my high expectations.

Right from the start of my NQT, I had been told that I should never fall in the trap of becoming a 'Scooby Doo' teacher; a type of teacher who would mutter, 'If it wasn't for those pesky kids' at the end of every bad lesson. For a while I agreed with my NQT coordinator, but as the weeks and months went on, I realized that it was in fact those pesky kids who were messing my lessons up. Obviously not having the desired management backing on my side also compounded the problem.

In April 2006, Rav and I bought a new black Ford Focus. It was only right that I should add some of my character to it. So, I decided to buy a nodding Scooby Doo and I stuck it down on the dashboard. It was my way of telling myself that failure was totally unacceptable as well as reminding myself that pesky people did exist and that sometimes you just have to nod your way through life.

I lost a lot of faith in the management team during this period and kept my distance from them forever after. 'Were they trying to make me a teacher or break me as a teacher?' It was difficult to differentiate at times, but I knew that I would not be broken.

The problems that I was experiencing in the classroom may have also arisen because I was just trying too hard. It was obvious, the reason I was struggling was because I took things too personally. I tried to be friendly, I tried to be me, but sometimes in the classroom, you have no choice but to be someone else. In this instance, my NQT coordinator was quite correct when he said that teaching was all about acting. However, all that became irrelevant once my father passed away. I had no choice but to put on a different face. An act is exactly what I had to put on every second I stood in front of all my students. I had to put on a mask. Inside I was hurting but on the outside I had to show that nothing could upset me. There were some occasions when my mask would slip and my emotions would get the better of me as I would lose my cool but I would quickly try to regain my composure. It took time but eventually I reached a point where some of my own personality began to leak into my acting and once the students had gotten to know me more, things became better. I was being tested, but I knew I just had to keep performing.

Most of the science groups I had been given in my first year as an NQT were simply quite horrendous in relation to some of the students within them and their overall behaviour. Thankfully, mixed in between these groups were rays of light that I knew I couldn't give up on. Fantastic hardworking students who would try their best at all times, even in the midst of the chaos that was regularly going on around them. I tried my very best every day for these conscientious students. Sometimes I would really get frustrated with myself, knowing that I was letting them down because I could not engage with them as I had hoped. Their voices too quiet to hear and their confidence sapped by the louder ones when they tried to speak. I saw so much frustration in the eyes of these students who wanted to learn but were being held back by those that tried to make out that they didn't care. It used to break my heart. On most, occasions it wasn't even the not so intelligent ones that caused the problems. The biggest problems came from the supposedly intelligent ones. This made the act of actual teaching even more frustrating. They just wanted to show off all the time, and in the process brought everyone else down with them. I would take it personally. Sometimes I would see my father in their eyes and remember how he also used to struggle when things didn't go his way. I didn't want to let them down. Every child mattered and every child deserved a chance, yet I was finding it increasingly difficult to do what I wanted to do: teach. I tried my hardest and I tried my best and I knew I couldn't give up on them. The fact that I took so very little time off work showed how much I tried. In my mind, I convinced myself that I shouldn't complain. I was an NQT and the way I saw it was that whether my father had passed away or not, the first year at John Port School would have been difficult. If this was the worst it could or would ever be during my whole teaching career, then so be it. All I had to do was survive and get through it. If I could succeed and complete my first year then my future teaching days would be so much easier and better for it. 'Surely school life would be a little easier having already completed one year?' I kept telling myself, 'No matter how bad things get. Never give up, there is always hope,' just like the underlying message in J.R.R Tolkien's The Lord of the Rings trilogy. No matter how bad it gets, there is always hope in the face of great darkness. I had been thrown in at the deep end and all I had to do was keep my head above the water.

I was not the only teacher being let down by misbehaviour. Every teacher I knew experienced it no matter how many years they had been in the job. Those who had been in the job the longest just learned to adapt. In most cases I didn't even have to bring the matter up as it would be regularly discussed in the science staffroom. From my customary position in the corner I would hear enough to know that I was not alone in my predicament. I just had to get on with it; what else could I do? Although I was being supported at school, I never truly felt the management backed me.

I had to carry on. I was going through hell, but I just needed to keep going. KBO as my great hero, Sir Winston Leonard Spencer-Churchill used to say.

As the weeks and months passed, my spirits began to lift a little and every now and then, whenever a chance arose, I would tell my students to keep pushing on and not give up. I would remind them of the words of Churchill and Shackleton. Why was I doing this? Maybe I wanted to somehow share my own struggle with them without actually revealing my own difficulties in life.

All my students were well aware of Sir Winston Leonard Spencer-Churchill and for those that didn't know who Sir Ernest Henry Shackleton was ... well, it was always a great privilege for me to recount Shackleton's story of endurance and absolute defiance.

Sir Ernest Shackleton was an Anglo-Irish Antarctic explorer, best known for leading the Endurance expedition of 1914–6. In 1914 he began his third trip to the Antarctic with the ship Endurance; planning to cross Antarctica via the South Pole. However, in early 1915, Endurance became trapped in the ice and ten months later sank. Fortunately, Shackleton's crew had already abandoned the ship to begin living on the floating ice. In April 1916, the entire crew was forced to set off in three small boats, eventually reaching the uninhabited Elephant Island. Taking five crew members with him and leaving the rest behind, Shackleton went to find help. In a small boat called the James Caird, the six men spent 16 days crossing 1,300km of ocean to reach South Georgia. They then trekked across the island to a whaling station. The remaining men from the Endurance were finally rescued in August 1916. Astonishingly, Shackleton's extraordinary leadership skills contributed to saving the lives of 28 of his stranded men, including himself. All of them successfully braved the Antarctic for nearly two years. Not one man died under Shackleton's heroic leadership. Not one was expected to survive. Nobody expected them to ever return. Shackleton would not be defeated.

'Fortitudine Vincimus – By endurance we conquer'
Shackleton Family Motto.

I had no choice but to continue my enforced optimism. Another thing that helped me a great deal were the books I was reading during this time. I was reading up on people who had persevered through their own personal hardships in many cases against insurmountable odds or public ridicule. Their stories of defiance began to settle in the corners of my mind and displaced the darkness. I knew that I too had to endure like Shackleton and Churchill did before me. Their stories of defiance would spur me on in my own most difficult of times. They allowed me to see the faintest light at the end of the longest darkest tunnel. They stopped me from thinking bad thoughts. They kept me from thinking about giving up.

Churchill used to have a black dog. This black dog then became my own ever-present companion. It was only right that I spoke so highly of his master.

As the academic year went on, things began to gradually get a little easier. The butterflies in my stomach had also, by now, settled down. It was still hard work and sometimes I would come home after a long day and just drop exhausted onto the sofa. I would then take a little nap, whether it was for one minute or ten. I would then wake up and feel invigorated. It was almost as if I was rebooting myself. However, sometimes I would have a bad nap and after the sleep inertia had worn off I would be snapped straight back into my existence: I would forget about everything then suddenly remember, acknowledging to myself again, 'My dad's dead.'

My most satisfying memories in my first year revolve around the parents' evenings. Although, the lead up to them was filled with anxiety. Once I had sat down and got going, I was in my element. It was never in my nature to give bad reports. So I would always make sure I was positive about the students. Even if some of them had been, at times, little rascals in the classroom. I wanted to fill their parents with hope. Something, they could then pass onto their child, who may then actually realize their full potential. On many an occasion a student would come up to me the day after a parents' evening and thank me for their report. Even though they knew full well that their behaviour and attitude during lessons needed to improve, some students never did change, but at least I gave them the tiniest glimmer of hope, and make them believe that they did have the potential to change their ways. I knew full well how the tiniest bit of encouragement could do wonders for somebody's self-confidence.

During the last few months of the 2005–6 academic year, Dave Sankey helped me out a great deal by keeping me distracted. He was only a couple of years older than me and he was always someone I enjoyed passing the time with. Just before the 2006 World Cup kicked off we both began collecting stickers for the Panini FIFA World Cup Germany sticker album. Initially swapping stickers between ourselves, we then began swapping stickers with the students too. Sometimes I would come into school with handfuls of Panini Sticker packets, sit myself down in the corner of the science staffroom and then begin ripping the packs open; sorting all the stickers into little neat piles, ready to be stuck in or put aside on the swap pile. Other teachers would look on smiling at my childish nature, but it didn't matter. They could see I was happy. There I was a 26-year-old man behaving like a big kid. I didn't care; it reminded me of how I loved to collect stickers during my Pear Tree and Village school years. It took me back. Back to Pear Tree and happy days. Whenever I would reach the point where I would have too many swaps I just gave them away. Swaps were even carried out in class to the amusement of my other non-collecting students. Dave also formed a 2006 World Cup Match predictor competition. I didn't do very well at predicting the scores but it was good to see myself making a late rise up the table like a phoenix as the tournament came towards it's inevitable end. Dave and I also participated in the school's Fantasy Football League competition, competing against all the other students and members of staff who had picked their own line-up of Premier League players. It was all great fun. Shackleton Endurance ukFC was the name of my team.

Towards the end of the 2005–6 football season, Dave and I also went to watch Derby County play against Millwall in a league match at Pride Park. Derby won the game 1–0 and in the process relegated Millwall.

Before this game I had only ever watched one live Derby County football match at home. A fixture between Derby County and Oxford United in the Football League First Division that took place on the 30th April 1994 at the old Baseball Ground. It would become a memorable game for me because prior to the kick off the club announced the Derby County Player of the Season. This award was voted for by the club's supporters and the trophy was named in honour of Jackie Stamps, a Rams legend who had scored two goals for Derby County in the 1946 FA Cup Final victory against Charlton Athletic. On this particular day, goalkeeper, Martin Taylor became the recipient of the Jack Stamps Trophy.

It was only during my time at the University of Leicester that I really became a big Derby County fan. The connection to my team back home suddenly began to mean so much more to me. However, even after returning to Derby from Leicester I never went to any matches. It was quite a simple reason why; I just never had anyone to go with, or anyone that I knew who really supported the Rams. During that time, I had oddly seen more Leicester City F.C. games whilst working as a steward at Filbert Street than I ever did watching as a fan of Derby County at Pride Park. Although I was at the Leicester City vs. Derby County game as a steward on February 23rd 2002, when Derby County thrashed Leicester by three goals to nil. Fortunately for me, all the goals were scored in the second half and I watched them all go in, as I sat behind Ian Walker's goal, trying my best to contain my smiles. At the end of the game I was walking past the tunnel when I noticed Fabrizio Ravanelli poking his head out from within. He hadn't played that day and was a little surprised when he noticed me and my big wide smile, walking over to him to shake his hand. He must have been even more surprised when I then told him I was a Derby County fan even though I was dressed in a Leicester City F.C. steward's jacket and tie.

In the July of 2006, I finally found out that I had passed my NQT year. They had literally left it to the last couple of weeks of the academic year to put me out of my misery. I had done it. I had persevered. I had endured for my father. I had won. I was proud. I was now a fully qualified science teacher. I was giving something back to my community. To my people: the people of Derby. Once I knew that I had passed my NQT year I began to relax completely. The summer holidays were now only around the corner. The faint light from the end of the once long dark tunnel was no more. It had now become incandescent and I could now thankfully see the end.

In the final week of the academic year I had a bit of fun with my students. Although none of them knew anything about what I had gone through, I did try to leave them with a few last messages of encouragement for the years they had ahead of them. I did this by hiding motivational passages in the word-searches I had created for them. For every group I had I created a wordsearch in which they had a list of every child's name in their class. Now that was simple enough, but then I also told them that if you then circle all the remaining letters and put them in order from left to right moving downwards as you did so. A secret message would reveal itself. For the younger Year 7, 8 and 9 students I hid a passage from Roald Dahl's, 'The Swan'.

'The Swan' was a deeply moving short story that I had first come across when I read a book called 'The Wonderful Story of Henry Sugar and Six More' by Roald Dahl. A story about the indomitable spirit of people who never give up in life no matter what obstacles are placed in front of them.

The little passage I quoted from is found towards the end of the short story. It always lifted my spirits in times of darkness, even though the whole story itself made for uncomfortable and upsetting reading.

I included the same hidden message in the wordsearch for my other two Year 10 groups as well as some helpful advice in the form of another hidden message to make them realize the importance of always working hard and never becoming complacent.

'You can take a thirsty camel to a waterhole. But you can't make it drink from it.'

Those that finished the wordsearch inevitably got what I was getting at.

The last day of the academic year finally arrived. I had survived and the summer holidays were now ahead of me.

During these six weeks off Rav and I decided to get away from Derby and spend some time in Scotland. So we decided to drive up to Edinburgh in our new Ford Focus. She deserved just as much of a break as I did. But once again trying to kill two birds with one stone, I decided to also meet up with my cousin, Satnam, and his wife, Natasha, who were now living in Glasgow, and had previously invited us up.

I have always had a habit of trying to do as many things in one go as I could possibly get away with. On our honeymoon in 2005, Rav and I went to California and spent a week in

Los Angeles and then a week in San Diego. My cousin, Jeeta, originally picked us up from the LAX airport, as he was living nearby in Van Nuys. In that first week we spent some time in his family's company. It was good to see them all again.

Satnam and Natasha were now working in their own family restaurant. It was called 'The New Turban Tandoori' and was in a small town called Giffnock, the birthplace of the politician Gordon Brown. Having originally set off from Derby we initially stopped over for the night at Rav's parents, in Ingleby Barwick, near Middlesbrough. The next day we set off for Edinburgh. The plush green scenery that revealed itself the further up north we went was quite beautiful to the eye. It was a lovely long drive all the way to Edinburgh and our arrival just so happened to coincide with the start of the 2006 Edinburgh Fringe Festival, although that was not the main reason we decided to go to Edinburgh.

The 2006 Edinburgh Fringe Festival began with a little controversy, thanks to an old friend. That year it became the first Fringe following the introduction of the new legislation banning smoking indoors. Winston was not happy. During a photo call at the Assembly Rooms, the actor Mel Smith who was playing Winston Churchill on stage decided to light a cigar, flouting the ban. Mel Smith was adamant that he would continue to smoke during the first performance. However, the controversy soon subsided when he decided not to go through with his initial decision.

During our time in Edinburgh, we stayed at a hotel on York Place, not too far from the Scottish Nationally Gallery, where Rav and I managed to see an exhibition put on by the Australian hyper-realist Sculptor, Ron Mueck. We both found his work and attention to detail quite breathtaking.

Ron Mueck's work epitomized the hyper-realsitic sculptural representation of the human body, concentrating entirely on the human figure, tracing the human passage through life from birth to death, sculpted with an obsessive attention to realism, right down to the pores in the skin and the hair on the body. At times his sculptures looked so real that it was hard to believe at first sight that they were not. The only giveaway was that the size and scale of his creations did not always match the true proportions of the human body.

Not for one second did I ever not think about my father; from the moment I woke up to the moment I went to sleep.

Occasionally he would fleetingly appear in my dreams too, it was good to see him again.

One night whilst staying in another hotel room, in Glasgow after visiting Satnam and Natasha, I couldn't get to sleep. Rav had quickly nodded off and I remained awake in the darkness. I picked up the Powerball that I had brought with me and decided to give it a spin.

A Powerball is a gyroscopic wrist exerciser. My particular model came with a digital counter that counted the number of revolutions made by the rotor inside. It also featured a dynamo connected to LED lights within the body that flashed as the rotor inside, spun.

I managed to get it spinning in the dark with the use of the little string that came with it. I then lay down flat on the bed with my right arm pointing towards the ceiling as I continued to manoeuvre my wrist and maintain the spin of the rotor. The dynamo immediately kicked in, which then enabled the LEDs to emanate a blue light. This blue light began flashing around the walls of the room like a rotating police beacon. By now not only was it producing light, but it was also producing a faint whirring sound as the rotor inside spun.

Making sure that it would not lose its gyration, I continued to spin my little Powerball for a good 20 minutes. I wasn't looking for how many rotations I could do, or how fast. My only aim was to keep the lights flashing and the sound whirring until I could do no more. Rav carried on sleeping undisturbed as the sound and light produced from the rotating Powerball was not enough to wake her from her sleep. However, anyone looking in from outside our hotel window would have noticed these flashing blue lights and wondered whether the TARDIS was materialising inside. Maybe the hypnotic flashing of the lights convinced me that it would. Maybe I was wishing it would. Maybe I was calling in a favour from my Doctor. This current predicament made me think about my life. 'Where was I going to go from here?' 'School would restart again within a month and I would have to do everything all over again?' 'Was I prepared for another year?' 'Could I cope with another year?' I began to get anxious again. I realized I had to change my ways. I had to snap out of my moments of deep anxiety and insecurity. I had to stop this cycle of negativity that was consuming me and bringing me down. I needed to get out of the darkness and step into the light. 'Tomorrow would be another day and I must change my ways,' I thought to myself. I had no choice. I then decided to stop spinning my Powerball as I lowered my arm back down towards my chest and then leant over to the bedside table to place the Powerball down. It continued to spin and illuminate its immediate surroundings. The purple Post-it notes that I had placed on the coffee table earlier were now also being illuminated. I watched on as the light began to slowly dissipate and the whirring sounds began to fade. Just as the light was about to vanish I caught sight of some words that lit up in the fading blue light. I then realized what I had written as the lights went out and I lay back down on the bed to contemplate the message.

'Never reject your own community no matter what faults you find within it.'

It was the same words I had written for my father's obituary in the Derby Evening Telegraph. 'But what did that even mean?' I began questioning myself. 'Who was that message actually for? Was it for my father? Was it a message he actually lived by? Was it for me? Was it a message I was living by?' I was confused. 'But then if I was confused by it now, what would all the other people who had read it originally, have made of it?' 'Hold up, he died because he did reject his community. He died because he didn't want to live any more. He died because he gave up on life; right?'

No. No. That was not the message. The message was not for him. It may have been once, but it was not in the end. It used to be his message, but that message was shattered when mental illness corrupted his mind. It then hit me like a bolt from the blue. The message was for me. The original message had been deeper than I initially thought. It was a message to myself, my future self. To never reject my own community of Pear Tree in Derby, because if I ever did, not only would I be forgetting who I am and where I came from, but also, I would be well on the road to forgetting who my father was and where he had come from. It could never happen. I would not ever let it happen.

'No matter what happens in your life, never reject your own community. It is in that community that you will find your salvation.'

From that moment on I knew that I would never forget my father's memory, provided I never rejected the community I came from. It would become my own new mantra in life.

Surprisingly and unexpectedly in February 2014 at the age of 88, after a lifetime of maintaining that she would never publish another novel. Harper Lee's lawyer released a statement confirming publication of a second novel: a novel written in the mid-1950s, which served as the original draft for 'To Kill a Mockingbird'. On the 14th July, 2015, the follow up to 'To Kill a Mockingbird' called 'Go Set a Watchman' was released.

Thus my original message in the obituary was to take on an extra meaning. All these years I had thought that it applied to Atticus Finch, the father figure. Reading 'Go Set a Watchman' made me realize its true significance and whom it really related to.

'Never reject your own community no matter what faults you find within it.'

It was me, my father's child.

I thought back to the day at Village Community School when my English teacher, Mrs Dancer, first handed out our new curriculum-set textbooks. I looked down at my copy of the book and quickly realized that it had seen better days. It was a dreary-faced, beaten-looking book, which had a picture of a tree on its front cover that I initially thought was a bird-hunting manual. I took a closer look. 'To Kill a Mockingbird – A Novel by Harper Lee.' I had never come across the book or the title before, in my life. I turned it over to read what else was written about it.

'Shoot all the blue jays you want, if you can hit 'em. But remember it's a sin to kill a mockingbird.'

So my first impressions were correct. It was a bird-hunting manual! How wrong I was to judge a book by its cover.

Harper Lee's novel changed my life forever and now here I was in Scotland, the homeland of my former English teacher who had first handed it to me. The message I had been searching for all along had been hiding in plain sight within me all along.

'Never reject your own community no matter what faults you find within it.'

I then shot out of bed and turned on the bedside lamp. I reached out for the Post-it notes. What else had I written? I turned over the first page and the words behind it gave me further insight and clarity.

Spirit – Community – Pride – Vision – Derby

These words lifted my spirits. There was my answer to what I had to do. I would not give up on life. I had a reason to live. My quest for happiness had begun. I gratefully turned off the light and went back to bed. I then closed my eyes and saw Brian Clough smiling back at me through the darkness.

*

Gian Singh VC
Born 5th October 1920
Sahabpur Village, Nawanshahr
District of Jalandhar, Punjab.

Victoria Cross 2nd March 1945
Married Hardyal Kaur (Died 1995)
Three Sons, Two Daughters

Died 6th October 1996

Never Give Up
Never Give In
Never Surrender

Fight till your last breath
Fight back like a tiger

***
**
*

A FATHER IN TIME AND SPACE

My first fixed memory of watching Doctor Who with my father was when we watched Episode 4 of 'The Caves of Androzani' together. It originally aired on the 16th March 1984 and I would have been four-and-a-half years old at the time. At the end of this particular episode, the fifth incarnation of the Doctor, Peter Davison, regenerated into the sixth, Colin Baker. I guess at the time, it would have been my first experience of death. Yet, this death was different as the Doctor didn't die, but he regenerated into another body. As a Punjabi Sikh I found this all quite logical.

Sikhism was founded by Guru Nanak in 1469. Successive Sikh Gurus then established Sikhism over the following four centuries. Over the course of this time there were 11 Gurus in total; ten human and the eleventh or current and everlasting Sikh Guru, became the integrated Sikh scriptures known as the Adi Granth and then later the Sri Guru Granth Sahib, the living word. The name 'Nanak' was used by all the Gurus who added any sacred text in the Sri Guru Granth Sahib. Each Guru, in succession, was then referred to as 'Nanak' and as 'Light', making their teachings equivalent. Hence all the Gurus are referred to as 'Light of Nanak'.

In my warped way of thinking, I recognized that the Gurus, like the Doctors, also had numerous incarnations and regenerations. Sikhism preached a message of devotion and remembrance of God at all times, truthful living, equality of mankind, social justice and the denouncement of superstations and following blind rituals. The Doctor's message was in his morality. He was an archetype of courage, values and a belief in goodness.

I was so happy when Doctor Who returned to our screens in March 2005. I thought Christopher Eccleston had done an amazing job in portraying the ninth incarnation. Although I was initially very disappointed with him when he said that he would give up the role after the first series. What made this revelation even more difficult to stomach was that he dropped this bombshell straight after the transmission of episode one of the new series. I could not believe it. I was not happy. Would this be the end of Doctor Who again? Thankfully it was not. Christopher Eccleston's portrayal of the Doctor drew me back in effortlessly, as the series went on. In the end, I was delighted that he had done such a great job in bringing the show back. After this I knew full well that whoever got the role, as the tenth incarnation would join a show that was in good hands. At the end of series one, the Ninth Doctor regenerated into the tenth incarnation of the Doctor, David Tennant, and we would begin the cycle of life all over again.

I have loved science fiction for as long as I can remember. Even before my father's death, some of my most lasting memories in the genre have always revolved around father and child relationships. In every case, it is about a child travelling in time and space to try and save their father.

My final fixed memory of watching Doctor Who with my father was when we watched 'Father's Day' on the living room sofa together. This episode aired on the 14th May 2005 on BBC One and I would have been just over 25-and-a-half years old at the time. It was episode eight out of thirteen in the new first series of Doctor Who, which began on 26th March 2005. It would be the last ever episode of Doctor Who my father and I would watch together.

The first episode of the series 'Rose' marked the end of the programme's 16-year absence from episodic television format following its suspension of production in 1989. This first series featured Christopher Eccleston as the ninth incarnation of the Doctor accompanied by Billie Piper as his main companion, Rose Tyler.

'Father's Day' written by Paul Cornell.

In 'Father's Day' Rose asks the Ninth Doctor to take her back to 7th November 1987, to witness her father's death so that he wouldn't be alone when he is killed in a hit-and-run accident. However, when Rose is faced with the reality, she impulsively rushes forward and saves her father from being run down. This then results in a change in history, causing a temporal paradox that damages all of time thus causing catastrophic effects on the TARDIS. Destructive reapers then begin to sterilize the wound in time by devouring everything in sight. Later in the episode Peter figures out that Rose is his daughter. However, when he hears what an ideal father he's been, he realizes Rose is only lying to cover up the fact he was supposed to have died. Peter's paternal instincts are then awakened; he bids Rose and Jackie an emotional farewell then deliberately steps in front of the car that should have killed him, dismissing the Reapers and putting time back on track. History is then changed to a small degree as the Doctor allows Rose to rush to her father's side. This also results in the driver of the car not fleeing the scene. In Peter's last moments Rose is able to hold his hand whilst he dies. Just before death Peter smiles whilst gazing at his daughter's face. Rose and the Doctor then walk hand in hand back to the restored TARDIS. The episode then ends with a flashback similar to the opening scene, as Jackie explains to a young Rose that Peter didn't die alone and that there was a young woman who stayed with him until his end.

'I should have been there that morning with him. If only. If only I had a TARDIS.'

As a science fiction fan and knowing that the Doctor's TARDIS could travel in time did it ever cross my mind: if only I could go back in time to stop him. Of course it did. I could have used the TARDIS to go back in time to save him. An hour after it happened I could have gone back, a month after I could have gone back. Years after? No. I was never going to go back. I had to accept that time moves on and I must live with my grief and accept the road that I must travel. It would not be possible. All 'wibbly wobbly, timey wimey stuff' aside and the fact that Doctor Who is primarily a British science-fiction children's television show, nothing was ever going to physically bring my father back. Nor would there be any regeneration.

The last Doctor Who episode I watched whilst my father was still alive was 'The Christmas Invasion' which aired on 25th December 2005. In this episode, Rose and the newly regenerated Tenth Doctor return to Rose's house. Where Rose, her mother Jackie and her former boyfriend Mickey carry the Doctor inside to rest and fully recover from his traumatic regeneration from the previous episode at the end of series one.

The next time the Tenth Doctor returned to our screens on 15th April 2006 in the episode 'New Earth', my father, like Peter Tyler would also be dead. From then on I watched the series very intermittently. There were some episodes I watched and some I missed altogether. I say watched. In most cases the TV was on, but very little was being assimilated regarding the plot and what was happening. For a few years after the death of my father I stopped watching as I once religiously did. But I knew deep down in the back of my mind that, one day, I shall come back. Yes, I shall come back. I would return and so would my Doctor.

The blue police box would not be coming to my rescue but a metaphorical TARDIS would. My TARDIS to the past would be my memories. Memories that would forever take me back to Pear Tree and happiness.

END OF PART ONE

ABOUT THE AUTHOR

Born in Derby in 1979,
Kalwinder Singh Dhindsa attended Village
Community School – a short walk from his childhood
home in Pear Tree. He then graduated from the University
of Leicester with an Honours Degree in Physics with
Astrophysics followed by a PGCE Secondary
Physics.
These days
he works as a
science technician at
Littleover Community School and
an activity facilitator at the Enabled Centre in Derby.

As well as a safety steward at his beloved Derby County F.C.

54400951R00227

Made in the USA
Charleston, SC
04 April 2016